THE DISPOSSESSED

Other books by George Grant

Bringing in the Sheaves:
  Transforming Poverty into Productivity, 1985

In the Shadow of Plenty:
  The Biblical Blueprint for Welfare, 1986

To the Work: Ideas
  for Biblical Charity, 1987

THE DISPOSSESSED: HOMELESSNESS IN AMERICA

George Grant

DISTRIBUTED BY
CROSSWAY BOOKS • WESTCHESTER, ILLINOIS
A DIVISION OF GOOD NEWS PUBLISHERS

The Dispossessed: Homelessness in America. Copyright © 1986 by George Grant. Published by Dominion Press, P.O. Box 8204, Ft. Worth, Texas 76124.

Distributed to the bookstore trade by:

Crossway Books, a division of Good News Publishers
9825 W. Roosevelt Rd., Westchester, IL 60153

First Printing, 1986

Printed in the United States of America

Library of Congress Catalog Card Number 86-71355

Bookstore trade: Order From Crossway Books: ISBN 0-89107-411-2

Direct Purchase: Order From Dominion Press: ISBN 0-930462-11-4

To Dad
who gave me a home
and
To Karen
who made me a home

AUTHOR'S NOTE

All the stories in this book are true. In some, names have been changed; in others, editorial liberties have been taken to combine certain events for purposes of clarity or illustration. But, in all instances, the events and conversations underlying the stories are absolutely factual.

Most of the stories come from a single investigative visit to New York City, April 22-26, 1986. But lest anyone get the impression from this book that I threw caution to the wind and struck out alone and unguarded in the Wilds of New York, let me clarify: During the time I was on the street I was in constant communication with professional contacts in New York, local police, and family members back home; I never entered into an unsafe area without first taking the precaution of notifying authorities; at particularly sensitive times I had a "guardian angel," a friend, follow close behind me; I scouted out the areas I was going ahead of time so that I would not go into a situation "blind"; I had read and researched extensively so I knew what to expect pretty well; I prayed *constantly* and had the support of my Church at home in constant vigil. The point of my relating all this is to warn anyone against trying to duplicate my sojourn on the streets without similar preparation and precaution. The streets are lethal and should not be taken lightly.

CONTENTS

ACKNOWLEDGEMENTS

"Composition is the easiest thing in the world," Mozart is reported to have boasted. "All you have to do is write down the music you hear in your head."

Easy for him to say!

The melody for this book has been playing in my head for years. But for some reason when I sat down to write, it did not flow forth in a torrent — lyrical, lustrous, and lilting. The melody was still there, but it had betangled itself betwixt and between harmony, rhythm, dynamics, tempo, and timbre. The writing process became quite difficult, mind bogglingly laborious. Without the help of a number of philanthropic virtuosos, this performance would *never* have seen the stage.

Mel and Dorra Hunter, the dedicated researchers who turned a backroom enterprise into the most informative newsletter on the United Nations available anywhere, were most cooperative. They let me pour through their old files of *The U. N. Insider*, from which I gleaned my best sources on the International Year of the Homeless, and without which this book would have been impossible. The cessation of their newsletters' publication schedule due to Mel's recent bout with cancer is a great, great loss.

The Hunters' New York neighbor, Bill Holiday, also assisted me immeasurably by giving me access to his extraordinary library of antique books on theology and the social sciences. I could never have found the valuable sources necessary for a book of this sort without his help.

Robbie Breckenridge also aided my research, giving me a home away from home while I was in New York. He steered me in the right direction when time, money, and encouragement were all of the essence.

James B. Jordan is a benevolent maestro who smoothed out the rough edges and disharmonies of the manuscript when and where he could with a passionate but compassionate abandon. A better editor and a better friend could hardly be found.

Great thanks is also due to David Dunham who has believed in my ability to complete this project from the start. His patience and kindness have been unparalleled.

And of course, I can't even begin to express the gratitude I feel to my Church and my family who put up with my sequestered and single minded estate during the months of composition and consummation.

Mozart had only to depend on his genius. I have had to depend on my friends and loved ones.

My music may not be as brilliant as his, but I still think I got the better deal.

The 8th Sunday of Pentecost
Humble, Texas

FOREWORD

by James B. Jordan

"And as they were going along the road, someone said to Him, 'I will follow You wherever You go.' And Jesus said to him, 'The foxes have holes, and the birds of the sky have nests, but the Son of Man has nowhere to lay His head'" (Luke 9:57-58). With this statement, our Lord called attention to His condition of homelessness during His ministry on earth. Jesus' remarks are a continuing challenge to His people, for they indicate that "homelessness" is, in one particular sense, a mark of true discipleship. Indeed, just a couple of verses later, we read: "And another also said, 'I will follow You, Lord; but first permit me to say good-bye to those at home.' But Jesus said to him, 'No one, after putting his hand to the plow and looking back, is fit for the Kingdom of God'" (Luke 9:61-62).

From time to time in the history of the Church, strange sects have arisen that misinterpret our Lord's words. With a literal-mindedness that totally rejects the Biblical context of Jesus' statements, they insist that the true Christian will drop out of society and become a wandering beggar or nomad. Such movements were numerous and influential toward the end of the Middle Ages, and in our own time we have seen something similar in parts of the "Jesus Movement" of the 1970s.

There is an implicit cruelty in such an interpretation, for if physical homelessness is a mark of spirituality, then clearly we should do nothing to house and shelter the homeless. We don't want to diminish their spirituality, after all! Let them remain homeless — it is better for them.

Obviously this was not our Lord's intent. Rather, Jesus was calling men to make the New Home of the Kingdom of God their first priority, and not to cling to their fallen, ruined Adamic homes.

Adam had been given a home in Eden, a garden to dress (beautify) and keep (guard). As George Grant points out in chapter 13 of his book, in his fall Adam essentially gave his home over to Satan. As a result, he was cast out. God did not leave Adam homeless, however, but promised him a New Home to be built by a Deliverer. When Jesus called on men to forsake their homes and follow Him, He was announcing that the Kingdom had arrived and the New Home was being established.

Jesus told His disciples that the New Home was not centrally located on this earth, but rather in heaven. "In My Father's House are many dwelling places; if it were not so, I would have told you; for I go to prepare a place for you" (John 14:2). In the Old Covenant, the Angel of the Lord had gone before the people to prepare the land of Canaan (Exodus 23:20). This was a figure for the Kingdom of Heaven that Jesus would eventually bring. Referring to the exodus, Jesus assures the disciples that their New Home is being prepared, and that they will be guided to it.

"My Kingdom is not of this world," said Jesus to Pilate (John 18:36). The Kingdom of God is *in* the world, but its *root* is not in this world. Located in heaven, the New Home for God's people cannot be assailed by men, nor can it be corrupted. It is perfectly secure.

Yet we pray, "Thy will be done on earth, as it is in heaven," and the promise of the Gospel is that there is a foretaste of the heavenly Home even here on earth. Its primary manifestation is in the Church, the new Family of God and the Home of believers. Beyond that, however, the world is progressively restored by Gospel influences and becomes more and more home-like. Where the Gospel goes, peace and security follow, and men are restored to homes. Homelessness declines and even disappears from society.

"Out of sight, out of mind," says the proverb. The saints in heaven are not aware of the pain and anguish experienced by the homeless souls in hell. The separation of tares and wheat, of sheep and goats, is complete. Those who have moved into the heavenly Home have no responsibility for those who refused the Gospel and are consigned to eternal homelessness.

As we noted above, the central blessing of the Gospel is that God's will is done on earth as it is in heaven. In a Christian society, the homeless tend to be out of sight and out of mind. There is no shame in this; it is a benefit of the Gospel. After all, in a Christian society, those who wish a home can find one in the Church and her provisions. Those who reject the Gospel, and choose to "gnaw their tongues" in hatred rather than repent (Revelation 16:10-11), *deserve* to live in homelessness even in this life.

At the same time, however, we are not yet living in heaven. In this life, we are not always supposed to give people what they *deserve*, but to manifest the longsuffering mercy of God. We are called to forsake some of the blessings of the Gospel, sacrificing some earthly joys in order to "seek and save that which is lost." A significant incident that bears on this is recorded for us in John 9. "And as He passed by, He saw a man blind from birth. And His disciples asked Him, saying, 'Rabbi, who sinned, this man, or his parents, that he should be born blind?' Jesus answered, 'It was neither that this man sinned, nor his parents; but it was in order that the works of God might be displayed in him. We must work the works of Him who sent Me, as long as it is day; night is coming, when no man can work'" (John 9:1-4).

In fact, it would seem that this man's blindness was part of the judgment on human life that stems from Adam's fall. In a sense, his blindness was indeed due to his parents' sins, his first parents being Adam and Eve. Yet Jesus informs us that this fact is secondary. Human suffering actually presents an opportunity for the Kingdom, an opportunity for the Church to labor at the work of restoration. This is the most important thing.

Thus, even though homelessness is a judgment of God against sinners, Christians are still obliged to labor to help alleviate the situation as much as possible. This is all the more the case because our society is no longer a very Christian one. The faith has been waning in influence for over a century now, and one of the results in recent years has been a startling increase in the number of homeless and destitute people in our society. For most of us, these people are blessedly out of sight and out of mind; but George Grant calls us to set aside this blessing, to sacrifice some degree of our Christian comfort, and imitate our Lord in seeking the lost. We are not yet living in heaven, and we still have earthly work to do.

Jesus forsook his home in Nazareth and lived a homeless life for three years. This is not a pattern for the Christian. Rather,

Jesus was taking upon Himself the curse and judgment that we deserve, the curse of homelessness and exile. His homelessness was substitutionary, and ours can never be. We cannot die for the sins of the world, and we cannot suffer for the sins of others. We are indeed to break from our old homes, as Jesus called men to do, but that is for the purpose of joining the New Home of the Church, not for the purpose of becoming nomads. We are not to despise "sabbath rest and festivity," but rather we are to appreciate and enjoy the blessings Christ has earned for us. Imitating Jesus does not mean forsaking our families and other responsibilities.

A useful rule of thumb is the tithe. God calls us to give ten percent of our income to Him for His work, which includes care for the poor. Beyond that, we are to give alms. The remainder is ours to keep, to use to build up the world. We are, after all, still called to "dress and keep," that is, beautify and protect our homes and our culture. Thus, while Job remembered the poor (Job 29:12-17), he did not thereby cease to be "the richest man in the east" (Job 1:3). He kept his wealth and influence intact, that he might do the more good with it. Such is the balance we are to maintain, unless we are called to a special fulltime ministry to the poor.

In this valuable and eye-opening book, George Grant shows us the plight of the impoverished and homeless in America today. He discusses the causes and the effects of this condition. He displays false cures, and contrasts them with the true hope offered by the Gospel. He calls upon us as Christians to take part of our time and effort and devote it to the ministry of poor relief. For most of us, these problems are "out of sight, out of mind," but that must not continue to be the whole story. Only God's people can provide a real cure for the problem of homelessness, for only the Church can display God's New Home to men on earth.

Give me your tired, your poor,
Your huddled masses yearning to breathe free,
The wretched refuse of your teeming shore.

Send these, the homeless, tempest tost to me,
I lift my lamp beside the golden door.

Inscription on the Statue of Liberty

INTRODUCTION

"I never imagined that one day I'd be homeless," she told me. "I mean, it's not like I fit the bag lady profile or anything."

Sean Ballard was striking. Some would say beautiful, with her immaculately clear complexion and neat, shoulder length auburn hair. Recently divorced, she lives with her three children —nine, seven, and four—in a tiny but tidy room in one of New York's Welfare Hotels: temporary shelter for the city's "family homeless." She was right. She didn't fit the bag lady profile but she was homeless, all the same.

"I had big dreams when I was a kid. Real idealistic. But then I got pregnant in my second year at Ohio State. I dropped out. And . . . well, it's not been too terribly good since."

Until fairly recently though, Sean had been able to get by. She and the children lived in a nice, two bedroom apartment in the Long Island suburbs. "I worked a waitress job, and with tips and all . . . well, it was okay."

But then the owner of her apartment complex sold out to an investment company that adopted an "all adult" policy for the property. "They gave me a month-to-month lease and took me to court."

Her search for other apartments was frustrated by her lack of credit references and the size of her family. "The landlords would say the apartment was too small or my wages weren't sufficient or whatever. I didn't know where to turn. So I decided to move into the city. The kids and I could stay in a hotel for a couple of days. I'd find a new job. We'd make a clean start of it. That's what I thought, anyway."

So, with $800 saved up, Sean moved to Manhattan. But jobs were scarce. The money quickly ran out. "I'd applied for welfare and subsidized housing. I hated to, but . . . with the kids. . . . 'Course, it takes a while for that stuff to get processed, and with no address, it takes even longer. Bureaucracy. So when the money was gone, we had to pack up and go."

That first night, she and the kids slept in Grand Central Station. "A policeman gave us blankets and a couple of dollars for food. We bought chips and Coke. That's all we could get there in the station. I felt so foolish. I felt so helpless. The kids were cold. And hungry, and confused. It was awful."

Tears welled up in her eyes and dribbled unnoticed down her smooth, pale cheeks. "I always thought that only winos and criminals wound up on the street or in these dive hotels . . . homeless. I never imagined that it could happen to me. Never in a million years."

Homelessness. Unimaginable, but all too real. An ugly fact of modern American life.

It is estimated that there are anywhere from 250,000 to three million people just like Sean in our nation today.[1] They live on the fringes, taking meals and shelter when and where they can.

Some are old. Filthy and suffering, they stuff the pockets of their tattered jackets and their shopping bags with their every earthly possession — with all the litter and rubbish they collect and live on.

Some are what modern men call "mentally ill." Twisted and worn, they wander an urban wasteland muttering, twitching, moaning, and shuffling. Just barely existing.

Some, like Sean, are young. Displaced and disenfranchised, they wait. They yearn for a better day. Someday.

The New Mendicancy

From the post-war forties to the pre-stagflation seventies, these dispossessed souls were nowhere to be found. Stories like Sean's simply didn't exist. The nation was enjoying unprecedented prosperity. Homelessness was not just unimaginable. It was unconscionable.

Between 1945 and 1970, median family income (dollar denominated) in the U.S. more than doubled.[2] Twenty-one million new homes were added to the nation's overall housing stock, increasing the supply by 50% and outpacing new household formation 3 to 2.[3] The proportion of families owning their own homes jumped from 43.6% in 1945 to 62.9% in 1970.[4] Dire privation was limited to small rural enclaves in the south, the west, and Appalachia and to inner city skid rows.[5] Actually, once the great travail of the depression era had passed, the only people who persisted in homelessness were a few hoboes, drunks, bowery bums, vagabonds, and derelicts.[6] Certainly, there were no Sean Ballards on the streets.

But then with the advent of stagflation in the seventies, a radical transformation took place in the ranks and numbers of the homeless.[7] They began to spill over the boundaries of traditional skid rows. A new mendicancy appeared. Suddenly, sidewalk psychotics began turning up everywhere in increasing numbers.[8] Massive migrations of runaway teens gave new meaning to the phrase "street person."[9] Almost overnight, hippies seemed to replace hoboes, drug addicts seemed to replace alcoholics, and lice-infested communes seemed to replace lice-infested flophouses.[10] Women began to show up with greater frequency, and a whole new social category appeared: bag ladies.[11] And with them, a whole new social concern was created: the feminization of poverty.[12] Even children seemed to be joining the ranks of the homeless in alarming numbers.[13] Previously ebullient, the economic forecasters were shocked by the magnitude and the intensity of the crisis. The problem seemed to spring up without warning. Like some black plague, it horrified them, terrified them, and trapped them between the devil and the deep blue sea.

The Political Debate

The dramatic shift in the nature of the underclass coincided with an equally dramatic philosophical mood swing all across the nation. Old traditional liberalism began to die a slow and painful death.[14] Four out of five presidential elections were won by Republicans. Exorbitant social spending programs fell into disfavor. Campuses became places to study and learn rather than stages for radical unrest. Yippies went out. Yuppies came in. "Conservative" was the banner flown high over a culture grown weary of untethered socialism and international wimpesence. The old liberals claimed that there was a direct correlation between the two trends. Homelessness, they said, was an all-too-obvious result of this new pebble-hearted stinginess.[15] Conservatism, indeed! We had become a "me generation": selfish, greedy, and power mad. They cited mountains of statistics, and volumes of facts and figures, charts and graphs, demonstrating beyond a shadow of a doubt that increased military spending combined with entitlement program crackdowns had led inexorably to the impoverishment of not hundreds, not thousands, but millions — count them — millions of Americans.[16]

The new conservatives chided the old liberals for their emotional over-simplification of an extremely complex problem.[17] They too cited mountains of statistics and volumes of facts, figures, charts, and graphs, demonstrating beyond a shadow of a doubt that it was the old liberal "war on poverty" that had failed.[18] They argued, in fact, that the "war on poverty" had actually *increased* poverty and had led to the situation where the poor were forced out into the streets.[19]

When homelessness reached crisis proportions in the early eighties, the debate between the old liberals and the new conservatives rose to a fever pitch. Charges and counter-charges were hurled back and forth in the political arena like so many pigskins on a Sunday afternoon. Reputations were won and lost.[20] Congressional hearings were staged.[21] Press conferences were held.[22] Campaigns were launched.[23]

The media began to inundate us with vivid and lurid tales of the victims of homelessness.[24] They showed us people living on park benches and street corners, under bridges and loading docks, in public shelters and abandoned buildings, on subways and heating grates, in bus stations and old cars, thus attempting to up the moral ante and stir the moral outrage.

Then came the United Nations. That august body jumped into the fray on the side of the old liberals by declaring 1987 "The International Year of the Homeless," and unveiling a comprehensive, decade-long social and political agenda.[25]

New studies were commissioned.[26] Monographs were written.[27] Agencies were established.[28] Dissertations were presented.[29]

The old liberals gleefully debunked the findings of the new conservatives.[30] The new conservatives then promptly returned the favor.[31] Tit for tat.

Homelessness began shaping up as one of the hottest social issues in recent memory, ranking right up there with abortion, taxes, government deficits, and military rearmament.[32]

Who would have ever imagined that the day would come when Lucille Ball would portray a bag lady on network television;[33] or that Martin Sheen would star in a major miniseries about a shelter operator;[34] or that rock stars would stumble all over one another for the chance to deflect a little of their cherished limelight on the hungry and homeless of our land?[35] Who would have ever imagined that the day would come when a clumsy, Victorian-era, Dickensian word — "homelessness" — would leap back into prominence, snatched from oblivion by the uneasy conscience of a public made suddenly aware of a long-hidden secret? Who would have ever imagined that the day would come when *The New York Times* would devote 43 articles,[36] *The Los Angeles Times* 62 articles,[37] and *The Washington Post* 105 articles,[38] all in just one year, to such a dismal subject? Who would have ever imagined that the day would come?

But it has. That day is here. Now.

"No one likes gadflies: From Socrates on down, their assaults on conventional wisdom have been sometimes brilliant, sometimes silly — but always irksome."[39] Those are the hazards of the trade.

That being as it may, this book is designed to play the part of the gadfly: debunking the "conventional wisdom" of the humanism of the new right and the humanism of the old left. In fact, the primary thesis of this book is that virtually everything that either brand of humanism has come up with in order to combat homelessness has only added to the problem.

The deinstitutionalization of the "mentally ill" was supposed to help. It only hurt.

Feminism was supposed to help. It only hurt.

Rent controls and redistribution of resources were supposed to help. They didn't. They only hurt.

Farm subsidies were supposed to help. They too, only hurt.

Federal welfare programs and the "war on poverty" were supposed to help. They only hurt.

On and on the litany of failure goes. Every hope, every dream, every program, and every proposal that the two humanisms have devised have only added to the anguish of the poorest of the poor.

A Third Way

Amidst all this hoopla, one sector of society has been strangely silent. For nearly twenty centuries the Church had set the parameters for the social welfare debate.[40] She had been unrivaled in her care for the poor, the homeless, and the dispossessed.[41] No discussion of the issue could even be considered without placing the Church at the center of its purview. Of course, times change. Due to new theologies, aberrant both Biblically and historically, the Church has dropped out of her place of prominence and yielded either to the old liberals on the one hand or to the new conservatives on the other.[42] Instead of leading the way, the Church finds herself tagging along, forced to swallow either the absurdities of a humanism on the left, or the follies of a humanism on the right.

This book is an attempt to cut through all the rhetoric and all the propaganda. It is an attempt to move past the left-right debate, to debunk the "conventional wisdom." It is an attempt to cut a new path toward solving the dilemma of homelessness, to set the Church at the forefront of the issue once again.[43] It presents a "third way," the Scriptural alternative to both humanisms.

But even more than this, it is the chronicle of my personal experience with the homeless. So despite the fact that it contains plenty of statistics and facts and figures, this book is first and foremost a story. It is the story of one Christian's struggle — one churchman's struggle — with this vital issue, for these vital people: the dispossessed.

In Part I, the dimensions of the problem are assessed and ascertained. Who are the homeless? Where did they come from? How many are there? Why has their plight become such a hotly contested political issue? How can conservatives and liberals look at the same data and come up with such dramatically divergent perspectives?

In Part II, the various causes of homelessness are examined. Why are so many of the dispossessed "mentally ill"? Why have the numbers of women on the streets increased so dramatically? What roles have urban renewal, rent control, the farm crisis, and the federal welfare system played in either aggravating or alleviating homelessness? And what about alcohol? Are most of the street people just a bunch of unredeemable winos and derelicts?

In Part III, solutions to the problem of homelessness are addressed. What does the Bible say about hapless, helpless sojourners in our midst? What are our responsibilities to them, and how can we implement appropriate care? What is the possibility of real and tangible success? Can what has worked in the past be adapted to present circumstances?

Finally, in Part IV, the Biblical hope for the future is established. Jesus said that the poor would be with us always. Will the homeless always be with us as well? Can the policies, trends, and movements that put thousands and even millions out on the street be controlled or reversed? What will the future bring?

A Way Out

At the end of our conversation, Sean Ballard looked at me with woeful eyes and said, "There's got to be a way out for people like me. There's just got to be."

Her gaze pierced me, through and through.

"Yes," I agreed, "There's just got to be."

PART ONE

LIFE ON THE STREET

Faust: First, I will question thee about hell. Tell me, where is the place that men call hell?

Mephistopheles: Under the heavens.

Faust: Ah, but whereabouts?

Mephistopheles: Within the bowels of these elements, where we are tortur'd and remain for ever: Hell hath no limits, nor is circumscrib'd in one self place; for where we are is hell, and where hell is, there must we ever be: and to conclude, when all the world dissolves, and every creature shall be purified, all places shall be hell that are not heaven.

Faust: Come, I think hell's a fable.

Mephistopheles: Ay, think so still, till experience change thy mind.

Christopher Marlowe
Doctor Faustus, Act X

Over that art
which you say adds to nature, is an art,
that nature makes.

William Shakespeare

ONE

THE DRAWING OF THE DARK: A PERSONAL LOOK

The snow fell in flurries. Dusting the door stoops and flocking the storefronts, its crystalline whiteness seemed somehow to bestow a pristine purity on the busy street corner.

Covering over the ugly, obscuring the dull, and taming the pretentious, the damp blanket began to transform midtown Manhattan before my very eyes. Were it not for my feet, aching and raw from three days' calculatedly aimless wandering, I might have actually taken pause to marvel. Were it not for the blustery cold, cutting mercilessly through my thin and ragged jacket, I might have actually reveled in the wonder of it all. Were it not for my soggy socks, my chafing skin, my weary limbs, and my wary disposition, I might have actually enjoyed it.

The moist flakes twinkling past New York's neoned hustle and bustle cast a spell of transfixing beauty over the entire cityscape. But I had no eyes for beauty. The dispossessed seldom do.

My homelessness was supposed to be a pose. An act. A temporary accommodation to journalistic integrity. But somewhere along the way, I had crossed the threshold of tolerance. The ordeal had torn me from my aloof vantage and plunged me into a mirthless daze.

Just then though, a lyric, luxuriant refrain drifted across the hard edge of my tiredness. It was an odd verse to recall in this dismal moment. Odd consolation. "And he pitched his tent having Bethel on the west and Ai on the east: and there he builded an altar" (Genesis 12:8). The words rang in the hallows of my disquiet and calmed me. Ever so subtly.

Like Abraham, I had staked a bivouac between the "house of God" and the "house of man," if only for three days.

I was in New York for the sake of research. I was "undercover." Having donned filthy, ill-fitting clothes, grown a scruffy, scraggly beard, and taken to the streets, I was attempting to infiltrate the ebon and tuberculin world of the homeless. I ate with them. I slept with them. I wandered the urban Negev with them. I cast my lot with them, if only for three days.

I had become convinced that in the past five years, as I had worked with the poor, and especially with this unique sub-sect of the poor, I had really only scratched the surface of their world. And I needed to go deeper. I needed to know more. I needed to see more.

So, here I was.

If only for three days.

Like Abraham, I was straddling two realities. I was camped between Bethel and Ai. I had sojourned between promise and plague. I was caught amidst the wild fracas: blessing versus cursing, good versus evil, covenant of life versus covenant of death.

If only for three days.

In this moment it was consolation to see the Abrahamic parallel. It was confirmation.

"Quite a sight, ain't it? Nothin' like a spring snow. Beautiful, huh?"

I turned to meet the eyes of one of New York's finest. He was beaming.

"Puts everyone in a glorious mood. Thankful just to be alive."

"Yeah, I guess so," I replied, "thankful just to be alive."

So, This is Home

My baptism into street life had come just seventy-two hours earlier. The airport transit bus from Newark, after struggling through turnpike traffic and Lincoln Tunnel congestion, dropped me off with a dozen or so shuttle commuters at the Port Authority terminal, just blocks from the Hudson River. That first night I would sleep in the West End YMCA, but I had a lot of territory that I needed to stake out in the few remaining daylight hours, so I immediately took to the street. I wanted to make certain that my time in New York was fruitfully spent. I would catalog, map out, and prioritize the sites that seemed to me to be the most promising for research, for interviews, and for investigation.

At least, that was the plan.

The first sight that greeted me was a street fight. A small crowd had gathered in front of an addict rehabilitation center called Daytop Village to watch two emaciated black youths lunge and slash at each other with cheap gravity-blade knives. The onlookers seemed to divide their attentions between the petty struggle before them and the prospect of a hustle around them. They made for a motley crew.

Pimps bedecked in gold chains and gaudy velour, widebrimmed hats, and $200 Italian shoes preened along the edges of the crowd while their girls seduced the young and the vulnerable. "Party babe? Show ya' a real good time. How 'bout it, hon? Come on, handsome."

Several teens wove in and out of the spectators peddling everything from pot to heroin. "Got coke, man. Good coke. Ludes. Reefer. Dust. You name it man, I got your high. Ups. Downs. Got what ya need. Got it, man. Best price."

Oblivious to this litany of debauchery, two overworn middle-aged men circulated through the disinterested and restless throng, distributing handbills for a new topless bar on Broadway. Most of them fell to litter the sidewalk after only a moment or two.

It seemed as if everybody was working some angle or another.

So, this was Hell's Kitchen.

I moved on, checking the location of several shelters that I might need to return to tomorrow. On West 40th there was The Dwelling Place, a small, 5-story tenement walk-up where a bedraggled contingent of nuns were caring for homeless women, bag ladies. Two blocks away was Covenant House, a large immaculate haven for teenage runaways. And three blocks from there was The Lighthouse, a shabby old mill converted into a storefront mission to alcoholics and derelicts. I watched broken souls listlessly wander in and out of each of them and a dull and aching dread washed over me. Tides of apprehension.

I crossed over to 42nd and made my way toward Times Square. It was almost dusk now, and the streets were just starting to come to life. A garish kaleidoscope of flashing lights mixed with the wheedling jive of hawkers and the choked cacophony of rush hour. From 9th Avenue to the ticket island on Broadway, I counted twelve porno shops, three live sex theaters, seven peep show parlors, and fourteen X-rated movie houses. There were twenty-two bars, all full, and seven shops specializing in "street gear": knives, chains, chukka sticks, belo balls, handcuffs, machetes, ninja stars, slam jacs, and cudgels.

My head was swimming. I could scarcely take it all in. This would be "home."

Crazy Red Basque

Seven o'clock Mass is a popular attraction for the homeless on cold mornings. St. Patrick's Cathedral is the first warm building to open anywhere in New York. So, though I was reluctant to leave my spare but comfortable accommodations at the YMCA, I knew I'd best be there on time, if I were to meet up with any of my new compatriots.

The cold cut through me like a knife. And the sidewalk slush soaked quickly through my old shoes. I noticed several men rousing themselves from park bench slumber as I passed through Central Park, their mounds of blankets and overcoats obviously soggy from their overnight ordeal. The sight sent frigid shivers up and down my spine. And I walked on, anxious for the warmth and the solace of St. Patrick's.

The huge bronze doors admitted me to the cathedral's insular domain: vast aisles, soaring cross vaults, magnificent stained glass, thousands of sputtering, flickering candles, and incongruently, several dozen homeless men and women scattered here and there among the other early morning patrons. I stood, gawking at the sight.

"So. You need a tour guide, or what?"

Startled out of my wonderment, I turned to face my inquirer. I don't know what I was expecting; certainly not what I now beheld. He looked like a derelict Santa, long white beard matted and stained, jolly countenance scarred and weather-beaten.

"Red Basque," he declared, thrusting his unwashed and calloused hand toward me in greeting. "Crazy Red Basque, they call me. You Catholic, or just gettin' warm?"

"Uh, . . . just getting warm," I replied as I took his hand.

"You're green. I can always tell. New to the streets. That's why I made the offer."

"The offer?"

"Tour guide. Show you the ropes. A few tips. Trade secrets. All that."

"Oh, I see. Well . . . thanks."

Red was a ten-year veteran of the streets. So he really knew the ropes. In the next few hours I would learn more about homelessness than I had in five years of serious research — a gift of insight given me in the house of God.

He showed me the best places to eat, to sleep, and to pass the time of day. "They say beggars can't be choosers. They's wrong."

He guided me through the labyrinthine steam tunnels running under Park Avenue, long known on the streets as a hobo's haven. "This is the one place jackrollers is at a disadvantage. Us skels has got 'em over a barrel here."

He taught me how to bypass the subway turnstiles and pointed out all the most lucrative scams, hustles, and cons. "Just don't mess with the books or the montes."

And he warned me away from the public shelters and the horrid welfare hotels as well. "You got a better chance at makin' it on the streets. It's safer."

Red had worked for the city in the parks and recreation department for six years. "But then the city went bust and they laid me off. City's okay now I hear. Now's just me that's bust. Me an' all the other skels."

After a hearty lunch scrounged from a restaurant wholesaler's surplus, Red bade me farewell. "Got me business to attend to. Stay away from the shelters. See ya at Mass, huh?" And he was off, checking the pay phones for forgotten quarters, checking the trash barrels for abandoned treasure.

I never saw him again.

Third Street Men's Shelter

Despite Red's insistence, I knew that I needed to visit the public shelters. I wanted to see for myself the vineyards where today's grapes of wrath are stored. So, I made my way toward the Bowery on the lower east side.

After only a few blocks, I decided that I just couldn't walk another step, so I opted for the subway. A ragged man was working the southbound No. 2 train, cadging change. He stumbled down the aisle, shoving his dixie cup under every nose. At the Times Square Station, a putrid-smelling, vacant-looking man asked commuters for a nickel as they climbed the stairs to 42nd Street. In the lee of a doorway at Town Hall, an old fellow in a knitted cap, with a paper sack containing an empty Thunderbird bottle at his feet, addressed the ambivalent passers by with the plea, "Help. Help me out." It seemed everywhere I looked, at every station, the dispossessed were posted like sentinels, watchmen on the walls.

It was midafternoon by the time I reached New York's main intake center for homeless men, at 8 East 3rd St. It provides meals for about 1,500 people every day and shelter for about 3,000 more. On this day, cold and wet as it was, the building was full to overflowing. Men greatly outnumbered chairs.

Up the front steps and to the right — past a man reading aloud from a Gideon New Testament, and several hucksters peddling loose Marlboros for a nickel, and over two men sprawled asleep on the linoleum — was the end of a long line that I took to be admissions. A paralyzing fear rose up in my throat as I looked up and down the line. It was as lost a collection of souls as I could have ever imagined. Young and old, fit and lame, they were uniformly pathetic. Grimy from head to toe, scratching, wheezing, and moaning, they were here as the final resort, the last stop in a long downward spiral. They shuffled across the floor, littered with styrofoam cups and old newspapers, at a snail's pace. But they were unbothered by the wait. They had nowhere to go.

The air was heavy with a powerful stench. Thunderbird wine, urine, sweat, stale tobacco, vomit, marijuana, and disinfectant. It was stifling. Overwhelming. I had to force myself to take a place in line.

After about an hour I reached the glassed-in partition. I traded a bit of biographical information for a voucher: a three-by-five card with my name, a case number, and a stamp good for ten days' food and shelter. The clerk then pointed me toward another, more crowded line which was slowly making its way fifty feet across a dayroom and down some dark, filthy stairs to the basement cafeteria.

As I passed into the large open space at the bottom of the stairs, a cook handed me a plate over the steam table. I was pleasantly surprised. Warm, filling, and good, the meal consisted of two slices of white bread with two pats of margarine, rice, chopped beets, some kind of stew with a few pieces of meat and a good many beans, over-sweetened coffee, and for dessert, two stewed prunes. Several security guards patrolled the cafeteria, and diners who sat too long in front of empty plates were urged out the door and back onto the street. I finished in less than ten minutes.

I felt refreshed and was beginning to wonder why Red had been so wary. But then I heard a ruckus in the street. A huddle of broken humanity watched from the doorway as three young black street toughs—jackrollers—accosted an old derelict. They threw him down into a frigid puddle of slush and began rifling his pockets. A few coins spilled out onto the asphalt. The old man was whining and pleading and covering his head, but the jackrollers continued to pound him mercilessly. No one made a move to help. I was horrified and began to shout for the security guards. When I turned back around, the jackrollers were casually picking up the coins and turning to leave. Happy-as-you-please. The old man was slumped, bloody and unmoving beneath a sign that read, "CLIENTS: PLEASE DO NOT DISTURB THE NEIGHBORHOOD." Still, no one made a move to help. I was flabbergasted.

"So what's the problem, Bub?" A security guard had finally made his way over to where I was standing.

I excitedly related the entire incident. The guard's bored expression never changed. It was as if this sort of thing were an everyday occurrence.

It is.

"Okay, okay. So don't get your bowels in an uproar, Bub. Everything's cool."

"Look!" I exclaimed, "If you're gonna catch the guys that did this, you're gonna have to hurry! They can't have gotten far yet! Just around the corner!"

The guard just chuckled. "Right!" he said. "Just around the corner!" Then he turned to the gawking onlookers and shouted, "Okay, skels. Outta here. Move on. Everybody waitin' for the buses, up to the second floor. Let's go. Move on."

And that was it. We were shuffled off like cattle, while the old man in the street continued to lie there, untended and unnoticed.

Hell's Color

Once again on the second floor, there were many more men than chairs, so there was a lot of sitting on the stairs and slouching against the walls. One wizened and irascible old codger seemed especially disturbed by the close quarters. He shook his crutch and traded immensely profane insults at those who came too close. Another, in a drunken stupor, stumbled and fell down a flight of stairs, hitting his head against a radiator. No one even looked up. Still another proceeded unabashedly to urinate on the wall. He had been mumbling nothing much at steadily increasing volumes, and this vile act of exhibitionism and bravado seemed to be his last-gasp attempt at securing the room's attention. Still, no one even blinked an eye. No one noticed. Resigned, the man quietly retired to a vacant spot against the wall.

I scanned the stuffy room. I scrutinized every face. The untouchables. America's pariahs. Surplus. Disposable.

They all looked groggy and bleary-eyed — some apparently from drink, some from drugs, some from lack of sleep, many from all three. Most seemed so ravaged by illness, addiction, madness, and sheer neglect that I could not imagine them ever making their way back into society's mainstream. They were hopelessly lost. And a dark cloud of misanthropic gloom descended over me.

"Ain't a pretty sight, is it?" The small man beside me had been fidgeting constantly since we'd entered the room. He spoke slowly, hesitantly. "I never knew hell came in this color."

I smiled. Quite a line. Black comedy. But the man remained humorless, looking at me in dead seriousness. He had not meant it as a joke.

Immediately in front of us, one man suddenly grabbed an empty chair and attempted to break it over his neighbors' head. They were shouting and wailing at one another. In my haste to get out of the way, I jostled a sleeping drunk on one side of me, and fell across the small disconsolate man on the other. Everyone was yelling now. I was terrified.

It took almost fifteen minutes for the guards to untangle the mess. The strong bullying the weak. The hale brow-beating the halt. Everyone taking advantage of the scuffle, releasing pent-up frustrations, venting harrowed tensions, jockeying for position.

When it was all over, the small man beside me, obviously shaken, still fidgeting, turned to me. "It's like the soaps. Same damn story every day. Never endin'. Keeps you guessin'. Keeps you hoppin'. Keeps you on edge. Gotta stay on top of it or you don't make it. Remember that."

I said I would.

I do.

At Deviant's Palace

Of the nearly 4,000 homeless men who were sheltered by the city that night, only 17 actually got beds at East 3rd street. They were in the infirmary, on the 2nd floor. The rest of us went to one of the five shelters—the Ft. Washington armory (525 men), the Ward's Island asylum (810 men), the Williams Avenue school in Brooklyn (350 men), the 8th Avenue school in Harlem (121 men), and Camp La Guardia (965 men)—or to one of six Bowery flophouses, ranging in population from the Palace Hotel (423 men) to the Stevenson Hotel (62 men).

Transportation to the various shelters was by bus. But the buses didn't arrive until 11 P.M. at the earliest. That meant that I would have to wait in that second floor tinder-box of humanity for another four hours. At least. Then and only then would I be allowed to take my vermin-infested cot for the night. And that was a prospect that I just couldn't bear. So I decided to go downstairs and put in for a transfer. I could walk to the flophouses—they were all right there in the Bowery—and thus get a good start on a full night's sleep.

The clerk downstairs looked at me as if I had a hole in my head. "You sure you wanna transfer, man?"

I nodded "yes."

"Okay, man. It's your neck." He reassigned me to the Palace and gave me brief directions.

The Bowery at night is not exactly what you'd call a "nice neighborhood." In fact, it is not all that hot in the daytime either. For most of our nation's history its name has been synonymous with skid row, and for good reason.

As I walked in the frigid night air to the Palace, I noticed that the commerce in the district was limited almost exclusively to pawn shops, liquor stores, resale shops, hole-in-the-wall saloons, firetrap flophouses, and a few dive restaurants. Along the way I passed a dozen or more men sprawled out on the sidewalk amid shards of broken bottles. Several had no coats or jackets. Two were barefoot. But they seemed beyond caring.

The city-contracted dormitories occupied two floors of the Palace. The rooms appeared to me to be a jumble of furniture: dilapidated beds, broken down metal lockers, torn mattresses, and a few bare-spring chairs. The smell was overwhelming, worse even than the East 3rd Street reception room. My head began to reel.

I could barely see — four dim light bulbs provided the only illumination in my room, perhaps 40 by 80 feet. But I could see enough to know that I would not care to spend the night here. No matter how tired I was. No matter how desperate. Many of the beds had no mattresses, the naked metal rack covered only with a scrap of carpet or a piece of corrugated cardboard. Those that did have mattresses were black with dirt and grime and pockmarked with innumerable cigarette burns. There were no sheets or blankets or pillows in sight. But perhaps worst of all, the whole room was literally crawling with lice. Vertigo gripped me.

I couldn't get out of there fast enough.

Now I understood what Red was getting at when he warned me against the shelters and flops.

He was right.

You're better off taking your chances in the streets. It's safer.

I took the subway back to uptown and checked into the YMCA. I immediately proceeded to take the longest and most strident shower of my life.

The dirt, the grime, the grit, and the grease of a hard day on the streets washed down the drain. But try as I might, I could not wash away the memory. Try as I might, I could not sanitize my psyche.

Where the Shadows Fall

I slept fitfully that night. Dark dreams danced morbidly on the distant horizons of my shallow unconsciousness.

Dark voices: "Fiery the Angels fell . . . deep thunder rolled around their shores; burning with the fires of Orc."[1]

Dark visions: "I've seen things . . . seen things you wouldn't believe . . . Attack ships on fire off the shoulder of Orion bright as magnesium . . . I rode on the back decks of a Blinker and watched C-beams glitter in the dark near the Tanhauser Gate . . . All those moments . . . gone . . . like tears in the rain."[2]

Dark vagaries: "Home again, home again, jiggedy-jig. Good evening, J. F."[3]

I woke with a start.

The next morning I was up and out early — out where the shadows fall — out where pitches beck and call.

The snow had turned to drizzle, sloppy and wet. I salvaged a copy of the *Times* from a dumpster near the Julliard School and after a quick glance at the headlines — "Reagan Readies for Summit," "Two Men Leap from Empire State Building," "AIDS Increases Toll" — I tucked it into my shirt for insulation. Still, it was cruelly cold.

I began simply to wander. Quite aimlessly. I no longer adhered to a plan. I had no goal. I had no reason to be anywhere at any time. I was beginning to fit into my element. I tried not to think about it.

On the Upper West side I saw a homeless man dangerously dodging traffic in the center of Broadway tracing imaginary designs in the sky with a splintered old cane.

In a small park near the Hudson River piers, a homeless woman lay sprawled out on a handball court madly babbling to herself — or to some invisible spirits — with soiled and tattered gardening gloves tied to her otherwise bare feet.

In Central Park a homeless man stood still and silent, staring intently into blank space, for how long I'll never know — I grew impatient and drifted on after about 20 minutes.

Along 5th Avenue a homeless man accosted strangers with dire warnings that "sidewalk gamma radiation" was endangering their lives, their very existence. He approached me with a knowing, confiding wink. "Ethyl methane sulfonate is an alkylating agent," he whispered to me, "a potent mutagen. It creates a virus so lethal . . . so lethal . . ." he trailed off momentarily, ". . . and look at them . . ." he waved his arm toward the throngs of commuters, "they're totally unaware." He shrugged and returned to his dutiful warnings.

On the Staten Island Ferry I met a homeless woman who waxed philosophical about "life, the universe, and everything."

Her garbled dissertation ran from the genius of Mozart to the hazards of Mediterranean fruit flies, from the liberal bias of Dan Rather to the parasitic fleas carried by Atlantic gulls. In summary she gazed into the sky, grey and mottled like cigar ash, and said, "But to have a place to sleep, warm and dry. That's the onliest thing. That an' havin' someone to love who'll love you back. That'd be even onlier."

My final 36 hours on the streets became a collage of such chance encounters — encounters that moved me, shook me, frightened me, compelled me, hurt me, and exhausted me.

When at long last it was time for me to return to Newark for my flight home, it was snowing again. I traded my street disguise for my regular clothes and immediately felt refreshed.

It was then that my mind returned to ponder the Abrahamic parallel, "And he pitched his tent having Bethel on the west and Ai on the east . . ." and I remembered the policeman's commentary, ". . . thankful just to be alive."

It was quite late when I arrived home. The house was warm and dry. I would sleep soundly. Thankfully. "That's the onliest thing," I thought. Karen, my wife, had tried to wait up for me. She groggily wiped sleep from her eyes and gave me a welcoming embrace. And I realized, "That's even onlier."

The further one travels
    the less one knows
For in the Duende Dancehall
    agony unmasqued bestows
A ghostly gleam
A mystic sheen
To all the breadth, the depth, the pall
    in sinful minds reshow.

William McAllister

DUENDE DANCEHALL: THE CRISIS

They have always been with us. They are with us still.

Shriveled and weatherbeaten, dispossessed vagrants begged for alms from passing pilgrims outside ancient Ephesus. Today those same timeworn faces and pleading hands can be found along Fifth Avenue in New York, still thirsty for wine.

Disoriented and feebleminded, dispossessed ragmen pillaged the grimy alleyways of eighteenth century Vienna. Today, those same desperate and delirious souls collect tattered bits of rubbish in cherished shopping bags on Peachtree Street in Atlanta.

Bruised and abused, dispossessed women slept in the dreary haunts and sewers of Victorian London. Today, those same broken lives bed down along Colfax Avenue in Denver, still alone in the cold and the dark.

Wild-eyed and atrophied, dispossessed waifs scoured the nightside markets of 19th century Paris ever alert for a hustle, a con, or a debauched jaunt. Today those same youngsters, riven with rootlessness, cruise Castro Street in San Francisco, like flies on parade.

Homeless and hopeless, dispossessed farmers fled depression-racked Oklahoma in droves, only to huddle together in ramshackle "Hoovervilles" and labor camps down the San Fernando Valley. Today, those same discouraged and disillusioned families crowd into tin-and-tent towns along the bayous and under the bridges in Houston.

They have always been with us. They are with us still.

And ironically, they seem to be with us in greater numbers than at any time since the Depression.

Anecdotal suspicion has given way to irrefutable evidence. Social service agencies and institutional charities around the country are swamped beneath an avalanche of need. And this, despite a blossoming economic recovery and unrivaled unemployment lows. From New York to California soup lines are longer, beds are being filled up more quickly, and there are more people living on the streets.

New York City provided shelter for twice as many families in 1983 as they did in 1982.[1] In 1984 the need doubled again.[2] And in 1985, those numbers rose astronomically, doubling every four months.[3] In Los Angeles shelter requests rose 10% in 1983, another 20% in 1984, and still another 20% in 1985.[4] In Detroit, despite the recovery and surging auto sales, soup kitchens and shelters are reporting a startling 70% increase in emergency aid over the last four years.[5] And in Milwaukee, reported homelessness rose 50% during the same period.[6]

"From California to the New York Island, from the redwood forest to the Gulf Stream waters. . . ."[7] The story is virtually the same. No region has been spared. Scattered throughout the land like so much cast-off and unsightly litter, they are with us still. In our alleyways, warehouses, and public parks, they are with us still. Crowded into tent cities, living out of the backs of cars, under bridges and in abandoned buildings, they are with us still.

The situation has grown to crisis proportions.

In Chicago, where in 1984 sixteen out of every one thousand home loans were in some stage of foreclosure[8] and rental evictions were the highest in the nation,[9] homelessness claimed an estimated 20,000 to 25,000 individuals.[10] And according to the director of the city's Emergency Services Department, "the numbers are increasing" not decreasing, as time goes on.[11] "We are finding more and more people," he says, "who live on the streets involuntarily."[12]

In New York the situation is equally dire. The city currently shelters more homeless adults than it did in the depression spring of 1932.[13] According to most estimates there are between 30,000 and 36,000 people living on the streets on any given night.[14] "You can't go anywhere in the city without being forcibly confronted with their existence," says one shelter operator. "They are everywhere: the bag ladies in Grand Central Station, the drunks in the bowery, the indigent musicians along Broadway, the lame, halt, and blind around Washington Square, the beggars down in the subways, and the angry young street toughs up in Harlem. You can't get away from them. They are everywhere."[15]

In Washington, D.C., the fact that the President's nearest neighbor on Pennsylvania Avenue is a shuffling, twisted, filthy shell of a man sleeping fitfully on a sidewalk heating grate has become epigrammatic of the problem.[16] He, and the other 10,000 to 13,000 displaced and dispossessed like him in the nation's capitol, symbolize the magnitude of the problem.[17]

It is a national problem.

"Homelessness is a massive epidemic," a congressional committee report declared recently, "so overwhelming that the problem must be treated as a national emergency."[18]

According to George Getschow of the *Wall Street Journal*, "Across the United States, tens of thousands of families and individuals . . . have joined the ranks of the homeless, jobless, and dispossessed."[19] He goes on to say, "A recent report by the U.S. Conference of Mayors says thousands of families have been evicted from their homes and are living in cars, campgrounds, and rescue missions."[20]

The motley ranks of America's homeless have swollen to outlandish proportions. In Cincinnati, where according to the City Housing Assistance Program 29% of the citizens were found to be in need of sheltering aid,[21] there are approximately 2,000 homeless men, women, and children.[22] In Tulsa, a city that has boasted one of the lowest unemployment rates in the nation, homelessness has continued to climb to an estimated 1000 persons today.[23] Denver has gone from boom to bust and back again so many times over the last decade that the fallout and shakeout has resulted in a homeless population of about 2,500.[24] Cleveland, where the Salvation Army has been forced to open five new soup kitchens just since 1982, all in predominately blue collar neighborhoods, is facing a homeless population of nearly 1,500.[25]

"Sunbelt" cities, especially hard hit by the exodus of workers from the "rustbelt," face catastrophic conditions. Houston has between 15,000 and 20,000 homeless.[26] Santa Monica has 3,000.[27] Orlando has 3,000.[28] San Antonio has 23,000.[29] Atlanta's first shelter opened its doors to the homeless in 1979.[30] Now the city has twenty-seven different operations.[31] Salt Lake City's mayor complains that his city has become a "blinking light" for dispossessed transients.[32] In Tucson and Phoenix, officials are worried about the hoards of vagrants that have descended on Arizona.[33] And state officials in regions as wide-ranging as Oregon[34], Texas,[35] Florida,[36] and Vermont[37] have been forced to entertain legislation to deal with tent cities, skid row encroachments, and embarrassingly public vagrancies.

The director of New York State's Office of Mental Health recently asserted that homelessness is "the single greatest problem . . . facing us today."[38] Sociologist Ira Bolston, in his seminal work on transience concurred saying, "If we fail to deal with this dilemma we may find social policy in the nineties entirely stymied, economic capacities mercilessly paralyzed, and cultural productivity dramatically undermined."[39] And political analyst Ray Wittengsten has argued that "homelessness is a national disgrace of monumental proportions. More disconcerting even than Watergate, Koreagate, and Abscam is the fact that millions of our citizens—the hungry and haggard, the restless and ragged, the displaced and disenfranchised—wander our streets, bent and twisted by the downward curve of dispossession and desperation."[40]

The Numbers Game

Other than the seriousness of the current crisis, there is little about homelessness that can be established irrefutably—not the causes, not the solutions, and certainly not the exact numbers. In fact, the issue of how many people *really* are down and out in the U.S. has become one of the hottest topics of contention in recent memory.

Some say that there may be as many as three million.[41] Others harrumph that a more reliable range would be between 250,000 and 350,000.[42] Liberals and homeless advocacy groups quite predictably tend to favor the former estimate, while conservatives and government officials tend, with equal predictability, to favor the latter.[43]

The discrepancy in figures is due to more than simple ideological disparity however. The task of measuring an undocumented and transient sample is subject to myriad obstacles and difficulties. And according to Ellen Baxter and Kim Hopper, researchers for the Community Service Society of New York, even the most meticulously obtained figures are "subject to wild discrepancies depending upon the methods of estimation used, the source of the figures, the time of the year, and . . . the purpose for which the numbers are put forth. The kinds of living arrangements defined as 'homeless' may also vary considerably, adding a further element of uncertainty, and making historical and cross-regional comparisons hazardous."[44] Is it any wonder then that social scientists are more prone to play percentage point ping pong than they are to attempt to arrive at workable solutions to the problem?

But, as Heritage Foundation policy analyst Anna Kondratas has argued, "Sound public policy requires that we have some reasonable idea of the scope of a problem before we attempt to rectify it."[45] That is why, despite all difficulties and uncertainties, studies are continually conducted. And that is why, despite all our reservations and hesitations, we must take each of those studies into account as we try to bring focus to the issue of homelessness.

Probably the two most important surveys of homelessness conducted of late are those of the U.S. Department of Health and Human Services (HHS), and the U.S. Department of Housing and Urban Development (HUD). Of the more than one hundred and some-odd additional studies of homelessness over the past five years,[46] these two have proven to be the most representative, the most respected, and the most often cited.[47]

The HHS report concluded that advocacy groups were probably not far off the mark with their two to three million "guesstimates,"[48] while the HUD report, released just six months later, concluded that the low range figure of 250,000 to 350,000 "was more likely."[49]

So, which was right?

In all probability, *both* studies accurately measured their samples. It is just that they measured two *different* samples, thus highlighting two *different* aspects of the homelessness problem.[50]

The HHS study was conducted in the dead of winter when most of the homeless are driven indoors by the elements. Crowded into soup kitchens, storefront missions, and public shelters, the normally dispersed and mobile population of the dispossessed were then accessible and countable.

The HUD study, on the other hand, was conducted during the late spring. All but the most infirm and disabled of the homeless had by that time vacated the shelters for the freer domains of the parks, the streets, and the highways. And many, unable to work in winter, were reemployed shortly after the spring thaws in agricultural, resort, or construction jobs.

The HHS study was based upon the records, estimates, and projections of service providers and advocacy groups. Any and all benefits rendered to clients considered "homeless" were included in the overall count. Definition of terms was left to the discretion of the providers.

The HUD study, in contrast, was based upon literature reviews, interviews with local experts, and spot site counts. Limited resource or service allotments were not included in the overall count and definition of terms was enforced uniformly without regard for varying local conditions.

The HHS study had no "recurrence pattern" stipulation and no "cross check requisite" purge, thus leaving open the possibility of considerable overlap: The homeless that alternately frequent more than one agency could be counted more than once.

The HUD, conversely, had rigid "recurrence pattern" stipulations and adhered to careful "cross check requisite" purges, thus eliminating many short term homeless or sporadically homeless from the count. Since as many as 84% of the dispossessed fall into this category, variance could be dramatic.[51]

The HHS study was based upon "actual" counts and projections, city by city. Averages and extrapolations were accepted only for sparsely populated regions where homelessness is generally not at all prevalent.

The HUD study was based upon averaged and extrapolated figures over vast "commercial marketing units" or "metropolitan trade areas," thus inflating the populations' denominator and shrinking the homeless sample.[52]

The short of all this is that the HHS study was prone to measure general, short term, and peak homelessness while the HUD study was more likely to measure specific, long term and chronic homelessness. The HHS study tells us that at any given time, especially during the winter months, there may be as many as two to three million people on the streets. But the HUD study tells us that the vast majority of those people are *not* chronically homeless, that in fact, they will be able to remedy their dire situation in short order. The HHS study tells us that thousands upon thousands of Americans briefly hit rock bottom every year. But the HUD study tells us that only 250,000 to 350,000 never recover from that calamity.

Thus, when considered together, these two seemingly contradictory surveys of homelessness actually bring clarity and definition to the crisis at hand in a way that neither alone could ever bring. Together they provide a profile of the dispossessed heretofore entirely unavailable.

First, taken together the two studies demonstrate irrefutably that the problem of homelessness has reached crisis proportions. There are only 91,000 shelter beds available nationwide.[53] So, even if the most conservative estimate of total homelessness is accepted as normative, at least two thirds of the dispossessed could not come in out of the cold even if they wanted to. "Even with all our shelters open and every bed filled, we're meeting less than half the need," says Betty Knott, who operates a church shelter in Atlanta.[54] The numbers then are incidental. The studies agree: Homelessness is an encroaching crisis.

Secondly, taken together the two studies demonstrate that there are two very different categories of homeless. There are the chronic, hardcore, permanently dispossessed and there are those who have hit the skids only recently, only temporarily. Kim Hopper and Ellen Baxter vividly describe this clear contradistinction in their disquieting book, *Private Lives/Public Spaces: Homeless Adults on the Streets of New York City.* "A tattered appearance, bizarre behavior, belongings carried in plastic bags or cardboard boxes tied with string, swollen ulcerated legs or apparent aimlessness: these are the obvious features which distinguish the homeless from other pedestrians and travelers. But there are also those who have been able to maintain a reasonable good personal appearance and whose behavior betrays no apparent sign of disorder, and they are often overlooked by casual observers. Their presence during late night hours when commuters have gone home and stores have closed, and especially their repeated presence in the same sites days or weeks later, is the only telling sign."[55]

Common sense indicates it. Observation supports it. And the HUD and HHS studies taken together confirm it. There are two very different categories of homelessness.

Chronic Homelessness

The ranks of the chronically homeless are populated almost exclusively by men, usually older white men, most of whom suffer from serious mental or physical disorders.[56] They live in a listless, aimless world, void of hope, ambition, direction, or bonds. It is a world populated by the remnant casualties of pathology, psychosis, perversion, and privation.

As early as 1890, Jacob Riis identified the chronically vagrant as the culprit in 80% or more of the crimes against property and person.[57] In 1960, they accounted for more than 50% of all arrests, and in 1968 for 38%.[58] For the chronically vagrant, life is an endless cycle of arrest, detention, arraignment, conviction, incarceration, release, and re-arrest punctuated only by periodic psychiatric confinements and sprees of drunkenness.

"I've worked with hardcore street people for over 27 years," confided Dr. Ambrose Polk, "and quite frankly, there is very little that we can do for them. Keep them out of trouble, maybe. Keep their medical problems down to a bare minimum. That sort of thing. But as far as long term recovery . . . well, the prognosis is not too terribly good."[59]

According to Dr. Elbert Hillerman, another sociologist who has devoted his carer to the chronically homeless, "It is next to impossible to help anyone who really does not desire help. The most that we can do is to try to protect society from their irresponsible antics, and perhaps more frequently, to protect them from themselves."[60]

He goes on to conclude, "It is indeed fortunate that their numbers are few. Ants always outnumber grasshoppers, the careful outnumber the slothful. Thank God for that."[61]

Temporary Homelessness

Despite the popular conception that most of the homeless are these hardcore vagrants and derelicts, the evidence says otherwise. A vast majority taste only briefly the grapes of wrath. Most were, until the economic and political cataclysms of the seventies, solidly entrenched in the work force, actively pursuing the "American Dream." Many were skilled industrial workers.

"In Tulsa," says Roland Chambless, the Salvation Army Commander there, "most of the people we fed a year ago were derelicts and alcoholics, but today it's unemployed oil field workers, mothers, and small children . . . families."[62]

Sergeant E. D. Aldridge of the Houston Police Department's Special Operations Division has said, "It used to be that most of the homeless on the streets were alcoholics and things like that.

Now, if you talk to them, most seem quite intelligent, middle class types. They're just flat out and down on their luck."[63]

A recent New York City survey of those staying in shelters there found an extremely high percentage of families and first time applicants. The number of families seeking help increased 24% between 1981 and 1982, and then doubled the following year.[64] By the end of 1984 over 3,000 families a night sought such accommodations.[65] The same survey determined that more than half of the homeless were high school graduates with some college.[66] They were primarily middle-aged secretaries unable to find work, or young construction workers who had been laid off due to the soft building market, or department store clerks who had never been unemployed before.[67]

Gary Cuvillier, who operates a family shelter in New Orleans says, "Most of the folks we deal with day in and day out are from the fringe of the middle class. Many owned homes before the big layoffs. None had ever known real want before."[68]

"Lots of long-time indigents are out there in the streets," says Michael Elias, who administrates a shelter near Los Angeles. "But so are a whole new class of people . . . families from Michigan and Ohio . . . middle class people . . . it's a tragedy."[69]

The average age of these temporarily homeless adults has been estimated to be thirty-four.[70] Add to that an additional 300,000 runaway teens and you've got an incredibly young homeless population, hardly what you'd expect.[71]

Clearly, there are two very distinct categories of homeless: the chronically dispossessed and the temporarily dispossessed. The twain meet in the shelters, the flophouses, and the gutters of our cities.

The Bible and the Dispossessed

Not surprisingly, this differentiation in the ranks of the homeless has a direct correspondence in Scripture. It is not simply an artificial sociological determination or an accidental demographic phenomenon that divides the dispossessed into two distinct categories. The distinction reflects a reality clearly delineated by Biblical definition.[72]

According to Scripture, the poor are divided between the "oppressed" and the "sluggardly."

The oppressed are the objects of God's special care.

When Jesus began His ministry, His attentions were especially devoted to the oppressed. He dwelt among them (Luke 5:1-11); He ate with them (Luke 5:27-32); He comforted them (Luke 12:22-34); He fed them (Luke 9:10-17); He restored them to health (Luke 5:12-16); and He ministered to them (Luke 7:18-23). When He summarized His life's work, He quoted Isaiah, saying,

> The Spirit of the Lord is upon Me, because He anointed Me to preach the gospel to the poor, He has sent Me to proclaim release to the captives, and recovery of sight to the blind, to set free those who are downtrodden, to proclaim the favorable year of the Lord (Luke 4:18-19).

But while the oppressed are the objects of God's special care, the sluggardly are the objects of His special condemnation.

Sluggards waste opportunities (Proverbs 6:9-10), bring poverty upon themselves (Proverbs 10:4), are victims of self-inflicted bondage (Proverbs 12:24), and are unable to accomplish anything in life (Proverbs 15:19). A sluggard is prideful (Proverbs 13:4), boastful (Proverbs 12:26), lustful (Proverbs 13:4), wasteful (Proverbs 12:27), improvident (Proverbs 20:4), and lazy (Proverbs 24:30-34). He is self-deceived (Proverbs 26:16), neglectful (Ecclesiastes 10:18), unproductive (Matthew 25:26), and devoid of patience (Hebrews 6:12). A sluggard will die for the lack of discipline, led astray by his own great folly (Proverbs 5:22-23). Though he continually makes excuses for himself (Proverbs 22:13), his laziness will consume him (Proverbs 24:30-34), paralyze him (Proverbs 26:14), and leave him hungry (Proverbs 19:15). A sluggard's wasteful and irresponsible behavior will ultimately land him in the gutter. His moral catatonia will drive him over the edge of responsibility, prosperity, and sanity.

The Christian's Duty

As Christians, we are commanded to show charity and to exercise compassion to both the oppressed poor and the sluggardly poor—to both the temporarily dispossessed and the chronically dispossessed. It is not enough simply to acknowledge their existence. It is not enough to be able to make distinctions between them. It is not enough to compare government studies and Bible verses. We must respond. We must respond charitably.[73]

The Bible tells us that if we obey the command to be generous to the poor, we will be happy (Proverbs 14:21), God will preserve us (Psalm 41:1-2), we will never suffer need (Proverbs 28:27), we will prosper and be satisfied (Proverbs 11:25), and even be raised up from beds of affliction (Psalm 41:3). God will ordain peace for us (Isaiah 26:12), bless us with peace (Psalm 29:11), give us His peace (John 14:27), guide our feet into the way of peace (Luke 1:79), be ever and always speaking to us (Psalm 85:8), and grant peace to the land (Leviticus 26:6).

Of course, charity to the oppressed poor of necessity will be different from charity to the sluggardly poor. Just as we must make distinctions between the various kinds of dispossessed, so we must make distinctions between the various kinds of help we can offer.

Charity to the oppressed involves loosening "the bonds of wickedness," undoing "the bonds of the yoke," and letting "the captives go free" (Isaiah 58:6). It involves dividing bread with the hungry, bringing the homeless poor into safe shelter and covering the naked (Isaiah 58:7). It involves transforming poverty into productivity by any and every means at our disposal.

Charity to the sluggardly, on the other hand, involves *admonition* and *reproof* (2 Thessalonians 3:15; Proverbs 13:18). It involves a reorientation to reality through the preaching of the Gospel (John 8:32). The compassionate and loving response to a sluggard is to *warn* him. He is to be warned of the consequences of immorality (Proverbs 5:20), and of sloth (Proverbs 6:11), of deception (Proverbs 11:24), of boastfulness (Proverbs 14:23), of slackfulness (Proverbs 19:15), of drunkenness (Proverbs 21:17), of gluttony (Proverbs 23:21), and of thievery (Proverbs 28:22). Charity to the sluggardly equips and enables him to move *beyond* dependency, beyond entitlement.

Christians have the responsibility — the inescapable responsibility — to exercise both kinds of charity with all diligence and zeal.

Conclusion

According to President Ronald Reagan, "There is . . . one problem that we've had, even in the best of times, and that is the people who are sleeping on the grates, the homeless. . . ."[74]

Clearly it is a problem that has grown and grown and grown —to monstrous proportions. Just as clearly it is a problem that eludes nice, neat, easy definition.

The worst of it is that this gargantuan, elusive crisis at hand is not just impersonal facts and figures. It is not just numbers. It is not just messy charts and graphs marring the immaculate and impeccable record of our once proud chambers of commerce. This crisis is people. It is people—drawn into a common stew of indignity and sheer animal horror. It is people—mocked and jeered by a kind of devil's comedy. It is people—tossed to and fro by the waves of passion and travail far beyond our imagining, just the flotsam of the general ruin of ugliness and want. It is people—needful not of our speechless pity nor our heart-racked sympathy, but our diligent charity.

There is a crisis at hand.

It demands our best efforts. It requires our greatest care, our deepest commitment and our surest love.

Because "it" is "them."

Let those who care for the interior
    . . . despise and neglect
    All that is without
And raise for their own use buildings
    Shaped to the form of poverty
    Making hay unto prideful debasement.

                        William of St. Thierry

MAKING HAY:
THE U.N. RESOLUTION

The crisis of contemporary homelessness is not limited to the urban centers of the United States. It is a global problem.

In Western Europe, as many as 2 million dispossessed drift around the countryside or wander urban streets, finding shelter when and where they can.[1] One might expect that the European nations with their comprehensive welfare systems designed for cradle-to-grave protection would escape such problems. But such is not the case. In fact, as socialistic policies have become more predominant, homelessness has increased.[2]

According to the European Economic Community's Commission on Poverty and Homelessness there are as many as 10,000 homeless in Paris with a 7% annual rate of growth.[3] Add to that another 35,000 throughout the rest of France and you have a telling indictment of the effectiveness of that country's socialist experiment.[4] West Germany has more than a quarter of a million homeless with a 10% annual rate of growth.[5] Tiny and relatively affluent Denmark has 15,000[6] while Holland has 30,000.[7] Great Britain where the unemployment rate reached 13.6% in 1986 has nearly 200,000 homeless.[8]

"Comparatively few of the homeless in Europe are hoboes or drifters, the sort who might be found on the streets even in the best of times," says Debbie Tennison of the *Wall Street Journal.* "Just as in America, the derelicts have been joined by thousands of young people who have never held jobs; by people who have worked too little to qualify for unemployment benefits; by self-employed workers who have gone bankrupt; by released prisoners and mental patients; and by people who, even with government benefits haven't enough income to hang on to their homes."[9]

"More and more middle-aged people lose their jobs and then

can't pay their mortgage," notes Bob Widdowson, director of The Shelter National Housing Aid Trust in London. "And young people leave home and have no place to go. It's certainly gotten worse in the last eighteen months."[10]

As in America, homelessness in Europe has reached crisis proportions.

The Third World's Trauma

If the state of affairs in the U.S. and Western Europe seems dismal, the plight of many Third World nations is downright depressing.

It is now conservatively estimated that one billion of the Third World's two-and-a-half billion people do not have permanent housing.[11] Of these, approximately 100 million have no housing whatsoever.[12]

In Latin America, nearly 20 million dispossessed children and youths live and sleep in the streets.[13] In the cities as many as 50% of the inhabitants live in cardboard and tin squatter settlements.[14] Mexico City has almost 550,000 homeless squatters.[15] Rio de Janeiro has 700,000.[16] Lima has 400,000.[17] And Bogota has 140,000.[18]

The future offers little hope that the squalor of these homeless settlements will improve. In fact, the rapid urbanization of the Third World makes "hope" seem an absurd notion altogether. It is estimated that by the year 2000, approximately one in two Third World inhabitants will be living in cities.[19] What this means is that in less than fifteen years, the population of those cities will more than double — from 900 million to 2.1 billion.[20] Of these more than 2 billion urban dwellers, about 500 million will be living in sixty cities of more than 5 million inhabitants.[21] And the population of a few of those already humongous cities will bloat beyond the bounds of even the wildest imagination. Consider for instance that, if present trends continue, by the year 2000, Mexico City will have 31 million inhabitants,[22] São Paulo, 25.8 million,[23] and Bombay, 16.8 million.[24]

Where will they all then live?

Many will have to settle for a cardboard box or a tin hovel amidst the mud, waste, and squalor of a shanty town slum. Many will have to settle for even less than that.

A Harvest of Wrath

Even more dismal than the horrid specter of Third World and Western European homelessness is the vast hoard of homeless refugees, set loose on the seas of uncertainty by political oppression.

Besides the more than 150 million people who have been slaughtered outright by communist governments the world over,[25] another 6.5 million have been exiled from their tortured and imprisoned homelands.[26]

More than 1.5 million Cambodians died in torture camps, resettlement compounds, and random executions when the Communists seized control of their country in 1975,[27] while another 500,000 escaped only to find themselves impounded in refugee camps with thousands of exiles from the other captive communities of Asia: Vietnam, Laos, China, North Korea, South Yemen, and Afghanistan.[28]

The Soviet Union and its satellite states in Eastern Europe have exiled more than 2 million of their citizens.[29] A full 10% of Cuba's population have fled Castro's reign of terror.[30] At least 225,000 Nicaraguans have been forced out of their homes by the Sandanista insurgency.[31] And in Ethiopia, where the communist government deliberately created famine conditions in order to stifle freedom fighters in the provinces, not only have over 250,000 starved to death,[32] but another 1.2 million have been forcibly resettled by the government,[33] and still another 900,000 have poured over the borders into Chad, Djibouti, and The Sudan.[34]

Despite all the barbed wire, closed borders, guard towers, restrictive travel policies, and comprehensive police surveillance that the communist prison states have instituted, people desperate for freedom continue to breach the iron curtain at an astonishing rate. To risk death, privation, and homelessness is apparently a risk that millions are willing to take.

The U.N. Declaration

Recognizing the monstrous proportions of global homelessness, the United Nations' General Assembly designated 1987 as the International Year of the Homeless.[35] According to the U.N. Center for Human Settlement office in Nairobi, the purpose of the year—and the "application and implementation" years to follow—is to "highlight the plight of the millions of people with no home—the pavement dwellers, those who must sleep in doorways, subways, and urban recesses . . ." as well as those "hundreds of millions of others who lack a real home—one which provides protection from the elements; has access to safe water and sanitation; provides for secure tenure and personal safety; is within easy reach of centers for employment, education, and health care; and is at a cost which people and society can afford."[36]

The Commission on Human Settlements office in Istanbul was more forthright about the goals of the year, saying that the Secretary General's office would work to "ensure political priority and commitment" to implement a "globally prescribed set of options" utilizing "the coordinated force of the United Nations Children's Fund (UNICEF), the World Health Organization (WHO), the United Nations Center for Social Development and Humanitarian Affairs (UNSDHA), as well as the United Nations Center for Human Settlements (HABITAT)."[37]

Interestingly, the U.N. plans to focus the brunt of that force on the U.S. According to Leland Burns, a professor in UCLA's graduate school of architecture and urban planning, the U.N. declaration will be received primarily "as a call for ways to deal with the rapidly growing numbers who live unhoused in the U.S.'s cities."[38] He says that the reason the U.N. plans to level all its political clout on the U.S. is that "Private institutions and governments of the Third World countries . . . have made remarkable progress in attacking the problem. In that respect, they are far ahead of the U.S."[39]

Interesting, isn't it?

Somehow we are supposed to believe that the 250,000 to 3 million homeless in the U.S. constitute a greater failure of public policy than the 100 million to one billion homeless in the Third World. Somehow, we are supposed to believe that the U.N. in its infinite benevolence has nothing in mind here but sheer philanthropy.

Burns concludes saying, "The U.S. response to the U.N.'s admonition 'to insure improvements in the shelter and neighborhoods for all the poor and disadvantaged by the year 2000' may depend on how effectively knowledge gained from the Third World is translated into action."[40]

In other words, the U.N. wishes for the U.S. to adopt for itself "Third World models for helping the homeless."[41]

And what "models" does the U.N. have in mind? The Center for Human Settlements recommends three: the Nicaraguan model, the Sri Lankan model, and the Tanzanian model.[42] These great "successes" are the paradigms the U.N. hopes to persuade us to emulate.

The Nicaraguan Model

The "success" of the housing program in Daniel Ortega's Nicaragua is readily apparent. As of 1984, approximately five years after his Sandanista communists seized power, statistics for the capitol, Managua, showed that more than 20% of the population were still homeless, another 15% inhabited crude slapdash shanties, and a further 30% lived in one-room huts.[43] Before the insurgency, on the other hand, only 8% of the city's population was homeless with another 12% living in sub-standard dwellings.[44]

Quite a record, isn't it? Two steps forward . . . three steps back!

One of the reasons that the Sandanista's "success" has been so dramatic is that immediately upon ascension to power, the regime reduced rents in the capitol by 50% to 60%, with high standard housing being rented at up to 5% of its fiscal value per annum.[45] Since such reductions did not even cover the tax base, the Sandanistas were "forced" in many cases to confiscate the properties "on behalf of the tenants."[46] But, with this practical abolition of property ownership in Managua, many properties fell into abominable disrepair and became uninhabitable. In fact, between 1980 and 1986 the housing stock in the capitol has diminished 35% despite a population increase of more than 20%, making for a total shortfall of 55%.[47]

This is what the U.N. calls a "success." And this is the model they wish to foist upon the American homeless.

The Sri Lankan Model

It is not surprising that the U.N. singled the "successes" of Sri Lanka out. It was the Sri Lankan Prime Minister, Ranasinghe Premadasa, who first suggested to the 35th session of the United Nations General Assembly in 1980, that consideration be given to designating an International Year of the Homeless.[48]

The whole idea was his "baby" and he has superintended the project from its inception.

Premadasa was also the architect of one of the most comprehensive non-Marxist experiments in national socialization in modern history.[49] Serving under the previous regime of Sirimaro Bandaranaike, he moved the small island nation south of India from a parliamentary democracy to a total welfare state with an economy socialized to 90%.[50]

Every citizen, rich and poor, received two "free" kilos of rice monthly from the state. All staples — bread, flour, and sugar — as well as textiles, household goods, and shelter were provided through a massive government subsidy program. Education from elementary school to university, as well as medical care and legal counsel, were provided as citizen entitlements.

By 1977 Premadasa and Bandaranaike's expensive experiment collapsed. The treasury was drained and no more foreign capital could be obtained. And ultimately, the government fell.

Re-aligned with a new party and distanced from Bandaranaike, Premadasa rose from the ashes of his failure and regained power.[51] Immediately he set forth to re-socialize the housing industry. In Colombo, where nearly one-third of the 600,000 residents are either homeless or subsisting in squatter settlements, he initiated three massive urban renewal projects in cooperation with the United Nations Center for Human Settlements.[52] The focus of the projects was not only to provide "improvements to poorly distributed and derelict amenities" but also to insure "regularization of ownership" and "community organization."[53] Translated that means state control of land ownership, the abolition of private property, and the collectivization of urban populations.

Thus far, the projects are still in the "pre-implementation phase" of "deed centralization and clarification."[54] So, despite the rhetoric and the political power plays, the homeless are no better off than before, except that now they cannot claim exclusive rights to the label "dispossessed." They have been joined in that category by former property owners.

Quite a "success."

This is the model the U.N. wishes for us to emulate.

The Tanzanian Model

Over the past ten years, the government of Julius Nyerere has gobbled up $2.7 billion in aid from the U.S. and the World Bank.[55] But apparently the aid has done little to alleviate the dire conditions of Tanzania's poor. Per capita income remains at less than $250 per year for the 20 million inhabitants.[56] More than 90% of those live barely above the level of the stone age.[57]

Even so, Tanzanian "experts" recently joined researchers from Ecuador, Ethiopia, Mozambique, Zambia, Nicaragua, and Sweden to host a five-day U.N. seminar on "successful socialist housing policies" entitled "Gender-Aware Research on Housing in Third World Countries."[58]

It is doubtful that these "experts" mentioned the fact that of the 800,000 residents of the capitol city of Dar-es Salaam more than 600,000 live in unspeakable squalor in spite of (or perhaps due to) universal socialism, the absence of private enterprise, and the negation of property owners' rights.[59] Instead, they probably beamed over the great "successes" in urban renewal that their visionary leader has brought to fruition.

Actually, Nyerere has four major urban renewal projects on the drawing boards. But that's where they've been for the last six years — on the drawing boards — despite expenditures of more than $220 million.[60]

This is the U.N.'s grand-glorious Third World model for alleviating homelessness worldwide.

The Abolition of Private Property

In practical terms what would the adoption of these "Third World models" mean? Perhaps Europe's response can help us answer that query.

Utilizing the U.N. declaration as its platform, the member states of the European Economic Community met in September, 1985, to hammer out specific measures of compliance. The Commission on Poverty and Homelessness adopted a comprehensive legal program that "operates in full cognizance of the Nicaraguan, Sri Lankan, and Tanzanian models."[61]

The program asserted first, that "housing is a fundamental human right," and therefore as an initial step, "the right to shelter — shelter of a minimum standard, without time limit, and in small scale facilities — should be enforceable by law."[62]

Secondly, the program argued that "eviction is contrary to this right of shelter."[63]

Thirdly, the program allowed for intervention in the private sector so that the first two provisions could be enforced. "In situations of housing shortages, the member states must be prepared," the program says, "to intervene in the free market to regulate rents and provide financial assistance to individuals unable or unwilling to pay for private sector accommodation."[64]

Finally, the program called for a comprehensive legal overhaul of member-states: the repeal of vagrancy laws, the decriminalization of trespassing laws, universal legal, medical, psychiatric and educational services, and the establishment of a "minimum social guarantee."[65]

In short, the commission called for the abolition of private property, and the complete socialization of the European Economic Community.

Landlords would no longer be able to set rent values on their properties commensurate with the market. They would no longer be able to protect the integrity of those properties through eviction or selective leasing. And, they would more than likely no longer be able adequately to maintain those properties due to decreased income and increased socially directed taxes.

That is the crux of the Third World models.

And this is what the U.N. wishes for us. This is, for all intents and purposes, the whole reason the U.N. declared 1987 the International Year of the Homeless: to centralize control over property worldwide in general, and to centralize control over property in the U.S. in particular.

Thanks. But, no thanks.

The Origin of the Specious

Clearly homelessness is a serious problem, even a crisis. To advocate reform is certainly commendable. To struggle on behalf of the dispossessed is a worthy cause. But the U.N. has long shown a unique ability to warp worthy causes, twisting them to malevolent ends.

Consider the cause of peace.

The U.N. was founded in 1945 as "man's *last* hope for peace"[66] a purpose somehow more blasphemous than noble. Certainly the maintenance of world peace is a worthy cause. But the U.N. has shown scant interest in its peace-keeping mantle. It has been much more interested in pursuing an agenda of bureaucratic centralism and socialistic globalism.[67] It has been much more interested in making political hay.[68]

So for instance, when the Soviet Union disrupted world peace in Hungary in 1956, in Czechoslovakia in 1968, in Vietnam in 1975, and in Afghanistan in 1979, the U.N. uttered nary a peep. Somehow the diligent peacekeeping delegates in the General Assembly overlooked the brandishments of genocide in Cambodia in 1975, the winds of war in Iran in 1979, the stench of triage in Ethiopia in 1984, and the legions of international terrorism in Libya in 1986.

Why? Because the worthy cause of keeping the peace has been subverted to serve other ends — the ends of a global awareness,[69] a global economy,[70] a global citizenry,[71] and a global government.[72]

Innumerable analysts and historians have long decried the globalist bent of the U.N., asserting that its designs on dissolving national sovereignties and its universalist claims would inevitably militate against its purported peacekeeping intent.[73] According to Paul Johnson, ". . . by the 1970s, the U.N. was a corrupt and demoralized body, and its ill-considered interventions were more inclined to promote violence than to prevent it."[74] Because the U.N. has been so fitfully jockeying for a "New World Order"[75] and "One World Government,"[76] it has simply not had time to play the pipes of peace. Because it has been so terribly busy establishing, subsidizing, and/or advocating organs of international centralization like The World Economic Community, The World Health Organization, the World Food and Energy Council, the World Bank, the World Council of Interdependence, and the World Affairs Council, it has simply ignored the world's hottest hot spots. Because virtually every powerful internationalist institution from the old line Council on Foreign Relations[77] to the New Age Aspen Institute[78] recognizes the U.N. as the perfect forum for the implementation of their disparate humanist ends, world peace has been shunted off the agenda. Thus, as Johnson says, "the U.N. has actually promoted violence rather than prevented it."[79]

The U.N. and its globalist conspirators worldwide have messianic aspirations, and everything, including the cause of peace, has been relegated to the sidelines while the power, influence, and bureaucratic control necessary for the realization of those messianic aspirations are focused and consolidated. World Peace has become, over the years, nothing more than a specious pretext for the establishment of the U. N.'s *real* goal: World Control.

The U.N. Legacy

The U.N.'s messianism, though more often than not veiled, has been evident from the start.

The U.N. charter in its Preamble announces its salvific purpose, declaring that "We the people of the United Nations determined to save . . . have resolved to combine our efforts to accomplish these aims . . ."[80] As R. J. Rushdoony has commented, "Man needs a source of certainty and an agency of control: if he denies this function to God, he will ascribe it to man and to a man-made order. This order will, like God, be man's source of salvation: it will be a *saving* order."[81]

How would the U.N. usher in its "salvation"? How would it bring about its grand "New Age" or "World Order" and "International Unity"? Very simply, it would institute a new canon of law. According to Rushdoony, "The U.N. holds as its basic premise a thesis which has a long history in both religion and in politics, the doctrine of *salvation by law*. It believes that world peace can be attained by world law."[82]

And what is the nature of this salvific law?

It is a law rooted in absolute egalitarianism, first and foremost. As Rushdoony has asserted, "The goal of all humanists, all advocates of the religion of humanity, is the unity and oneness of all men."[83] Thus, anything that divides or stratifies mankind, be it national boundary, economic condition, cultural diversity, or religious exclusivity, is wrong and must be criminalized. The salvific law of the U.N. would level all men everywhere, equally. The rich would be forced to distribute their wealth to the poor. The advanced would be forced to share their technology with the primitive. The blessed would be forced to contribute their advantage to the cursed. The powerful would be forced to dole out their might to the weak. Thus, egalitarian law is, according to Herbert Schlossberg, "The dual effort to raise the lower classes and debase the higher. . . ."[84]

Bowing its knee to the U.N.'s messianism, and obediently

submitting to the rule of this egalitarian law, the General Assembly has consistently and insistently attacked Western industrialized nations as "evil,"[85] and even "heretical."[86] This quickly became a primary test of "U.N. Orthodoxy," says Paul Johnson. "High Western living standards, far from being the consequence of a more efficient economic system, were considered the immoral wages of the deliberate and systematic impoverishment of the rest of the world. Thus in 1974, the U.N. adopted a Charter of Economic Rights and Duties of States that condemned the workings of Western economies. The 1974 U.N. World Population Conference was a prolonged attack on U.S. selfishness. The 1974 U.N. World Food Conference denounced America and other states, the only ones actually to produce food surpluses. The Indian Food Minister thought it 'obvious' they were 'responsible for the present plight of the poor nations,' and had a 'duty' to help them. Such help was not 'charity,' but 'deferred compensation for what has been done to them in the past by the developed nations.' The next February, the 'non-aligned' countries castigated 'the obstinacy' of the 'imperialist powers' in preserving the structures of 'colonial and neo-colonial exploitation' which nurture their 'luxurious and superfluous consumer societies,' while they keep a large part of humanity in misery and hunger."[87] And this, despite the fact that "during the previous fourteen years alone (1960-1973), official development aid from the advanced nations direct to the poorer countries, or through agencies, amounted to $91.8 billion, the largest voluntary transfer of resources in history."[88] The messianic U.N., wielding the double-bladed axe of egalitarian law, would not be satisfied until an absolute leveling of resources had been accomplished — until the West was reduced to the same ruinous chaos as the rest of the world.

This is why, when the U.N. stages International Years, the specious causes to which they are dedicated are nothing more than a pretext, a propaganda platform, for the advancement of the globalist, egalitarian, and messianic crusade.

The International Year of the Woman (1979), for instance, was simply an excuse to bludgeon the already guilt-racked West even more. One prominent feminist asserted: "This entire 'Year' business has proven to be a farce. Sure, there are still inequities and gross displays of unabashed chauvinism here in the West.

But despite these, women here enjoy extraordinary liberty and privilege. Meanwhile, our sisters across the globe suffer vile and grotesque injustices. So what does the U.N. 'Year' address? The problems abroad? The patriarchial oppression in the Third World? No way! The 'Year' has served only to wake us to the reality that the U.N. cares little for justice . . . it's only concern is for the advancement of its own socialistic and internationalistic agenda."[89] The International Year of the Woman was not designed to alleviate the genuinely dire difficulties of women worldwide. It was designed to further the cause of globalism—the cause of U.N. self-aggrandizement.

Similarly, the International Year of the Child (1982) was another propaganda ploy designed to undermine Western societal structures and to reinforce the aims of U.N. centralization. According to Child Welfare advocate Julia Weintraub, "The U.N. declaration has set us back immeasurably. All this attention to child abuse, child snatching, and children's rights is misplaced and misdirected."[90] Almost 98% of all the "missing children" cases, she says, "do not involve madmen rampaging our streets and neighborhoods, but rather conflicts between divorced spouses. That doesn't mean that there isn't a problem. There is. But the public has been propagandized on TV, in the grocery stores, and through PTAs and community organizations to the point that the *real* problem is utterly ignored: the breakdown of the family due to divorce and infidelity. . . . This is a direct result of the U.N.'s declaration and the incumbent media hype that followed the declaration . . . and it has hurt the cause of child welfare. The worst of it is that the U.N. has focused its closest scrutiny on the U.S. and Western Europe . . . as if the Third World and Iron Curtain nations had no child welfare crisis . . . it is absurd."[91] Her conclusion? "The U.N. was aiming at something else besides child welfare with this 'Year.' Perhaps its own political agenda."[92]

It is not at all surprising then, that the 1987 International Year of the Homeless has been similarly twisted. The reason the U.N. wants the U.S. to learn from and adopt "Third World models" is not that its benign bureaucrats actually believe that those "models" will alleviate privation. They are not fools. They know full well that the Nicaraguans, the Sri Lankans, and the Tanzanians have failed, and failed miserably. They want the

U.S. to adopt those "models" as the next step toward the egalitarian destruction of the West.

They want to dispossess us all in the name of the dispossessed.

Conclusion

Homelessness is a global problem. Recognizing that, the United Nations designated 1987 as the International Year of the Homeless. But far from being a benevolent attempt to spur real solutions to that global problem, the "Year" is simply another tool for the U.N. to capitalize on a worthy cause for the advancement of its own ends. The "Year" is simply an opportunity for globalists to make a lot of political hay.

Meanwhile, however, the problem remains unsolved, once again proving that humanism is the most inhuman of philosophies. While the bag ladies of Amsterdam, and the orphans of Calcutta, and the street urchins of Bangkok, and the squatters of Managua, and the refugees of Chad, and the wandering gypsies of Byelorussia languish in utter deprivation, the "advocates" for justice and equality launch ideological diatribes and spawn propaganda campaigns against their anti-globalist adversaries. While 100 million to one billion struggle against the ravages of homelessness in the Third World, they focus their righteous indignation against the U.S., with its 250,000 to three million homeless.

Why? Because the worthy cause of homelessness — like the other worthy causes the U.N. has deemed to champion — has been subverted to serve the U.N.'s own political and messianic aspirations.

PART TWO

THE FACT OF
THE MATTER

Now, what I want is Facts . . . nothing but Facts. Facts alone are wanted in life. Plant nothing else, and root out everything else . . . stick to Facts . . . In this life, we want nothing but Facts, sir; nothing but Facts.

Charles Dickens

Mine is the voice one cannot hear,
That whispers in the darkened heart of fear;
From one shape to another without cease,
And thus my cruel power I increase.

Goethe

FOUR

STILL CRAZY AFTER ALL THESE YEARS: MENTAL ILLNESS

His hand shook with emotion as he scrawled the words across dingy yellow pages in a well-worn spiral notebook.

The wind was a torrent of darkness among the gusty trees, the moon was a ghostly galleon tossed upon cloudy seas, the road was a ribbon of moonlight over the purple moor, and the highwayman came riding—riding—riding—the highwayman came riding, up to the old inn-door.[1]

He cast about, looking, muttering, and gesturing to whom or what I couldn't tell. Then a vacant grin slowly spread over his dull countenance and he returned to his labor.

He'd a French cocked-hat on his forehead, a bunch of lace at his chin, a coat of the claret velvet, and breeches of brown doe-skin; they fitted with never a wrinkle: his boots were up to the thigh! And he rode with a jeweled twinkle, his pistol butts a-twinkle, his rapier hilt a-twinkle, under the jeweled sky.[2]

The stark contrast was obvious at once. At least, it was obvious to most. But not to Raul. He continued to copy. Stanza after stanza, the small blue volume before him yielded up its passions and dramas to the small spiral. His spiral.

Over the cobbles he clattered and clashed in the dark inn-yard, and he tapped with his whip on the shutters, but

all was locked and barred; He whistled a tune to the window and who should be waiting there? But the landlord's
black-eyed daughter, Bess, the landlord's daughter,
plaiting a dark red love-knot into her long black hair.[3]

Raul laughed aloud, drawing the stares of others in the
room. Then with a sudden sober earnestness he scribbled out a
final stanza.

And dark in the dark old inn-yard a stable wicket
creaked, where Tim the ostler listened; his face was
white and peaked; His eyes were hollows of madness, his
hair like mouldy hay, but he loved the landlord's daughter, the landlord's red-lipped daughter.[4]

And with that he jumped up, out of his place, a stack of
books knocked askew. Grabbing his precious notebook and a
green garbage bag containing his every earthly possession, he
moved toward the stairwell as fast as his emaciated frame could
carry him.

I caught up with him one landing down and attempted to
draw him into conversation. But all I got was a snarled solilo-
quy. From Noyes.

Back, he spurred like a madman, shrieking a curse to
the sky, with the white road smoking behind him and
rapier brandished high! Blood-red were his spurs i' the
golden noon; wine-red was his velvet coat, when they
shot him down on the highway, down like a dog on the
highway, and he lay in his blood on the highway with a
bunch of lace at his throat.[5]

The inflection was perfect. But I had no chance to commend
his performance. Wild-eyed he spun on his heel and bolted down
the stairs, his filthy, flopping sneakers snapping sharply on the
white terrazzo.

As I stood there dazed, an incredibly eerie feeling swept over
me, like I'd just been made the brunt of some cruel, cosmic joke
—like I'd just been transported into the Twilight Zone. But this
was no joke. Raul was no jokester.

The New York Public Library is filled with such characters. Or so they say. Schizoaffective. Psychotic. Insane. Somehow though I never expected madness to be so frighteningly, so compellingly literate — Poe didn't occur to me at the moment. I could only think of Raul. I was flabbergasted. Transfixed.

So I set out to follow him. Just as I rounded the corner where the great stone lions stood sentry over the city, I spotted him. He was retracing the familiar route "home": over to the East River, down to the Brooklyn Bridge, in toward the Bowery, and up the stone landing to "The Haven."

It was an old-fashioned "3-S" (soup, soap, sermon) shelter offering "three hots and a cot." It was a dull and dilapidated old brownstone. And it was "home." His home.

Just inside the double-doored entrance, two disheveled old women traded disconsolate mutterings back and forth. Beyond them another thirty to forty lost souls were settling in for the night: shuffling, hacking, coughing, snoring, murmuring, and restlessly rearranging their meager possessions.

"No room," a strong baritone boomed, "No room tonight." And a firm hand spun me around. "No more beds. You'll have to go. Sorry."

He was a giant of a man, well over 250 pounds and standing a good 6′ 5″. Clad in a crisp security guard uniform all bedecked with ribbons and chrome, he struck an authoritative pose.

I quickly explained that I was not interested in a bed, I only wanted a chance to observe the shelter's operation, ask a few questions, and meet a few residents.

He looked me up and down quite doubtfully.

"Just twenty minutes. Give me twenty minutes and I'll be out of your hair."

After a long pause, he nodded a reluctant assent and proceeded to give me a quick cook's tour. The walk through coincided with his nightly inspection and collection, so it wasn't as if I had detoured his duties.

"Medicine check," he announced, as we threaded our way through the building. "Medicine. Right here." Holding a large brown bag open in front of him, he gathered up for the night a vast array of prescriptions — prescriptions for psychotropic wonder drugs to control the demons and delusions that haunted the residents: Thorazine, Stelazine, Lithium, Haldol, Mellaril, and

Prolixin. "Staples in the trade," he confided to me over his shoulder. "Can't imagine where we'd be if we didn't have the drugs to hold them at bay. They're all crazy, you know."

Raul dropped his prescription in the bag as we passed. Glaringly, he called out to me:

> Half a league, half a league, Half a league onward,
> All in the valley of Death rode the six hundred! Forward
> the Light Brigade! Charge for the guns! he said, and into
> the valley of Death rode the six hundred.[6]

The guard just smiled. "That's Raul for you. Yes, sir," he chuckled again, "That's Raul for you. Only talks in poems."

According to all the best estimates, a *large* percentage of all the dispossessed on our cities' streets are feebleminded, insane, delirious, or mad. Like Raul.

In 1980 the homeless men in Manhattan's sheltering system were carefully examined in an extensive study conducted by the N.Y. State Office of Mental Health in conjunction with the N.Y. City Human Resources Administration. The screening, which extended over several days, focused primarily on the psychiatric condition of the residents. The findings were astounding. Fully 70% of the men were diagnosed as mentally disordered to some degree; 60% of them, moderately or severely so and 9% were found to be in need of *immediate* hospitalization.[7]

Similar studies in St. Louis,[8] San Francisco,[9] Philadelphia,[10] Chicago,[11] Boston,[12] Denver,[13] and even in England[14] and Canada[15] confirm those findings. A clear coincidence of chronic homelessness and mental illness is characteristic of the dispossessed everywhere.

The National Institute of Mental Health asserts that at the very least, a third of the nation's homeless suffer from social and emotional dysfunction.[16] The Heritage Foundation,[17] the Community Service Society of New York,[18] and the National Coalition for the Homeless[19] all maintain that the percentage is even higher. "There can be no question," says Arlene Murdoch of New York's Office of Mental Health, "a large majority — a very large majority — of the homeless street dwellers in this nation have lost more than just a place to stay; they have lost their sanity as well."[20]

Raul was 18 when he was first diagnosed as being severely schizophrenic. The doctor gave him a prescription and sent him home to his alcoholic, epileptic, unwed mother. Two weeks later he was back, referred this time by the New York City Police Department. It seems that Raul had been making sport, bashing out the windows in his lower-east-side neighborhood with a flat-head shovel.

The doctor admitted him to the hospital, kept him heavily se-dated for a week, and then released him on his own recognizance. That became a constantly repeated scenario over the next several years. He was in and out of halfway houses, community centers, hospitals, and mental institutions as if they were revolving doors until about 18 months ago when he came under the care of a state mental-health counselor and a psychiatrist. From them he re-ceived the usual regimen of group counseling sessions and anti-psychotic drugs, and seemed to be improving ever-so-slightly. But then last spring, his "case management" broke down: The psychi-atrist transferred to another city and the counselor was promoted to another division. Raul was left to his own wits, such that they were. Thus, for the last nine months he has either been out on the streets or "at home" in the Bowery shelter. In all that time, no one has heard him speak a word of "normal" conversation. Not once. His every utterance is in verse, from poetry that he has committed either to his grubby little spiral or to his thoroughly distressed mind. Coleridge. Byron. Shelley. Keats. Tennyson. Longfellow. Kipling. Shakespeare. Browning. But never himself.

As darkness began to set in, I bid my guard-host at "The Haven" a cordial good-bye and headed back out to the street. Just as I reached the stoop of the old brownstone, Raul incau-tiously poked his head out the door. Then quoth he:

> Oh, East is East, and West is West, and never the twain shall meet, Till Earth and Sky stand presently at God's great Judgment Seat; But there is neither East nor West, Border, nor Breed nor Birth, When two strong men stand face to face, tho' they come from the ends of the earth.[21]

"And goodbye to you too, Raul," I replied. "Goodbye . . . uh. . . ." and I groped for the right words. Then dredged from the recesses, I remembered:

May there be no sadness or farewell, when I embark;
for tho' from out bourne of Time and Place the flood
may bear me far, I hope to see my Pilot face to face when
I have crost the bar.[22]

I suppose my message struck home somehow. Something inexpressible passed between us. Then, obvious glee spread across his face. He chortled happily and ducked back inside. Home. His home.

Deinstitutionalization

Raul is the product of a social service revolution. It is a revolution called deinstitutionalization. It is a revolution now mired in controversy, threatened with catastrophic failure.

In 1955, nearly 50% of our nation's hospital beds were occupied by mental patients.[23] At that time, there were approximately 550,000 people committed in our lock up wards, asylums, and institutions.[24]

Reformers within the psychiatric community felt that the situation was abominable. The quality of care was declining. Recovery rates were abysmal. Criticism was universal. The situation had to be remedied somehow. "Instead of locking them up and throwing away the key," said one early prominent reformer, "we must find and then implement an apparatus of rehabilitation so that they can return to their communities and live out normal non-institutionalized lives."[25]

The reformers, after a long and protracted lobbying effort, finally won the day when in 1963, President John F. Kennedy signed into legislation a comprehensive deinstitutionalization program. The goal of the legislation was naively hopeful, though certainly praiseworthy: release all but the most chronically ill mental patients from state-run asylums, and return them gradually to the community via halfway houses and the like.

Almost immediately the population of mental hospitals was slashed by 75%.[26] As many as 1,000 patients were discharged each day.[27] And new admissions were reduced to rates not seen in nearly seventy-five years.[28] Social scientists ebulliently heralded the program as a monumental success.

It was anything but.

As it turned out, once discharged, most of these mentally ill patients, these thousands upon thousands of emotionally and spiritually debilitated persons, had nowhere to go except the streets.

Only about 7% of those discharged were actually referred to the much-ballyhooed community based care centers and halfway houses.[29] Another 23% returned to their families.[30] But the rest were left to their own devices.

According to the National Institute of Mental Health, only about 290,000 patients are currently cared for in community rehabilitation programs.[31] Another 110,000 receive some kind of short-term treatment in hospitals, while still another 150,000 are permanently committed.[32] But that leaves approximately 1,100,000 others out and on their own.[33]

Is it any wonder then that so many of the homeless in our land are mentally ill? Is it any wonder then that their plight is so pitiful and pathetic?

The Failure of Psychology

The reason deinstitutionalization failed was not simply because the apparatus for care was never adequately implemented. Nor was its failure due to the utter unredeemability of the patients. The failure of deinstitutionalization was very simply the most visible manifestation of a much greater failure. It was the failure of modern psychology.

Deinstitutionalization was largely predicated on the therapeutic power of psychotropic pharmacology and psychotropic psychiatry. Neither has lived up to its high expectations. Both have been shamefully disgraced.

William Kirk Kilpatrick detonated a veritable bomb in the psychotherapeutic community when he wrote, "However good-intentioned and however nice, it is not at all clear that the psychological establishment knows how to help. Everywhere there are dark hints that the faith doesn't work. Despite the creation of a virtual army of psychiatrists, psychologists, psychometrists, counselors, and social workers, there has been no letup in the rate of mental illness, suicide, alcoholism, drug addiction, child abuse, divorce, murder, and general mayhem. Contrary to what one might expect, in a society so carefully analyzed and attended to by mental health experts, there has been an increase in all these categories. It sometimes seems there is a direct ratio between the increasing number of helpers and the increasing number of those who need help. The more psychologists we have, the more mental illness we get; the more social workers and probation officers, the more crime; the more teachers, the more ignorance. One has to wonder at it all. In plain language, it is suspicious."[34]

Here is an establishment psychologist, a tenured professor of educational psychology at a prominent Ivy League University who is actually suggesting that "psychology and other social sciences might be doing actual harm to our society," that in fact they may be terribly "destructive."[35]

The evidence seems to support Dr. Kilpatrick's claims.

As early as 1952, Hans Eyseneck reported that "neurotic people who do not receive therapy are as likely to recover as those who do."[36] Modern methods of psychotherapy, he found, were "not any more effective than the simple passage of time."[37] A flurry of new studies immediately after confirmed his results.

Later, Eugene Levitt of the Indiana University School of Medicine released a study that showed that "disturbed children who were not treated recovered at the same rate as disturbed children who were."[38]

Still later, in the extensive Cambridge-Somerville Youth Study, researchers found that "uncounseled juvenile delinquents had a lower rate of further trouble than counseled ones."[39]

A series of other reports, including the recent Rosenham studies, have indicated that "mental hospital staff could not even tell normal people from genuinely disturbed ones," and that "untrained lay people do as well as psychiatrists or clinical psychologists in treating patients."[40]

As for the "wonder" drugs that psychotherapists have so freely dispensed over the last twenty years, the evidence suggests that they too do more harm than good.

Thorazine, the most commonly used anti-psychotic, anti-emetic agent today, has a whole host of second and third degree effects that patients must endure. It provokes "drowsiness, dizziness, lethargy, a dulling of pain and other conditioned reflexes, increased appetite, blurred vision, diplopia, headache, nasal stuffiness, dry mouth and skin, constipation, urinary retention, hypothermia, peripheral edema, endocrine disturbances, reactivation of psychotic symptoms, bizarre dreams, hyperglycemia or hypoglycemia, convulsive seizures, respiratory depression, and jaundice."[41]

Dartal and Mellaril are two other commonly prescribed anti-psychotic tranquilizers despite similar dangers, as are Stelazine, Lithium, Haldol, and Prolixin.[42] In every case, after prolonged use the "cures" afforded by such psychotropic agents are worse than the "diseases" they were prescribed to control and contain.

With psychology practically and philosophically bankrupt, dependent upon the broken crutch of anti-psychotic drug use and abuse, it is no wonder that deinstitutionalization has been no more successful than previous policies of institutionalization.

The U.N.'s Answer

Mental illness, recognized as "a primary cause of homelessness, especially urban homelessness,"[43] has taken a high profile in the U.N.'s International Year of the Homeless. Naturally, the programs and the literature of the various agencies involved in the "Year" have focused much of their attention on appropriate responses, reactions, and solutions to "the scandal of unleashed and untreated insanity."[44]

So, what do they recommend?

More of the same, of course. Beat the dead horse. Only beat it harder, faster, and more often.

The U.N. recommends re-institutionalization.[45] More psychology. More psychiatry. More anti-psychotic drugs. More of everything that has failed so miserably in the past. And of course, more money to subsidize the whole vicious mess.

This comprehensive re-institutionalization plan was ultimately adopted by the European Economic Community's Commission on Poverty and Homelessness. The plan includes "a basic right" for all citizens "to appropriate medical and psychiatric services, including the right to hospitalization" and comprehensive care that is both "planned and long term, maximizing all-round health and not reliant on short term crisis solutions."[46]

The commission concluded by declaring its support for the U.N.'s mandate that the homeless be treated by a "holistic approach" to mental care, "involving innovative multi-disciplinary, psycho/socio/medico/logical services."[47]

More of the same. Throw good money after bad. If at first you don't succeed, try, try again. Try the same old proven failures again and again and again and again.

The Gerasene Paradigm

Jesus demonstrated to his disciples that there was an alternative to the 'round-in-circles approach to the mentally ill to which the U.N. and modern psychology have committed themselves.

He had just crossed the Sea of Galilee from Capernaum to "the country of the Gerasenes" (Matthew 8:5,28). "And when He had come out of the boat, immediately a man from the tombs with an unclean spirit met Him, and he had his dwelling place among the tombs. And no one was able to bind him anymore, even with a chain; because he had often been bound with shackles and chains, and the chains had been torn apart by him, and the shackles broken in pieces, and no one was strong enough to subdue him. And constantly night and day, among the tombs and in the mountains, he was crying out and gashing himself with stones" (Mark 5:2-5).

The Gerasene was a madman. Homeless. Jobless. Insane. Tormented. Hopeless. Dispossessed.

He had fled his family and friends to live on the fringes of the community (Mark 5:14-17), in the company of others similarly distressed and distraught (Matthew 8:28). He was so out of touch with reality that he not only flagellated himself with rocks and stones (Mark 5:5), but he cavorted about the caves and tombs where he lived entirely naked (Luke 8:27).

A classic schizophrenic. A classic paranoid psychotic. A demoniac.

So, what did Jesus do?

Rather than feeding the problems of the Gerasene after the manner of modern psychology, He confronted them head on. He confronted the demons that had long haunted the man, and exorcised them (Mark 5:8-13). But He didn't stop there. He cut to the heart of the dilemma, to the root problem that opened the man up to possession in the first place.

Whenever fallen men flee from their God- given responsibilities, they devolve into a vulnerable unreality. The farther they get from Him, the deeper they slide into a dark fantasy world of destructive behavior patterns.

All men are aware of the reality and presence of God (Romans 1:21). They are aware of His impending wrath against sin and its perpetrators (Romans 1:18). And they are aware of His Law, extending even to the penal particulars (Romans 1:32).

This awareness is woven into the very fabric of reality: in the warp and woof of creation (Romans 1:20) and in the very consciousness of the human mind (Romans 1:19).

Men cannot get away from this central reality, the reality that undergirds all sanity. But they try, anyway. They run from the truth of God by running from the world and running from themselves. Thus they become irresponsible, destructive, and suicidal (Proverbs 8:36). They open themselves up to oppression and possession (Proverbs 1:10-18; Ephesians 2:1-3; 1 Timothy 4:1-2).

This was the Gerasene's root problem. He had run from his responsibilities to God and his responsibilities under God in order to escape from the inescapable. In the process he had been taken captive by demons and driven to utter insanity. Jesus knew this and acted accordingly.

As Jesus was getting into His boat for the return trip, "The man who had been demon possessed was entreating Him that he might accompany Him. And He did not let him, but He said to him, 'Go home to your people and report to them what great things the Lord has done for you, and how He had mercy on you.' And he went away and began to proclaim in Decapolis what great things Jesus had done for him; and everyone marveled" (Mark 5:18-20).

The man wanted to *continue* his life of irresponsibility by tagging along with Christ's entourage. Long "dead" to his family, having followed a downward spiral of depravity and derangement to the tombs, he now wanted to perpetuate that revolt against maturity. Under the cover of religious devotion he wanted to proceed unabated with his frivolous, devil-may-care, unreliability.

Jesus refused his request.

Instead, He prescribed a simple, yet comprehensive, rehabilitation program for the man. First, he was to return home and take up his responsibilities. And second, he was to bear testimony of the grace and mercy of God.

The Word of Christ had freed him of the demonic enslavement. It had brought him to his senses, returned him to his right mind, and reoriented him to reality. But as miraculous as that first step was, it was only the first step in the Gerasene's recovery.

He needed to be rehabilitated through the discipline and routine of family life, through the reinforcement and encouragement of community life.

And he needed to comfort others as he himself had been comforted, by the Word of truth.

To the modern ear this plan for the treatment of chronic mental illness seems naively simplistic. (For a more detailed study of the Gerasene story and its relevance to schizophrenia, see Appendix 2). And yet the most technologically advanced testing has borne out time and time again that this "nouthetic therapy" based upon the Gerasene paradigm not only works, but it works phenomenally well.[48]

In a study conducted by the Lafler Institute for Psychopharmacology, nouthetic therapy was compared to "traditional" psychotherapeutic treatment for the severely psychotic. The patients who received no psychoanalysis, no psychiatric care, no drugs or psychotropic agents, but only "pastoral counseling" and "rehabilitative discipleship" had a 62% higher recovery rate than those treated "in accord with standard psychiatric operating procedures."[49] The study defined rehabilitative discipleship as . . . "confrontational and ethical discipline. The evangelical pattern of admonishment, encouragement, and community participation . . . as drawn from Scriptural analysis. . . ."[50] In other words, the "nouthetic" control group was turned over to local churches where their psychoses and delusions were confronted with the reality of God's transforming Word and God's reinforcing community.

And it worked. Better than the best that the professionals had to offer.

The various and sundry U.N. agencies charged with directing the International Year of the Homeless want nothing to do with the Gerasene Paradigm. Most professionals have never heard of it. And too many pastors have never thought to make use of it, either. The same study conducted by the Lafler Institute revealed that only 24% of all the pastors contacted in an eight state region "had even the slightest acquaintance with rehabilitative discipleship . . . or utilized even the most rudimentary fashion . . . of Biblical counseling in the course of their regular parish ministry."[51]

"All Scripture is inspired by God and profitable for teaching, for reproof, for correction, for training in righteousness, that the man of God may be adequate, equipped for every good work" (2 Timothy 3:16-17). Only the Bible can tell us of things as they *really* are (Psalm 19:7-11) because only the Bible faces reality squarely, practically, completely, and honestly (Deuteronomy 30:11-14). Thus, only the Bible can illumine genuine solutions to the grave problems that plague mankind (Psalm 119:105).

Counseling can appropriately and successfully be accomplished *only* within the Church, says Dr. Franklin Edward Payne, "because Scripture contains the only principles which truthfully govern life (Romans 12:2). Unbelieving psychotherapists and their theories represent 'conformity' to the 'foolishness' of the world (1 Corinthians 1:20). As such, they cannot perceive the obvious, elemental truths of Christianity: it is necessary to be 'born again' (John 3:5-8) and given a 'new heart' (Psalm 51:10); only the Spirit can illumine the mind (Judges 16:12-15; 1 Corinthians 2:12-14); the believer is able to live a transformed life only because of the indwelling Spirit (Philippians 2:12); and the Scriptures contain all that is needed to be 'thoroughly furnished unto all good works' (2 Timothy 3:16-17)."[52] And finally, says Dr. Payne, "The unbelieving counselor cannot pray for or with his client, nor can he use the spiritual resources of the Church."[53]

Technology, modern medicine, scientific advancement — they are all useful tools for the advancement of Christian civilization, but ultimately the ground upon which they all rise or fall, succeed or fail, is the Word of God. We can ply all the tools in the world on the desperate minds and lives of the mentally ill homeless, but without the application of the Gerasene Paradigm, without the Word of God, we are doomed to frustration. There is simply no other way to readjust the dispossessed to reality.

The Legacy of the West

Western culture has always anguished over the problem of how to care for the "moonstruck" — the "lunatic."

During the Middle Ages, the feebleminded were usually cared for in monasteries or at the large cathedrals where they would be given simple chores in exchange for room and board.[54] Surrounded by the community of faith, they adhered to daily disciplines, upheld personal responsibilities, and were continually taught, admonished, and encouraged by the pious fellowship of the saints.[55] In addition, their days were governed by the liturgical clock — Matins, Lauds, Prime, Terce, Sext, Nones, Vespers, and Compline — so that they were nurtured on a steady diet of the Word of God.[56] In other words, they were cared for "nouthetically," according to the Gerasene Paradigm.

With the gradual disintegration of the monastic movement during the early days of the Reformation came a gradual shift in the way the feebleminded were cared for. In the great revival cities of Germany, Switzerland, and Scotland for instance, the mentally infirm were most often cared for in the homes of pious merchants or tradesmen. Again, in exchange for apprentice chores and other simple tasks, the feebleminded would be provided room and board and a productive life within the community of faith. In addition, with the great Reformation emphasis upon family responsibility and family sanctity came a new level of family commitment to the "moonstruck." This trend carried over to the American continent and formed the basis of care until very recently.

Thus, contrary to popular notions, asylums, almshouses, and other institutions have *never* been the primary means by which Western culture has cared for its mentally ill.[57] Instead, the Church has always spearheaded a personal and "nouthetic" approach, discipling, rehabilitating, confronting, and encouraging, so that the feebleminded could take their place in the onward march of God's Kingdom in time.

Institutionalization, deinstitutionalization, and reinstitutionalization are all aberrations, historically, philosophically, and practically.

Conclusion

Deinstitutionalization is a scandal. But then, virtually every other modern means of treating the mentally ill has been equally scandalous.

There is only one proven effective means of rehabilitating the severely psychotic. But it takes care. It takes time. It takes energy. It takes commitment. It takes vast, vast reserves of love, joy, peace, patience, and kindness. It takes spiritual vitality, Biblical fidelity and the willingness to overcome adversities and setbacks over the long haul.

In short, it takes the Church, the Christian community, willing to do what it has been called to do.

And that's a lot.

You've come all this way; is it not true? So then, what is all this business about? Whence come the slanders that have been spread concerning you? Tell us the truth of it that we may not lightly judge your case.

Plato

FIVE

YOU'VE COME A LONG WAY, BABY: FEMINISM

Up until eight years ago, Kathi Tannenbaum was a traditional homemaker. She had dedicated herself to building a comfortable life with her husband Jacob and her son Aaron. For twenty-two years, she was the epitome of the committed and caring wife, mother, and housekeeper. She had a good life.

But then one day Kathi's whole world caved in. Aaron was killed in a tragic automobile accident and Jacob took to drink for consolation. "We were both devastated, of course. But Jake just never seemed to recover. He went deeper and deeper into his own dark little world and just shut me out," she told me. "We became strangers."

Three months after the accident, Jacob sold the family's small electrical supply business and two weeks after that he filed for divorce. "I just couldn't believe what was happening to us," Kathi said. "Grief . . . upon grief."

But that wasn't even the half of it.

The judge awarded Kathi an equal property settlement, but she was unable to demonstrate that Jacob had any other assets than the three-flat Brooklyn brownstone that had been their home for ten years.

"He had a fantastic lawyer and they were able to shelter the business assets. I didn't get a dime," she lamented, "and since New York has a no-fault divorce law, I wasn't entitled to any alimony."

Suddenly, at age 43, Kathi Tannenbaum was alone. She had

no job. No job history. No job skills. No job leads. No job references. Nothing.

Her share from the sale of the brownstone came to just under $45,000. But after paying her half of the back debts, she was left with a mere $39,000. And with that, she was to start a new life.

Kathi immediately moved into a small, one bedroom apartment and went to work as a waitress in a Brooklyn Kosher deli. She made about $900 a month, including tips. Jacob meanwhile, had quit drinking, gone back to the electrical supply business, and had remarried. His annual income returned to his pre-divorce level—nearly $65,000 a year—and he and his young new wife purchased a home in the Long Island suburbs.

"I'll admit it right off. I became very bitter at that point. Very bitter. Why he should have been able to just pick up and carry on as if nothing had happened just escaped me. Yes indeed," she said, "I was bitter."

Then, *she* began to drink for consolation. "At first, it was just a bit of sherry at night. But before long, I was hitting the bottle pretty hard."

When her work began to suffer, Kathi sought psychiatric help. "The doctor gave me some tranquilizers and listened to me ramble, but he never really gave me anything tangible. He never really gave me any help. I just decided, to hell with it. To hell with it all."

I met Kathi in the Riverside Clinic, a rehabilitation center in New York's upper west side that specializes in indigent women. "I just woke up one day in a welfare hotel and realized that I was on the road to becoming one of those shopping bag ladies. I was out of money. I'd lost my apartment and my job. I was a total mess. I thought, 'What's a nice Jewish girl like me doing in a place like this?' I decided then and there I was going to get the help I needed. Somehow. I was going to rebuild my life."

She checked herself into the Riverside program and began the long and arduous task of returning to the mainstream. "I'm still bitter. And that's something I'll have to continue to deal with. I know that it was my own irresponsibility that got me into trouble. The alcohol and all. But even so . . . it seems to me that women have been led down the primrose path. We've fought so hard to be 'liberated.' To be 'equal.' And here to find out, all that 'liberation' has only earned us more pain and more heartache. I wish to God that . . . well, I wish that I'd just known then what I know today. I feel used."

Martin LaTallia, director of the Riverside Clinic, told me that indeed, Kathi *had* been used. "Fifty years ago a situation like Kathi's simply could not have existed. But the social revolution ushered in by the womens' movement 'equalized' our institutions and expectations to such a degree that virtually all the social support systems designed to protect women were removed. You could almost say that feminism has actually backfired."

The Feminist Failure

The feminist movement *has* backfired. Just ask Kathi Tannenbaum. Instead of liberating women in America, it has set them back a generation or more.

Economist Sylvia Ann Hewlett has argued in her groundbreaking critique, *A Lesser Life: the Myth of Women's Liberation in America*, that "modern American women suffer immense economic vulnerability. They have less economic security than their mothers did."[1] A bevy of serious papers,[2] articles,[3] and books[4] have shown beyond any shadow of a doubt that feminism has done much more harm than good. It has broken down traditional family structures. It has contributed to epidemic irresponsibility. It has diminished courtesy, respect, and commitment. It has opened a pandora's box of social ills, not the least of which is the progressive impoverishment of the very women it was supposed to liberate.

Evidence of the feminization of poverty everywhere abounds. 70% of today's women in the labor force work out of economic necessity.[5] More often than not, they are single, widowed, or divorced.[6] And more often than not, they are poor. A full 77% of this nation's poverty is now borne by women and their children.[7]

The number of poor families headed by men has declined over the last fifteen years by more than 25%.[8] Meanwhile, the number of women who headed families below the government's official poverty line increased an alarming 38.7%.[9] Thus today, one in three families headed by women is poor, compared with only one in ten headed by men and a mere one in nineteen headed by two parents.[10]

According to the 13th annual report of the President's

National Advisory Council on Economic Opportunity, "All other things being equal, if the proportion of the poor in female-house-holder families were to continue to increase at the same rate as it did from 1967 to 1978, the poverty population would be composed *solely* of women and their children before the year 2000."[11] As it stands today, nearly one fifth of all the homeless are women,[12] 6,500 of those in New York City alone.[13]

Virtually every plank of the feminist platform has backfired, precipitating an economic catastrophe of astounding proportions for American women: abortion on demand, equality in the workplace, casual sex, and easy, no-fault divorce. Each has led inexorably to the feminization of poverty.

Abortion on Demand

It is now widely recognized that every abortion involves two victims: the murdered unborn child and the mutilated, uninformed mother.

Recently the Centers for Disease Control conducted a study of maternal deaths and discovered that abortion is now the sixth most common cause. The results of the study, released in the May, 1985, issue of *Obstetrics and Gynecology*, admitted that those abortion-related deaths may be under-reported by as much as 50%.[14]

According to a Johns Hopkins University study, nearly 20% of all mid-trimester abortions result in serious genital tract infections.[15] And in a study conducted by two UCLA OB/Gyn professors, this means that "abortion can be a killer. This is pelvic abscess, almost always from a perforation of the uterus and sometimes also of the bowel. . . ."[16] But even if the infections and abscesses do not prove to be fatal, they can cause serious and permanent medical complications. According to one physicians' findings, "infection in the womb and tubes often does permanent damage. The Fallopian tube is a fragile organ, a very tiny bore tube. If infection injures it, it often seals shut. The typical infection involving these organs is pelvic inflammatory disease, or PID."[17] Another physician, writing in the British Journal of Venereal Disease, noted that this occurrence affected nearly 15% of all those who submit to induced abortion.[18]

Other medical complications of abortion include sterility (as many as 25% of all women receiving abortions);[19] hemorrhaging (nearly 10% of all cases require transfusions);[20] viral hepatitis (occurring in 10% of all those transfused);[21] embolism (in as many as 4% of all cases);[22] cervical laceration, cardio-respiratory arrest, acute kidney failure, and amniotic fluid embolus (occurring in as many as 42.6% of all Prostaglandin abortions).[23] Clearly, though abortions have been legalized, they have hardly been made safe.[24]

Besides the nearly twenty million children slaughtered on the altars of convenience since 1973 in the U.S., untold thousands of mothers have been harmed irreparably in the abortuaries of our land.[25]

As a result, abortion has necessitated a massive increase in the cost of medical care for women in America. While the average costs of normal health maintenance for men has increased nearly 12% over the last eight years due to inflation, the average costs for women have skyrocketed a full 27%.[26]

Such is the cost of feminism: the loss of health and the loss of financial stability.

Ruthie Jaimenez was twenty-two when she had her first abortion. Eight months later, she had another. "The first one went okay I guess," she told me. "I mean, there was a little bleeding and some pain for the next few weeks, but then everything seemed fine."

But things weren't quite so fine with the second abortion. "They did what they call a 'D and C.' Kinda like scraping the baby out. Well, this time they scraped more than just the baby out."

Ruthie required two units of blood immediately, due to heavy hemorrhaging. Her uterus had been punctured. Infection quickly set in. Scar tissue in the cervix from the first abortion was further damaged. Even so, after a few hours, Ruthie was sent home.

That was four years ago, and Ruthie has yet fully to recover. In the process, she has been in and out of the hospital seven times. She lost her job. She was dropped from her insurance. And she had to give up her apartment.

"I was told that abortion was the only responsible choice in my situation," she said. "And now look at where I am. My life is ruined. Nobody told me I'd be imprisoned forever by this. Nobody told me abortion wasn't safe. Nobody told me nothin'. If this is womens' lib, I want nothin' to do with it."

Equality in the Workplace

It sounded like a good idea. It seemed as if it were the only fair thing to do. "Equalize the workplace," the feminists argued, "and women will have better opportunity."

But they were wrong.

Equality in the workplace has worked *against* women in innumerable ways. "Besides the loss of the social advantages that chivalry has traditionally afforded women," says business analyst Hardin Caplin, "the equalization of working conditions and benefits has stripped them of maternity leave options, sick child allowances, and day care considerations."[27]

"All the *special* benefits, allowances, and considerations that women once had in the workplace have been eliminated in the name of equality," Richard Levine, professor of social economics at Midwestern University, confirmed. "But equality in wages has never materialized, probably because without those benefits, allowances, and considerations women are perceived as risk liabilities; they are perceived as less reliable than their male peers."[28]

Equality, then, has been a two-edged sword, slashing at traditional womens' benefits and at the same time slashing at the wage scale. The terrible economic liability of this "sword of justice" is all too evident. Since 1960 the number of women in the workplace has doubled.[29] Fully 45% of the U.S. labor force is now female.[30] Even so, the gap between male and female earnings has only narrowed 1% in the last half century.[31] According to Sylvia Hewlett, "in 1984 the median earnings of women who worked full time year-round was $14,479, while similarly employed men earned $23,218. A woman with four years of college still earns less than a male high school drop out."[32]

Employers justify the wage gap, saying that whereas men can be counted on to pursue career goals regardless of family circumstances, women are 70% more likely to quit mid-career to tend to some crisis at home.[33] "Maternity leaves, sick child allowances, and daycare considerations once provided employers with a bit of insurance against the permanent loss of women employees," says Caplin. "But now with equalization and the removal of these special womens' benefits, employers simply can't be sure that women will be a good return on their investment."[34]

Feminism's demand for *absolute* equality in the workplace has not only adversely affected benefits for women, it has also stymied advancement. Despite the enormous expansion of the female labor force in recent years, only 7% of those women have advanced to managerial positions and only 10% earn more than $20,000 a year.[35] In 1984, 25% of all full time working women earned less than $10,000 a year.[36] Promotions are few and far between. And what about advanced education, where advancement for women might seem easiest? Well, after extensive documentation and statistical evaluation, Thomas Sowell in his book, *Civil Rights: Rhetoric or Reality* concludes: "In short, after several years of 'womens' liberation,' laws and lawsuits, women's proportion of doctorates was [in 1970] *almost* up to where it had been nearly half a century earlier."[37] So much for advancement!

Today as many as 45% of all the women in the labor force are single, divorced, separated, or widowed.[38] Because of their low earning power and lack of upward mobility, 35% of them fall below the poverty line.[39] Clearly they are in dire need of an advocate. And just as clearly, feminism is *not* that advocate.

Lucy Makowski was passed over twelve times in nine years for the management of a convenience store on Manhattan. "It would infuriate me to no end to have to train my own boss. But the company figured I was too unreliable, what with havin' five kids an' all. Unreliable! What a joke. I work for nine years and never miss a day! But y'know, it's typical. Same ol' jive. Somethin' ol' Gloria Steinem and Helen Gurley Brown can't relate to."

Clearly, the struggle for equality has wrought more inequality than ever before. "Whenever we attempt to muddy the distinctions—the God-given distinctions—between men and women, it is always the women who ultimately lose," argued 19th century journalist Peyton Moore.[40] As he so often did, Moore spoke with prophetic clarity. Feminism backfired.

Casual Sex

The womens' liberation movement helped to usher in a sexual revolution. Sloganeering for "free love," "sex without commitment," "recreational sex," and "casual sex," the radical feminists helped create a new sexual ecology that has fundamentally altered American society. Sex outside of marriage is now considered "normal."

There have been a number of unexpected results. Herpes. AIDS. Teen pregnancies. Family disintegration. Women-headed homes. Illegitimacy. Male irresponsibility.

According to the Department of Health and Human Services' National Center for Health Statistics, in 1985 more than 55% of all black children in the U.S. were born out of wedlock.[41] In 1940 only about 15% were.[42] In some cities, that percentage is even higher: 80% to 90%.[43] In 1965, only one out of four black families was headed by a woman.[44] Today, almost half are headed by females.[45]

This crisis of illegitimacy is not restricted to minority communities. 13.8% of all white births were to teenagers.[46] The birth rate for unwed white women rose by 25% in the decade from 1969 to 1979.[47] The increase for minority women was a comparatively modest 3.2%[48]

The sexual revolution spawned a situation where men freely accepted the pleasures and privileges of intimacy without having to accept any of its responsibilities. Women were left holding the baby.

"My boyfriend jus' uses me," says Aileen McDowell. "I know that. But that's the way men is . . . these days. Leastwise here in the projects."

I looked around the playground where her four small children cavorted gaily with several other "project" kids.

"I love my kids . . . but I gets bitter. Why does I have all the responsibility? Why does I have t'raise 'em? All by m'self? Why's he get t'love me an' leave me like that?"

Casual sex requires no responsibility. It is consequenceless. For men, that is.

Another feminist backfire.

Easy No-Fault Divorce

As devastating as abortion on demand, equality in the workplace, and casual sex have been to women, the easy no-fault divorce has proven to be far and away the most destructive "achievement" of the feminist movement.

Feminists fought long and hard to have divorce laws follow "gender-neutral rules"—rules designed to treat men and women "equally." In 1970, California capitulated to their demands and introduced the no-fault divorce. Before that time every state required "fault-based grounds for divorce."[49] Some kind of marital fault had to be demonstrated—be it adultery, abandonment, or cruelty—before a divorce could be granted. The California law changed all that. Within ten years every state but South Dakota and Illinois had followed California's lead.

The practical result of this legal and marital revolution was that divorced women, especially older homemakers and mothers of young children, were deprived of the legal and financial protections that they had traditionally been provided. More often than not, that translated into economic deprivation. According to Lenore J. Weitzman, in her book *The Divorce Revolution: The Unexpected Social and Economic Consequences for Women and Children in America*, "on the average, divorced women and the minor children in their households experience a 73% *decline* in their standard of living in the first year after divorce. Their former husbands, in contrast, experience a 42% *rise* in their standard of living."[50]

Thus, argues Weitzman, "the major economic result of the divorce law revolution is the systematic impoverishment of divorced women and their children. They have become the new poor."[51]

In 1940, one out of every six marriages ended in divorce.[52] Forty years later, 50% of all marriages ended in divorce.[53] And demographers are now estimating that by the year 2000, that figure might increase another 16 to 20%.[54] With no-fault divorce laws in place, depriving women of alimony, child custody support, or appropriate property settlements, we can expect the feminization of poverty to continue to escalate exponentially.

"You've come a long way, baby," is the epigram that feminists have adopted for their movement. It is all too apt. Women have come a long way. They have come a long way down the road to ruin.

Feminism has backfired.

Kathi Tannenbaum knows that now. She learned the hard way.

"When Jake left me, I figured I'd be okay. I figured life would go on. I figured the courts would make him take care of me for all the years I'd put in making a home for us." She choked back a sob. "I figured wrong."

Feminism has backfired. Instead of advancing the cause of women, it set them back more than half a century. It feminized poverty. As Mary Pride has asserted, "Today's women are the victims of the second biggest con game in history. (The first was when the serpent persuaded Eve she needed to upgrade her lifestyle and 'become like God.')"[55]

The U.N.'s Answer

Recognizing the alarming trend toward the feminization of poverty and the close correlation of the trend to homelessness, the U.N. has convened several workshops and seminars to examine the problem and to propose solutions.[56] "The International Year of the Homeless," says one brochure, "is of necessity an exploration of womens' issues due to the feminization of the problem."[57]

Though most of the seminar transcripts and reports are garbled to the point of unintelligibility by bureaucratese — sentences like, "Structuralized functionalism represents both a continuance of, and a departure from, functionalistic structuralism,"[58] — it is evident that most of the delegates favored rigid adherence to radical feminism's old party line.

Virtually all of the recommendations that came out of the meetings revolved around four major topics: "population control" (translate: "abortion on demand"),[59] "institutional access and infrastructure services" (translate: "equality in the workplace"),[60] "environmental, moral, and personal self determination" (translate: "casual sex"),[61] and "displacement recalibration" (translate: "easy no fault divorce").[62]

Same song, second verse. The logic is simple enough to decipher: "walk by faith, not by sight." Despite the fact that feminism has backfired, despite the failure of the entire program, U.N. loyalists hang on to the old creeds and dogmas of the faith with all the tenacity of a pack of pit bulls.

Do women have an advocate on earth who can plead their cause?

Widows and Orphans

Unfortunately, even the Church has failed to plead their cause effectively. As Sylvia Ann Hewlett and others[63] have argued, the Church has thrown women to the mercy of "two powerful and antagonistic traditions. The first is the "ultradomestic fifties"[64] with its powerful "earth mother cult";[65] the other is "the strident feminism of the seventies with its attempt to clone the male competitive model."[66]

The Church has failed to integrate carefully the glorious calling of women to "keep the home" (Titus 2:5) with their Kingdom mandate to "go to the uttermost" (Acts 1:8) "taking dominion over the earth" (Genesis 1:28; Matthew 28:19-20). Thus women are forced to choose a humanism of the right or a humanism of the left. The beauty of Biblical balance is left unmentioned and unknown. Women—and especially Christian women—have been "sold a bill of goods" says Mary Pride.[67]

And at a price they could ill afford. It has left many of them widows and orphans, finding themselves in the howling wilderness.[68]

But such has not always been the case in the Church.

Care for women caught in the clutches of poverty, homelessness, abandonment, widowhood, and distress is a central sign of faithfulness to God. According to Scripture, God Himself is their advocate.

"The Lord lifts up those who are bowed down; the Lord loves the righteous. The Lord watches over the sojourners; God upholds the widow and the fatherless" (Psalm 146:8-9).

But God doesn't simply leave it at that. He expects His covenant people to take up that advocacy as well: "You shall not afflict any widow or orphan" (Exodus 22:22). "Seek justice, correct oppression; defend the fatherless, plead for the widow" (Isaiah 1:17). "Religion that is pure and undefiled before God is this: to visit orphans and widows in their affliction, and to keep oneself unstained from the world" (James 1:27).

From Elijah (1 Kings 17) and Elisha (2 Kings 4) to Boaz (Ruth 4) and Moses (Deuteronomy 14), God's people have always shown the authenticity of their faith by caring for women and children in distress. Admonitions and illustrations of such occur repeatedly throughout the Bible: in Genesis,[69] in Exodus,[70] in Leviticus,[71] in Numbers,[72] in Deuteronomy,[73] in Ruth,[74] in 1 Samuel,[75] in 2 Samuel,[76] in 1 Kings,[77] in Job,[78] in the Psalms,[79] in Proverbs,[80] in Isaiah,[81] in Jeremiah,[82] in Ezekiel,[83] in Zechariah,[84] in Malachi,[85] in Matthew,[86] in Mark,[87] in Luke,[88] in Acts,[89] in 1 Timothy,[90] and in James.[91] The message is inescapable: God's people are to take up the cause of the orphan, the widow, the mother, the woman in travail. The Church is to be the dam, holding back the rampaging waters of destruction, the waves of the feminization of poverty.

God didn't tell the state to halt the demise of woman's place in society. He told the Church to.

The Legacy of the West

Despite much feminist rhetoric to the contrary, women in Western Civilization have always been held in the highest regard. Rarely have they been reduced to the kind of pauperism and deprivation that they are facing today. And when they were, it was due primarily to great political, social, economic, or philosophical upheavals, soon to be corrected. The Scriptural foundations of the culture necessitated reform whenever inequity became apparent.

In the fourteenth century the simultaneous transformations wrought by defeudalization and mercantilism were calamitously aggravated by a scourge of panic, famine, and death when the bubonic plague swept over Europe.[92] Between one-quarter and one-third of the entire population perished and another third was displaced.[93] Women especially suffered, widowed and without the protection of either the feudal manor or the mercantile guild.[94] But within two decades, due to the combined efforts of the Church and the "wheels of commerce," women were once again brought under the protective cover of society, honored as "the weaker vessel."[95]

The great worldview shifts in the fifteenth century with the onset of both the Reformation and the Renaissance, and in the eighteenth century with the onset of the Industrial Revolution brought great difficulties to women and their children.[96] But again, the surging Christianization of Western culture quickly remedied the basest abuses and set into motion reforms that quelled the rising tide of the feminization of poverty.

During the Reformation for instance, the great charitable works established by Calvin in Geneva and Knox in Scotland quickly spread throughout the continent of Western Europe and reached deep into Eastern Europe and portions of Asia and Africa as well.[97] And the great revivals sparked by Whitefield and Wesley in the eighteenth century catalyzed massive cultural and legislative reforms—in England through the sponsorship of Wilberforce[98] and in America through the sponsorship of Webster and Clay.[99] Due to the activism of the Church and the high profile of Scripture, orphans, widows, and destitute women were cared for and protected. Affluence was certainly never the norm, but then neither was the feminization of poverty.

If Western history can be taken as any sort of guide then, the pauperization of women today is an indication that first, we are in the midst of a major cultural and philosophical transformation — our civilization is being fundamentally altered; and second, the Church is simply not doing her job — reform has not taken root. In short, the feminization of poverty in our day is due to the fact that humanism has gained control of the reins of societal power,[100] and the Church has thus far been unable to pose an appropriate response.[101]

Conclusion

Poverty in America has taken on an increasingly feminine face. More and more women than ever are falling through the gaps in society's safety net. Much of the cause for this abominable situation must be laid at the door of the very movements that sought to liberate women: the abortion movement, the careerist movement, and the no-fault divorce movement. Through them, the structures once built into our cultural system, designed to protect women, have been systematically dismantled.

Dire poverty and even homelessness have become inevitable.

The solution to the feminization of poverty, and the feminization of homelessness thus does not depend upon the advocacy of feminism. Indeed, it can not. The solution lies with the Church.

It is incumbent upon the Church to take up the mantle of responsibility. It is incumbent upon the Church to forge in the fires of experience the Biblical alternative to the insidious cults of our day: the 50's earth-mother cult on the one hand, and the 70's Amazonian-feminist cult on the other. It is incumbent upon the Church to do her job: teach the truth, minister grace, enforce justice, and effect healing in the wings.

Then, and only then, will women have the advocate they so desperately need.

And so we've had another night
of poetry and poses.
And each man knows he'll be alone
when the sacred ginmill closes.

David Van Ronk

TIME IN A BOTTLE: ALCOHOLISM

"If y'can remember . . . y're . . . y're not drinkin' enough."

His eyes were milky and unfocused, his wry smile unconvincing, but his words carried an unmistakable intensity—an intensity rooted in knowing experience.

"Course, there's times . . ." he looked past me into distant space. "There's times when y' can't help but . . . remember . . ." He spoke in a distorted, disjointed drawl. But the words were distinct, forceful, not slurred or muddled. "There's times when there ain't enough whiskey in Texas to wash away the memories . . . but . . ." and he smiled that unconvincing smile again, like a badge on the uniform of his decrepitude. "But y'd sell what's left a' y'r soul for another go roun' anyways."

The mist rose between us from the sidewalk heating grate—his home. It cast him in an ethereal shroud, backlit by the street lamp, enclosed by the cold of the night, contained by the pathos of his frame. "That's why you should never . . . *never* ask a drunk on the streets to tell his story . . . to remember. He'll be rememberin' soon enough. No sense in speedin' up the process, causin' good whisky to go to waste." He smiled at his joke. Still as unconvincing as ever.

He wouldn't tell me his name, not at first. He wouldn't tell me where he'd come from, or why he stayed. "I'm tryin' m' hardest to forget all that. Some nights, with a little luck an' a full bottle, I almost do . . . I almost do. . . ."

A Bowery bum. Perfectly typecast. Nothing but a lush. That was my first impression. But now I was unsure. I wanted to know more.

Over the next few hours we just . . . talked. Slowly a bit of his biography emerged. A thumbnail sketch. A snatch at a time.

Enough to dash my easy and impulsive first impression. Not quite enough to keep me from guessing at the loose ends.

His name was Henry. I finally got it out of him. Hailing from a small farming community in South Dakota, he had made his way to New York as a teen to find his "fame an' fortune." But fame and fortune had to be put on hold shortly after he had arrived in the big city. He was drafted.

In Vietnam, fame and fortune were put on hold permanently.

"We'd hit it perfect." He was talking now — remembering now — without hesitation.

"Flames poured out a' every seam. Jellied gasoline turned the entire bunker into a ball a' fire . . . an inferno. One gook ran screamin' from the entrance wrapped in flames. An' his eyes . . . I'll never forget his eyes. Meltin' in their sockets. He fell face first, right in front of me an' I watched his arms an' legs drawin' up under him as the fire shriveled the tendons and muscles . . . shrinkin' 'em. Inside the bunker they was screamin' an' hollerin' an' wailin'. . . .'til all 'a sudden like, ammo began t' explode. Ripped 'em t'shreds. Silenced 'em forever."

It was cold out. And getting colder. The steam grate was little consolation. Still, Henry was sweating profusely — streams of tension rolling down his brow — as he recalled his terror.

"I was hung up. In the barbed wire. My leg here, twisted under me. Bone splinters tore through m' uniform. When the flames started t' move down the trench closer to me, I tried t' squirm away. I only got more tangled up, the wire eatin' into m' flesh. I was in shock, blood pourin' out a' hundreds a' cuts."

He was wide-eyed now. Wild eyed. I began to wonder if perhaps I shouldn't have left well enough alone. His voice rose.

"I was close t' passin' out when I heard voices. Gook voices. I looked up t' see this SVA with a flame-thrower. Russian made. He'd stopped hosin' the trench an' was lookin' for new targets when he'd seen me, caught in the wire. He looked me right in the eyes an' smiled, real slow like. Then he swung the nozzle toward me. Finger on the igniter, he took in the slack. . . ."

I was transfixed. I caught myself holding my breath.

He suddenly relaxed. "An' that was the last I remember. Woke up next in a transport. After that, it was one hospital after another. I never . . . really recovered."

He was quiet now. Broken. He looked tired. Not just tired from lack of sleep, tired from too much life and too much death.

"Dreams. Couldn' shake 'em. Nightmares. So I . . . started to drink."

"So you wouldn't have to remember?"

"Yeah. So I wouldn't remember."

"Did it ever work?"

"No."

"Well then, why . . . ?"

"Look . . ." he cut me off. "Leave me be. Will y' just leave me be? I never asked for no shrink. For no Good Samaritan either. Leave me be, okay?"

He turned away sullenly. A tearful glint caught the light in the corners of his weathered eyes.

"Henry . . ." I tried.

"Go! Now!" he spat savagely. "I told y' before. If y' can remember, y're not drinkin' enough. I already remembered too much t'night. Thanks t' you. So go! I got some serious drinkin' t' do t'night."

I left him there. On his grate. And walked on into the cold and the dark. Remembering. In a stupor of self-pity.

Alcoholism

Alcoholism has always been closely identified with the problem of chronic homelessness. When the dispossessed strike a pose in our mind's eye, our imagination naturally constructs a stereotype: a dirty, ragged, unshaven shell of a man slumped over an empty bottle of cheap liquor. Our image of homelessness is simply not complete without the craving for alcohol.

It has always been so.

In 1890 Jacob Riis published his classic work, *How the Other Half Lives*. There he described the "reign of rum" among the poor and dispossessed, saying, "Where God builds a Church the devil builds next door—a saloon, is an old saying that has lost its point in New York. Either the devil was on the ground first, or he has been doing a good deal more in the way of building . . . turn and twist it as we may, over against every bulwark for decency and morality which society erects, the saloon projects its colossal shadow, omen of evil wherever it falls into the lines of the poor. Nowhere is its mark so broad or so black. To their misery, it sticketh closer than a brother, persuading them that within its doors only is refuge, relief."[1]

Various studies of poverty and homelessness in our own day confirm the conclusions of Riis: When there seems to be no other solace, strong drink becomes the refuge of the dispossessed. As many as 60% of the repeat clients in a Houston shelter showed signs of alcohol dependency.[2] In a Salvation Army shelter in Cleveland that figure has been estimated at 75%.[3] A soup kitchen in Denver says that its clientele of chronic homeless are "almost universally afflicted with alcoholism."[4] In New York City's shelter system, estimates range from lows of 25% to highs of 55%.[5] Many thousands of the homeless find themselves in dire straits only temporarily. Surveys found that these short term temporary homeless — four months on the street or less — are 70% less likely to evidence drinking problems than the long term permanently homeless.[6] But even then, a full 30% of the short term homeless *are* troubled by alcoholism.[7] That is no small number! Alcoholism, then, is undeniably part and parcel of the problem of homelessness. The typical stereotype is at least partially correct.

But, once the correlation between alcoholism and homelessness — and especially alcoholism and chronic hardcore homelessness — is established, social scientists invariably turn to the question of cause and effect: "Did the alcoholism cause the poverty or did poverty cause the alcoholism?" In many ways, this is a fruitless endeavor, like asking, "Which came first, the chicken or the egg?" But in other ways, it is the most relevant of questions, one rife with ethical implications.

If the homeless are on the streets due to their own sloth, irresponsibility, and driving addictions, that is one thing. But if life on the streets is so wretched, so hopeless, so demeaning, and so debilitating that it drives the homeless to drink, then that is quite another.

So, which is it? The chicken or the egg?

Driven to Drink

All those who drink too much have a good excuse. Or so they say. They have reasons. They may be drowning sorrows, drinking to forget — like Henry. They may be doing battle against the ravages of guilt or envy or bitterness. They may be feeding the personal demons that lurk in their downtimed nightsides. They may be shutting out the clamor and din of their daily responsibilities, or lavishing adornment on their bland daily mundanity. Whatever. They have reasons.

One survey of alcoholics conducted by California's Neurodaeliaforcation Institute indicated that 27% attributed their drinking problems to family strife. 22% cited financial difficulties. 18% cited job pressures. 14% admitted to chronic guilt or bitterness. The other 19% identified general depression, bad memories, or a sense of sheer uselessness and hopelessness. Interestingly, 76% of those surveyed indicated that they felt like their reasons for heavy drinking were "good reasons." Only 24% said that they "could not legitimately justify" their alcohol abuses.[8]

They have reasons.

The dispossessed have reasons, too. Lots of reasons. And unlike many of the lame excuses uncovered in the California study, a number of those reasons seem to be good reasons.

On cold nights, with nothing more than a steam grate and a few tattered blankets to warm them, many homeless rely on alcohol. "There's many a night when I was sure to a' froze," Henry told me, "if I hadn' a' had some ol' belly fire." According to homelessness expert Dr. Ambrose Polk, "Alcoholism is undeniably a wretched vice, but there comes a time in the cold of winter when a bottle of rye is the best ally a street person can have against the ravages of wind and snow and time."[9] Dr. Elbert Hillerman concurs: "Alcohol consumption is often the only thing that stands between the homeless and death."[10]

In 1976, at least 671 homeless froze to death on our city streets.[11] In 1977 another 898 died.[12] In 1978 the number rose to 928.[13] And in 1983 the number rose over 1400.[14] Is it any wonder then, that many homeless take their comfort from a bottle in the dead of winter?

The homeless not only struggle against the frigid winds and harsh elements day by day and night by night, they must also fight the rapid deterioration of their health. Exposure to heat and cold, rain and snow for months, even years on end, takes a mighty toll on the dispossessed. Open wounds are not uncommon. Ulcerations of the hands, legs, and feet occur with regularity. Frostbite, windburn, staph infections, ringworm, bronchitis, and tuberculosis are everyday hazards. Add to all that the dull aching and deep down bone tiredness that comes from too much walking during the day, and too little sleeping at night, and you've got bodies racked with pain. Continual, unabated pain. According to Dr. Hillerman, "Alcohol is the only anesthetic the homeless have. If they don't drink before they get to the streets, they are quickly driven to it by the sheer anguish of their circumstances."[15]

Purposeless. Aimless. Hopeless. Nowhere to go. No one to see. No reason to live. Homelessness takes a heavy toll. Even without the winter cold. Even without the threat of nagging illness. The dispossessed take solace in cheap Thunderbird wine. Just to cope. Just to pass the time. "Of course," says Dr. Polk, "that just drives the wedge between them and reality all the more. They end up wandering around in a dazed stupor. Chronic homelessness is thus a life faced, when it must be faced at all, with distilled courage. Alcohol . . . it saves them and it destroys them . . . it keeps them going and it cripples them . . . it nourishes them and it poisons them . . . all at the same time. It's the devil's paradox. It's awful. But it's the way things are."[16]

"Give strong drink to him who is perishing, and wine to him whose life is bitter. Let him drink and forget his poverty, and remember his trouble no more" (Proverbs 31:6-7).

For many of the dispossessed then, alcoholism is not simply a jaunt into licentiousness and lasciviousness. It is a means to survival, an occupational hazard.

Driven to Poverty

While it may be that many of the homeless drink because of the hazards of the street, many others would never have had to face the hazards of the street if they didn't drink.

Alcoholism, especially in its most advanced stages, so thoroughly deteriorates a person that he is rendered fit for little but the gutter.

There are multitudinous physical consequences of heavy drinking. "Alcoholics need far more medical services than do nonalcoholics," says Dr. Louis Jolyon West of UCLA's Neuropsychiatric Institute. "One study reports two to three times as many illnesses and two to three times more expenses for health care. Alcohol abuse not only exerts direct toxic effects on the body, but it often leads to dietary deficiencies that result in more subtle biochemical imbalances."[17]

The digestive system is especially hard hit by alcohol abuse. Many alcoholics suffer from "gastritis, erosion of gastric mucosa, gastric and duodenal ulcers, bowel motility disorders, and malabsorption syndromes."[18] Additionally, they often are afflicted with chronic pancreatitis, hepatitis, and cirrhosis of the liver.[19]

In addition to these direct toxigenic effects, "heavy alcohol consumption is also a risk factor for cancer of the mouth, pharynx, larynx, esophagus, and liver—a factor further increased in heavy drinkers who use tobacco."[20]

If that were not bad enough, alcohol is implicated in a wide variety of cardiovascular disorders including phlebitis, varicose veins, angina pectoris, and even cardiac arrest.[21] According to Dr. Stewart G. Wolf, Regents Professor of Medicine at the University of Oklahoma, "In the heart, alcohol affects the mechanisms that regulate the heartbeat, producing a variety of rhythm disturbances that may result in sudden death."[22]

And that is only the tip of the iceberg. Alcohol abuse can cause cerebral atrophy,[23] polyneuritis,[24] diabetes,[25] endocrine disorders,[26] intestinal ethanolization,[27] vitamin deficiencies,[28] and anemia.[29]

In short, chronic alcoholism can lead to such serious crippling of normal bodily functions that an ordinary life, fulfilling ordinary responsibilities is no longer possible. Heavy drinking can lead to the gutter simply by process of elimination: all other options are eliminated by the alcoholic's ruined physical state.

Sadly, the degenerative downward spiral of alcoholism is not limited to physical illness.

"Alcoholism is also a cause of major mental illnesses," says Dr. West, "including acute alcoholic dementia, delirium tremens, alcoholic hallucinosis and . . . encephalopathy."[30] In fact, alcoholism is diagnosed in 20-30% of all cases admitted to state mental hospitals, and in most states it leads all other diagnoses.[31]

Alcoholism can dramatically affect memory, impair visual-spatial and perceptual-motor skills, provoke bipolar manic-depressive psychoses, and induce atrophic metabolic aberrations.[32]

Is it any wonder then that the alcoholic is prone to lose his job, alienate his family, squander his savings, waste his opportunities, lose sight of all reality, cut off all his options, and wind up in the streets, wandering aimlessly about, a shell of the man he once was?

The U.N. and the Mark of Cain

Regardless of whether a man drinks himself *into* poverty or drinks *because* of his poverty, it is clear enough that chronic homelessness and alcoholism go hand in hand. And so while many thousands may drift in and out of the ranks of the dispossessed unscathed each year — due to deinstitutionalization, divorce, or deindustrialization — it is apparent that the permanent street dweller is branded with this liability more often than not.

Odd then, that the U.N. fails to mention alcoholism at all — not even once — in the hundreds of pages of documents supporting the International Year of the Homeless. Why? Because alcoholism cannot be legislated away? Because alcoholism cannot be reformed, or socialized, or regulated, or standardized out of existence by judicial fiat? Because alcoholism is sin and the U.N. has no means to deal with sin? Perhaps.

Sometime in the night, during our long belabored conversation, Henry confessed, "I don't s'pos I'd be in this fix if I'd a' tooken care a' things right after 'Nam. If I'd a' not drunk so much tryin' t' forget. But then after a'while . . . well, y'get into a routine. Y'know? It's like . . . this . . . this mark a' Cain . . . right here . . ." and he tapped his forehead. "Right here. Maybe somebody'll figure how t'get rid a' the mark a' Cain an' there wouldn' be folks like me on the streets. Yeah . . ." and he held up his half empty bottle, "this here's my mark a' Cain." He took a long, slow, deep pull.

Could it be that Henry, a Bowery bum, had a keener perception of the causes and the solutions for homelessness than the social planners in the U.N.?

The Mark and the Bane

Unlike the U.N., the Bible has much to say about the correlation between dire poverty and drunkenness.

"Wine is a mocker, strong drink a brawler, and whoever is intoxicated by it is not wise" (Proverbs 20:1).

"Who has woe? Who has sorrow? Who has contentions? Who has complaining? Who has wounds without causes? Who has redness of eyes? Those who linger long over wine, those who go to taste mixed wine. Do not look on the wine when it is red, when it sparkles in the cup. When it goes down smoothly; at the last it bites like a serpent, and stings like a viper. Your eyes will see strange things, and your mind will utter perverse things. And you will be like one who lies down in the middle of the sea, or like one who lies down on the top of a mast. 'They struck me, but I did not become ill; they beat me, but I did not know it. When shall I awake? I will seek another drink'" (Proverbs 23:29-35).

There is a direct relation between the abuse of alcohol and poverty according to Scripture.

"Listen, my son, and be wise, and direct your heart in the way. Do not be with heavy drinkers of wine, or with gluttonous eaters of meat; for the heavy drinker and the glutton will come to poverty, and drowsiness will clothe a man with rags" (Proverbs 23:19-21).

Henry was right. Alcoholism is a kind of "mark of Cain." Under its bane the earth "no longer yields its strength" and the dispossessed is cast as "a vagrant and a wanderer on the earth" (Genesis 4:12).

Clearly, if chronic homelessness is to be addressed in any measure, the issue of alcoholism will have to be faced squarely. Whether the dispossessed are driven to drink by the hardship of life in the streets, or are driven to the streets by the crippling effects of alcohol, the solutions to hardcore homelessness must take this factor into account. It cannot be ignored.

Shelter is not enough. Money is not enough. Opportunity is not enough. Advocacy is not enough. International Year declarations are not enough.

George Gilder has asserted that "the only dependable route from poverty is always work, family, and faith."[33] Alcoholism ruthlessly attacks all three. Thus, the road to recovery for the chronically homeless must be paved, not with new and better government programs, but with rehabilitation, and repentance.

The Legacy of the Reformers

In describing the conditions of England before the great reforms of Whitefield and Wesley changed the nation forever, Bishop J. C. Ryle asserted, "It may suffice to say that dueling, adultery, fornication, gambling, swearing, Sabbath-breaking, and drunkenness were hardly regarded as vices at all . . . Wilberforce had not yet attacked the slave trade. Howat had not yet reformed the prisons. Raikes had not established Sunday Schools. We had no Bible Societies, no ragged schools, no city missions, no pastoral aid societies, no missions to the heathen. The spirit of slumber was over the land."[34]

The "spirit of slumber" was most especially evident in the abuse of alcohol among the poor and working classes. According to Thomas O'Calthairn, a contemporary of Ryles, "Before the reforms, great hoards of afflicted souls would wander about the streets of London and Bristol in a drunken stupor. Having forsaken home, family, and friends, they fell into horrid lives of absolute destitution living only for the bane of gin."[35] But then he says, "the miracle of the great reformers, Whitefield, Romaine, Rowlands, and even the Arminian Wesley, was the eradication of this blight upon the name of every Englishman, and this without the temperance societies and teetotalism so popular today. It was accomplished by the sheer power of the Gospel call to repentance and rehabilitation."[36] He concludes his narrative saying, "The poor we still have with us, and our Lord assures us we always will, but as for the gutter mipes and street waifs and the sodden vagrants, the Gospel reforms have all but made them extinct."[37]

Christ who is "the same yesterday, today and forever" (Hebrews 13:8) can accomplish for us in our day, what He did for them, in that day, if only we would set our hands at the task of reform.

The cure for the drunkard is to stop drinking in the world, and drink only in the Kingdom. The wine of communion retrains the converted drunkard to use alcohol properly. Later in life he may learn to use it at other times, but not until he stops drinking in the flesh and learns to drink only in the Kingdom.

Thus, only the Church and sacrament can offer a real cure and rehabilitation to the drunkard. Sheer abstinence can only offer a manichaean negation and fear of alcohol, fixating on the problem rather than on the solution. To create a void, a vacuum, never solves anything (Matthew 12:43-45). Christianity offers a *real* cure because if offers *real transformation*.

Conclusion

Anyway you cut it, alcohol abuse is a significant factor in the problem of chronic homelessness. Of those dispossessed living on the streets for more than four months, a large percentage are alcoholics. Some became heavy drinkers because of the rigors of street life. Others wound up on the streets in the first place because of the debilitative effects of alcohol on their families, their health, and their mental faculties. But either way, alcohol takes a high profile in the dilemma of dispossession.

It stands to reason then that alcohol rehabilitation and repentance should be a major plank in any platform for the recovery of the homeless. Unfortunately, most social service agencies that work with the dispossessed sluff over the issue. The U.N. in its International Year of the Homeless literature ignores it. And most church outreaches, shelter ministries, soup kitchens, and rescue missions are oblivious to it, or have given up trying to stop it.

Is that any way to solve a problem?

Joyeuse Garde, that rare estate;
    where lovers dwell;
    where friendships swell.
Joyeuse Garde, devoid of hate;
    gone now for 'ere?
    for lack of care?
The broken citadel, a home no more.
The broken citadel, no more a home.

Tristram Gylberd

THE BROKEN CITADEL: HOUSING REGULATION

They stared at each other from across the cavernous room in apparent recognition, in apparent disbelief. One of them, a huge, hulking man with a shock of blonde curls matted and skewed beneath a well worn Dodgers cap, was in the process of trading his dignity for a five pound block of cheese. The other, a diminutive, bespectacled man clad in immaculate work khakis, dignity already long since gone, was waiting rather impatiently in the long food stamps line.

When their eyes met, there in the New York City Social Services Center, they were both surprised. The big man was so surprised, he nearly dropped his teeth. And his cheese. The small man nearly dropped his file folder, filled to overflowing with the artifacts of his demise.

"Hey . . . Hey, ain't you Mr. Rodecker?" The big man caught him before shame sent him in flight.

Rodecker's stomach tightened into a knot. He wondered to himself how much more humiliation he would have to endure. "Yeah, I am. And you're . . . Walker. Kevin Walker, if I'm not mistaken."

"Well, I'll be! Hah! I'll be! What the hell you doin' *here*, Mr. Rodecker?"

With his cheese in tow, and a wad of USDA paperwork billowing from the right rear pocket of his Levis, the big man crossed the room toward a fidgeting, wary Rodecker.

"Look, Kevin, just leave me alone. Go away."

"Hey, that's no way to be *neighborly*, I just . . ."

"We're *not* neighbors."

"Yeah. Right. You made sure of that, didn't you? Took care of that *real* good."

"That was none of my doing. And you know it. Look, just go, will you?"

A long, tense silence hung between them. Then the big man choked out a laugh. "You made my day, Rodecker. Just seein' you here's made my day." He shifted the bulky case to the other arm and started off. Then with a nod toward the line, "Happy hunting!"

It was an odd encounter. A chance encounter. But it was an encounter that illustrated all too vividly, all to painfully the double victimization that rent controls have wrought in urban America.

Eight months ago, Norm Rodecker was a landlord. Kevin Walker was one of his tenants. One of his last tenants.

Today, both men are homeless. They spend their days bouncing from one social service agency to another like pinballs in an arcade. They spend their nights just making do — Rodecker beneath a pile of blankets in the back seat of his '81 Chevy, parked in the lot between a K-Mart and a Kentucky Fried Chicken on Long Island; Walker tossing restlessly on an army cot in the Ward's Island Keener Building.

Rent Controls

Housing is expensive. As many as 24% of all Americans are forced to spend one-third of their total income just to put a roof over their heads.[1] 10% must spend half their income.[2] And inflation has made this bad situation worse. Over the last fifteen years, basic housing costs have risen more than 143%[3] while family incomes have only risen 54%.[4]

Citing the hardship that these kinds of rent increases and rising rent-to-income ratios impose on households of modest means, more than 200 cities nationwide have imposed rent ceiling laws, rent stabilization laws, and direct rent control laws.[5] Somehow, someway, affordable housing has to be secured for the poorest of the poor. Homelessness can only be overcome if the dispossessed can be placed into homes. Obviously. Advocates of rent controls assert that the only way to accomplish that aim is to clamp down on the free market, to make it less free, but more accessible. Unfortunately, the measures have only made the housing problems worse. According to Peter Navarro, an economist at the University of California at San Diego, with rent control "you reduce the supply of new apartment stock, destroy the existing stock, erode the community tax base, create unemployment, and wind up discriminating against the very people you are trying to help."[6]

People like Kevin Walker and Norm Rodecker.

It is a simple matter of supply and demand. A price that is artificially suppressed below market-clearing levels will spontaneously create housing shortages. Thus, consumers like Kevin Walker cannot keep or obtain the rental housing that they are able to afford. And landlords like Norm Rodecker may be forced out of the market by unrecoverable maintenance costs and taxes.

Even so, most municipalities that have instituted rent controls have displayed tenacious resistance to change.

Rent controls were first introduced in New York City in 1942. The controls were to be "temporary," "emergency" measures in order to relieve wartime pressures.[7] Somehow those "temporary" measures secured permanent tenure in the legal ecology of the city. The Emergency Price Control Act signed by President Roosevelt has *never* expired or been abolished. Even so, New York politicians have long held to the myth that the measures were only "temporary." In 1955, after more than a decade of the controls, Governor Harriman asserted: "Rent ceilings do not bring roofs overhead. Rent control must be viewed as only a single aspect of a broader housing program and as an interim device until such time as an adequate housing supply makes it no longer necessary."[8] Rhetoric notwithstanding, rent control has been anything but an "interim device" in New York. The original measures have been affirmed or reinforced twelve times in the intervening years, including the Emergency Housing Act of 1950, the Emergency Housing Act of 1962, and the Emergency Tenant Protection Act of 1983.[9] All passed amidst "emergencies."

Somehow or another the community leaders and politicians in New York have failed to learn over the past half century that the "emergencies" that precipitated the enactment of still stronger rent control measures — housing stock depletion, housing stock deterioration, housing stock conversion, and homelessness — were *caused* by rent control measures.

Housing Stock Depletion

Every year a half million units of low rent dwellings are lost due to abandonment, arson, demolition, or attrition.[10] If those units are not replaced with new construction, rehabilitation, and conversion, then literally millions of people are thrown onto the streets with nowhere to go.

Unfortunately, in communities where rent controls have been established, new construction drops off by as much as 65%[11] and low rent rehabilitation and conversion ceases to exist at all.[12]

According to Paul L. Niebanck, professor of urban and environmental planning at the University of California at Santa Cruz, the existence of rent controls "actively discourages moderately priced new construction and encourages withdrawals from the lower priced rental inventory. . . ."[13]

"When you remove any incentive for profit, construction *has* to come to a halt," says New York building contractor George Talbot. "There's no such thing as a free lunch. I'm not gonna build if I can't make it pay. No one will. And of course, when an old property comes up for repairs, often it's just cheaper to shut the building down entirely, rather than pour new investment dollars into it."[14]

Michael Stegman, Deputy Assistant Secretary for Research in the Department of Housing and Urban Development, asserts that rent controls have the inevitable result "of diverting investment capital from housing into (other) sectors of the economy."[15]

That perhaps explains why New York has seen the total number of rental units in the city shrink by 33,000 from 1981 to 1984.[16] And why Washington has 8,000 fewer rental units since controls went into effect in 1978.[17] When low-priced rental properties cease to pay, they cease to exist.

Despite the fact that nationwide, lower interest rates, tax-exempt financing programs, and tamed inflation figures sparked a spree of construction starts in 1985 — the number of low to mid-income rental units completed that year was up a whopping 97% from 1982 — rent controlled markets still struggled. In 1986 the vacancy rate for apartments in Boston, New York, Washington, Los Angeles, and San Francisco never rose above 3%,[18] whereas in decontrolled cites vacancy rates remained quite high: 10% in Cleveland,[19] 11% in Phoenix,[20] and 9% in Dallas.[21] So whereas in the controlled cities prospective tenants had to search high and low and then just take what they could get at whatever price they could get, in decontrolled cities, they had choices. They could choose prices, locations, and services. And since supply was greater than demand, they could get *better* prices, locations, and services.

Thus, in the end, housing stock depletion due to rent controls hurts the poor more than any other sector of the community. Depleted supply means excess demand. Excess demand means lower mobility. Lower mobility means slower turnover. Slower turnover means even greater demand. And so forth.

The poor can ill afford to play this kind of game. They are unable to pay exorbitant finders' fees to landlords or apartment locators. They are unable to spend the time valiantly searching hither and yon. They are unable suitably to impress scrutinizing property owners. So, they are simply left out.

Housing Stock Deteriorization

Even when poor tenants do reap the benefits of rent reduction due to imposed controls or ceilings, those benefits gradually diminish over time. Anxious landlords, desperate to preserve their operating income, more often than not will slash the services they provide at the fixed price. Garbage services cease. Security arrangements are dropped. Parking privileges are rescinded. Maintenance is pared to the bare minimum. Roofing, siding, lighting, landscaping, cleaning, and repairing are all put off, postponed, or cancelled altogether.

A Sternlieb study in New York confirmed that maintenance dropped considerably and deteriorization increased considerably due to rent controls.[22] The city of Boston recently estimated that landlords spend an average of $50 a year less to maintain controlled units. Jim Breland, a New York landlord, says, "I don't fix anything anymore. Not unless it's just plain dangerous. I can't afford to." And Charles Isham, a property owner in Santa Monica, admits, "I haven't had the halls swept in eighteen months."

"The result," according to Oliver Black, a Minneapolis realtor, "is the slumification of good, viable properties. The poor are hurt especially by this. They pay the same price they did a year or two ago, but the apartment has deteriorated significantly."[23] But with the reduced housing stock, the poor tenant has no choice. He can't move to better quarters. There are none at a price he can afford. He is stuck.

Housing Stock Conversion

In order to escape the clutches of rent control and to insure a return on their investments, many landlords simply remove their properties from the rental market and convert to condominiums. In New York more than 57,000 rental units were converted to cooperative or condominium ownership from 1978 to 1984.[24] Nationwide, between 1970 and 1982, 1,116,000 single room rental units were converted, nearly half the stock.[25] During the same period, New York lost 87% of its total "SRO," or "poverty hotel" capacity.[26] Other cities have lost as much as 65% of their rooming units this way.[27] The poor are simply displaced because their landlords can no longer afford to subsidize their rents.

Social scientists have created the word "gentrification" to describe this displacement and conversion process. In a working paper prepared by the Community Service Society of New York for the Institute for Social Welfare Research, Kim Hopper and Jill Hamberg describe the phenomenon: "Unlike the Depression, when households doubled up and owners boarded up vacant units awaiting the return of prosperity, in the 1970's landlords and financial institutions gave up on the 'bottom' of the market — both the buildings and the people. At the same time, a growing number of young professional and managerial people, increasingly locked out of the first-time buyers market, began to outbid moderate-income tenants in a pinched rental market. The result is 'reverse filtering' where people — rather than buildings — filter down through the market."[28]

In short, in times of housing shortages, money talks. If a landlord knows that he can convert a marginally profitable, rent controlled tenement into a high profile condo development for young, upwardly mobile professionals, wild horses won't hold him back.

Rent controls then, simply cut off the bottom of the market. They eliminate low budget housing altogether. Rather than protecting the poor, the controls assail the poor, leaving many with no other recourse than the streets.

Poor Tenants and Poor Landlords

Not only do rent controls contribute to the displacement and impoverishment of tenants, in many cases they produce displaced and impoverished landlords as well.

Norm Rodecker bought a small Brooklyn apartment building as an investment for his old age. Because of rent controls imposed by the Emergency Tenant Relief Protection Act of 1983, he found he could barely turn a profit, so he cut services. He cut maintenance. He cracked down on late payments.

Due to his belt tightening measures, he was able to get through 1983 in the black. But then in 1984 he was hit with a 72% increase in property tax assessments. That same year, the Health Department informed him that the plumbing in the building was substandard and had to be replaced.

"I figured I could pay one or the other but not both," he told me. "So I went to try to get either the tax assessor or the Health Department to cut me some slack."

No such luck. Both agencies demanded instant satisfaction.

"I was caught in the middle. There was nothing I could do. Nothing. I had to shut down the building. Evict everybody. I had no choice; the property was condemned and I just couldn't afford to bring it up to code. A lot of good people wound up on the sidewalk with nowhere to go. If this city wants to help take care of homelessness, maybe they ought to take a good, hard look at their rent control policies."

But if Norm Rodecker thought that was the end of his woes, he had another thing coming.

"I'd lost over $200,000 on that deal. My life's savings. My future. My retirement. But I still had a small inheritance I could live on till I got back on my feet. At least, that's what I thought."

The tax assessor thought differently. Norm was liable for payment on his property, despite the fact that he had abandoned it. The agency forced him into bankruptcy proceedings whereupon he lost everything he owned except the shirt off his back and his car.

"I know now that if I had gotten a better lawyer, I probably would not be in this terrible situation. At least, I probably wouldn't be homeless. Hindsight is always better than foresight. But I can't afford to look back now. I've got to look ahead. Good grief, I'm 57 years old. And I'm penniless, living in my car, for heaven's sake!"

Oliver and Birdie Guiton, an elderly black couple in Berkeley, are in a similar bind. They too bought a small apartment house as a retirement investment. They too were financially crippled when rent controls went into effect. Now they are losing $10,000 a year. And they say that they can't live too terribly much longer under such debilitating circumstances.

Their state representative is Nick Petris, a powerful California Democrat. Swayed by their plight, and the plight of hundreds like them, Petris suddenly changed his tune on rent controls in early 1986. During his twenty-eight-year tenure, he has sponsored every "pro-tenant" law that has come across the floor of the legislative chamber. He has, in fact, led the fight over the years for rent controls. But no longer. "Under rent control, the oppressed are the landlords, and I'm fighting for them like I fought for tenants," says Petris. "Many of these mom-and-pop landlords are poor, and they live in fear."[29] So now, Petris says he will vote "anti-rent control" in the future.

"It's about time," sighed Oliver Guiton. "It's about time."

The U.N.'s Answer

But while many former advocates of rent control measures like Nick Petris are now looking to the free market for answers to the low-rent housing crunch and homelessness, the U.N. is looking in the opposite direction.

According to the United Nations Center for Human Settlements (UNCHS), the International Year of the Homeless has as a primary goal, "the securing of political commitment and effective action within and among nations to help the millions of poor all over the world . . . secure shelter . . . and to make it possible to integrate them with the process of economic development."[30] Hence, the emphasis in U.N. literature has been to call on "government, national and international," to be the housing "facilitator or enabler, focusing its attention on access to land, secure tenure, improved legislation, property reform, and regulation of ownership."[31]

Nicaragua, Sri Lanka, and Tanzania, held aloft by the U.N. as "model" nations, have translated this mandate for reform into the abolition of private property altogether.

"State control of all property is just the rent control mentality taken all the way to its logical conclusion," says political analyst Ruben Martinez, "so not surprisingly, its disasters are just the disasters of rent control multiplied and magnified proportionately."[32] If rent controls wreak havoc on the availability, affordability, and dependability of the low- rent housing market, then rent controls, hyper-extended to the point that they are in Nicaragua, Sri Lanka, and Tanzania, are bound to bury the poor altogether.

And in point of fact, they have.

State controls have proven to be incredibly oppressive in the U.N.'s "model" communities, but somehow the General Assembly and the various bureaucrats in the UNCHS haven't noticed. Thus, they continue to harp on the dinosaurs of socialization, regulation, and confiscation, driving the poor ever deeper into the morass of destitution.

Sanctioned Theft

The Eighth Commandment says, "Thou shalt not steal" (Exodus 20:15). There can be little doubt about the meaning of this command. As economist Gary North has asserted, "the biblical social order is a social order which acknowledges and defends the rights—legal immunities—of private property. This prohibition binds individuals and institutions, including the state."[33] Whenever anyone, an individual or a government, violates the sanctions of private property, he or it is guilty of stealing. He may call it "land reform," or "ownership regulation," or "market rehabilitation," or "land access management," or "economic redistribution," or "rent control," but God calls it "*theft*."

The fact is that land reform and rent controls do not benefit the poor. They only benefit the *employees of the state*. Politicians and bureaucrats have a personal interest in high property taxes and rent controls, because such policies bring more money into the coffers of the state. This means that the salaries of state employees can be raised, not to speak of opening up new avenues of graft and corruption. We have to remember that the state is not an abstraction, it is people. Good government is run by good people who have everyone's welfare at heart. Bad government is run by bad people who are seeking to line their pockets.

A striking example of just this type of injustice is recorded for us in Nehemiah 5. "Now there was a great outcry of the people and of their wives against their Jewish brothers. For there were those who said, . . .'We are mortgaging our fields, our vineyards, and our houses that we might get grain because of the famine.' Also there were those who said, 'We have borrowed money *for the king's tax on our fields and our vineyards*. And now our flesh is like the flesh of our brothers, our children like their children. Yet behold, we are forcing our sons and our daughters to be slaves, and some of our daughters are forced into bondage already, and there is no power in our hands because our fields and vineyards belong to others'" (Nehemiah 5:1-5, italics added).

The nobility in Israel, those who controlled the power of the state, were using their wealth and position to oppress the poor. They were using high taxes to force poor landholders and landlords into bankruptcy and slavery. Nehemiah was furious, and rebuked the bureaucrats, saying "The thing which you are doing is not good; should you not walk in the fear of our God because of the reproach of the nations, our enemies?" (Nehemiah 5:9). Happily, the nobility repented of their usury, and returned the lands to the poor.

According to North, "Covenantal Law governs the sphere of economics. Wealth flows to those who work hard, deal honestly with their customers, and who honor God. To argue, as the Marxists and socialists do, that wealth flows in a free market social order towards those who are ruthless, dishonest, and blinded by greed, is to deny the Bible's explicit teachings concerning the nature of economic life. It is a denial of the covenantal lawfulness of the creation."[34] The story of Nehemiah and the nobles of Jerusalem is a bane to Marxists and socialists, to the leaders of "model" nations like Nicaragua, Sri Lanka, and Tanzania, and to the various U.N. bureaucrats, because it turns the tables and shows things as they really are.

North concludes, saying, "Critics of the capitalist system have inflicted great damage on those societies that have accepted such (Marxist and socialist) criticisms as valid. Men have concluded that the private property system is rigged against the poor and weak, forcing them into positions of permanent servitude. Historically, on the contrary, no social order has provided more opportunities for upward social mobility than capitalism."[35] As Scripture so clearly demonstrates, it is the state controlled economy, the abolition of private property, the socialist system, that is rigged against the poor and weak.

The Legacy of England

Every socialist experiment in history has ended in dismal failure. At no time have land reforms, rent controls, or state interventions worked in favor of the poor and homeless. In fact, as

Igor Shafarevich,[36] Sven Rydenfelt,[37] Miron Dolot,[38] and many others have shown, whenever the free market is substantially tampered with, the poor are dispossessed altogether.

That is not to say that the free market is always entirely benevolent to the poor. In times of social and economic upheaval, quite the opposite has proven to be the case. If we look back at Nehemiah 5, we see that not only were the wealthy abusing their taxing power in order to oppress the poor, they were also taking advantage of a famine in order to dispossess them (verse 3). Nehemiah's rebuke covered not only their excessive taxation, but also the usurious interest they were charging people during the famine (verses 6-13). There is nothing wrong ordinarily with loaning money out at interest—a good free market principle—but in a time of famine or disaster, such a practice can be oppressive. Indeed, the Law of God states that the poor are not to be charged interest on charity loans (Ex. 22:25).

Moreover, a semi-free or mixed economy allows for even more abuses. In the sixteenth century for instance, the people of England lived for the most part, in villages and small rural settlements. They supported a quasi-feudal system under which they would work the fields for a "land-lord," paying him rent from their produce.[39] Obviously these peasants were poor, but what they lacked in affluence was more than made up for in security. A peasant who had a bad crop, or who had an accident, could go to his lord for help. Or, he could go to the Church, known for centuries as a refuge for the poor.[40]

But due to the great boom in mercantilist enterprises, the nation was undergoing a dramatic transformation. With wool manufacturing expanding rapidly all across Europe and demand for the raw commodity driving the price ever upward, the lords found that they could make much more money grazing sheep on their fields than from the rents they charged peasants.[41]

The free market went to work. By a number of devices like "enclosure" and "rack-renting," the peasants were evicted.[42] And for the first time since the panics of the fourteenth century plague era, the land was flooded with homeless wanderers.[43]

In time, however, the presence of these vagrant peasants sparked two important developments in English society that would form the backbone of its moral and economic supremacy for the next 350 years. First, the peasants became the natural constituency from which England's burgeoning Industrial Revolution would draw its laborers.[44] Had England been able to continue in a contentedly pastoral fashion, the rapid, almost urgent growth of its manufacturing sector would certainly not have occurred.[45] England would probably have lagged behind the pace of France and Spain, and modern capitalism would have taken an entirely different shape.[46] Through great economic growth and the advancement of emerging technologies, virtually all of the displaced peasants were soon employed gainfully and sheltered adequately. Free enterprise fitfully pushed past a rough stretch and began to stride forward once again.

Second, the public at large was forced to re-examine its faith, and the application of that faith to the world at large. Obedience to Christ was not limited, they now understood, only to "spiritual" matters, but affected all of life, including tough issues like the care of the poor.[47] As a result, a series of "social security" measures were implemented at the behest of the king and the parliament on the parish level, culminating in the Elizabethan Poor Laws in 1601.[48]

Clearly, the free enterprise system was not then, nor is it now "perfect." Nothing is in this poor, fallen world. But even in the midst of its greatest failures, the free enterprise system is able to adjust, to push ahead, to reform, and ultimately to emerge stronger and more beneficent than ever before. And that is a claim that socialism simply cannot make. Not now, not ever.

Conclusion

If homelessness is to be overcome in any measure, affordable housing must be made available somehow. That is a given. But how? Many cities and municipalities have tried to regulate the current housing stock through rent controls, hoping to contain prices to affordable levels. Many nations, like Nicaragua, Sri Lanka, and Tanzania have gone even further, actually confiscating lands and redistributing them.

Well intentioned or not, these measures inevitably hurt the very people they were supposed to help. When the opportunities afforded by the free enterprise system are subverted unbiblically through theft and regulatory interference, the poor are hurt most of all.

There is a crying need for low-income housing. Demand.

If left to operate freely, entrepreneurs will find ways to meet that need. Supply.

It has always worked that way in the past.[49] And it will continue to work that way because it is a scrupulously Biblical system.

But in the meantime, the issue of theft must be addressed. The issue of oppression and bondage must be addressed. Government regulators must be called to task. Our modern day nobility must be confronted in our Jerusalems. They must be met by modern day Nehemiahs.

You've come too late to sell your closing
      chapters, for our hands
Have written an epitaph in rust, on dusty
      steel
We've pulled aside and served with debts and
      overdue demands
By angry, ragged shapes that once were us;
      and when we pay
We'll wait in neatly ordered lines to
      sign our souls away.

Timothy Powers

EIGHT

EPITAPH IN RUST: UNEMPLOYMENT

His arms and body still showed signs of abnormal strength in the thin, narrow bands of muscle rippling beneath his T-shirt. But that strength looked entirely out of place in the sterile office. Stifled. Uneasy. He sat, placidly waiting, resignation etched on his face.

The woman behind the desk ignored him. She busily shuffled and sorted the papers and files that littered the room — artifacts of a hundred other failed lives. The office had a single window with a spectacular view of a garbage-strewn alley. In the room there were four filing cabinets, a single potted poinsettia, long since dead, two ashtrays, both full, and on the walls there were a few old shop safety posters, faded, water stained, and torn. Institutional. Musty.

"Now then Mr. . . . uh, Mr. Gallin," she said not looking up, "Let's see what we can do for you." Scanning a single sheet, she issued forth with a series of unconvincing "ums" and "ahs," and then, "Well, . . . right now, I'm afraid. . . ."

"I know! I know!" he cut in, "same ol' song an' dance . . . but hey, it's okay. No excuses necessary." He rose to go.

She now looked up at him. Her eyes met his for the first time. They were steely grey and opaque. Dull. Unseeing. "Sorry. . . ."

He was out the door before she could finish the all too familiar liturgy of condescension. She sighed. Setting the "Gallin" file aside, she reached for the next. "Only twenty more minutes till lunch," she thought.

Mick Gallin irresolutely made his way down the long corridor thinking, "Okay. What now?" Into the men's room, over to the bank of sinks, splashing lukewarm water on his face, he pondered the situation for the thousandth time. The haunting refrain of an old hymn rang in the hallows of his mind.

> When upon life's billows you are tempest tossed,
> When you are discouraged thinking all is lost,
> Count your many blessings, name them one by one,
> And it will surprise you what the Lord hath done.[1]

He ran a hand through his short-cropped sandy hair, its peppered flecks of grey growing in number — daily now. He examined his reflection between the fly specks on the sink's mirror. He barely recognized the face looking back at him. He had become a stranger to himself.

> Are you ever burdened with a load of care?
> Does the cross seem heavy you are called to bear?
> Count your many blessings, every doubt will fly,
> And you will be singing as the days go by.[2]

A businessman walked into the room. Or a lawyer. His suit, charcoal grey flannel with a nipped-in waist, looked as if it had been tailor fit. His oxford cloth shirt was pink, with a button down collar. His vest was a tattersall check, subtle and sophisticated, red and black on a cream background. His silk tie showed chic horizontal stripes to match, and his European cut shoes glistened smartly on the tile.

Mick Gallin caught himself on the sink as a gall of bitterness rose in his throat.

> When you look at others with their lands and gold,
> Think that Christ has promised you His wealth untold,
> Count your many blessings, money cannot buy
> Your reward in heaven, nor your home on high.[3]

He took a deep breath. And then another. Vertigo swept over him anyway. It came in wave after wave of jumbled feelings, impressions, and memories. He reached into the waistband of his baggy work pants and withdrew a small revolver. A Saturday night special. He fondled it in his grip.

So amid the conflict, whether great or small,
Do not be discouraged . . .[4]

His hands were shaking as he raised the gun to his brow.
Envy, self-pity, and pride drove him over the threshold. Faithless
and hopeless, he pressed ahead. "No stopping now," he thought,
slowly pulling the trigger.

Count your many blessings, angels will attend,
Help and comfort give you to your journey's end.[5]

A statistic. Another grim statistic. A headline. Another telling headline. And then forgotten.

Mick Gallin was but a statistic to his former employer, U.S.
Steel, one of 13,000 workers laid off one dark day in 1979.[6]

He was but a statistic to the unemployment office in Youngstown, one of more than 51,000 who had passed through their
doors that year.[7]

He was but a statistic to his union local, one of more than
4,100 members in a similar fix.[8]

He was but a statistic to the steely-eyed woman in the state
employment commission, one of an unnumbered throng, seeking but not finding.[9]

And he was but a statistic to the Youngstown police who
picked his broken body up off the floor and hurried it to the
morgue, one of eighteen similar suicides thus far that year.[10]

He was but a statistic whose eulogy would be soon forgotten,
his epitaph carved in rust.

The Post-Industrial Economy

"One doesn't have to be an economist," says political analyst
Randy Barber, "to observe what's happening to America's northern industrial corridor. A simple train ride on Amtrak's New
York to Chicago run provides convincing evidence of the crisis at
hand. Passing through towns like Erie, Harrisburg, Cleveland,
Toledo, Elkhart, and South Bend, a passenger needs only to take
a look out of the window to see what has happened to these once-
powerful industrial centers. While each city could once point to
some unique feature as its own particular claim to glory, there is
now a sameness to them all. Old factories, some a block long or

more, dot the sides of the tracks. Mostly deserted, their windows shattered or checker-boarded, they look like a scene from war-torn Europe. There is a dreariness to these cities. It's not a lazy kind of dreariness, but more a tired kind. There's no life, no anticipation. The squeaks and groans of the train wheels seem to pass judgment on it all."[11]

America's economy has changed. Down to its very foundations. And these basic structural changes have obviously not come without pain. The "gradual transformation" of our nation "from an industrial society to an information society," as John Naisbitt has described it in his mega-bestselling book, *Megatrends*, seemed anything but "gradual" to the men and women who made their homes, raised their families, and staked their lives on the northern industrial corridor.[12] It seemed anything but "gradual" to those men and women who were unwilling participants in the great economic shakedown of the late seventies and early eighties: plant closings, corporate disinvestment, and the dismantling of basic heavy industry.[13] It seemed anything but "gradual" to those people who watched their once vital manufacturing centers turn — almost overnight — into giant industrial ghost towns.[14]

It seemed anything but "gradual" to Mick Gallin.

During the 1960s, the nation's overall economic growth averaged 4.1% per year.[15] As a result, the gross national product (GNP) expanded by a hefty 50% over the decade, consumers were able to post a 33% gain in buying power, and industry claimed a whopping 25% share of the world's manufactured exports.[16] America had the highest standard of living in the world[17] and everyone expected *more* of the same. The sky was the limit.

But the 1970s were a different story altogether. The GNP grew a mere 2.9% each year, giving consumers only about a 7% increase in purchasing power.[18] Industry's share of the world market dropped below 17% and the American standard of living dropped behind Switzerland, Sweden, Denmark, West Germany, Luxembourg, Iceland, Abu Dhabi, France, the Netherlands, Kuwait, and Belgium.[19] Dreams were dashed. Illusions were shattered.

The reasons for the drastic turnaround in the economic strength and vitality of the nation were multitudinous.[20] But chief among them was a rabid fear of change.[21] Americans clung tenaciously to a rapidly sinking status quo. Some went down with the ship. Instead of accepting and even advancing the "gradual" transformation of the economy from a heavy industrial base to a high tech information or service base, most Americans fought the changes off with all their might.[22] We were basking in the victories of the 60s instead of bracing for the battles of the 80s. We failed to invest in more efficient manufacturing methods for fear of trimming jobs.[23] We continued to subsidize declining industries well beyond their legitimate life span in the economy.[24] We ignored the trends in the world marketplace — and covered it over obstinately with protectionist tariffs and trade barriers.[25] We stifled entrepreneurial activity and rewarded ploddingly conservative and predictably uncreative endeavors with special tax structuring, occupational licensing, and industrial regulation.[26] We caved in to union pressure to maintain archaic management, pension, and investment policies as well as seriously inflated wages, and minimum wage laws.[27] In the midst of the changes in the world economy that were occurring, and with the full weight of our industrial and government policy resisting those changes, everything slowed. Other nations like Japan, West Germany, and South Korea jumped into the place usually reserved for the U.S.[28] The economy was thrown into an odd and awkward stasis.[29]

Then in 1973, the bottom fell out with the energy crisis.[30] Declining industries that had been putting off the inevitable for far too long began to collapse.[31] Instead of going through gradual, natural transitions, American businesses were backed against the wall. It was do or die. A lot of them died. Instead of taking the opportunities afforded by the prosperity of the sixties to launch into the future, we maintained our safe and comfortable position in the past. We held on. We ignored the warning signs. We resisted the changes. Then, when push came to shove, and changes were *forced* upon us, we no longer had the option of making a smooth, easy, and voluntary economic evolution. We were faced with utter chaos and calamity. Massive layoffs ensued. What could have been, what should have been a "gradual transition," became a catastrophe.

During the last few years of the 70s and the first few years of the 80s, the nation's steel production capacity was slashed by 11%, automaking capacity was cut 8%, rubber manufacturing capacity dropped 14%, and consumer electronics manufacturing, despite a big boost from the video and computer revolutions, saw a 21% cut.[32] As a result, nearly 38 million jobs were eliminated from the labor force—once the pride of the nation, the envy of the world.[33]

Most Americans were totally unprepared for unemployment on that scale. We were shocked to see our neighbors and peers standing in lines to obtain USDA milk, cheese, and butter. We were flabbergasted by the sight of tent cities and overcrowded rescue missions. Fear gripped the nation.[34]

Of course, the transformation process continued unabated despite the cataclysmic deindustrialization. Without many of the declining industries to sap their strength, investors were able to capitalize a number of new endeavors more in keeping with market needs and directions. Thus between 1969 and 1976, twenty-five million new jobs were created, about 3.6 million per year.[35] And between 1977 and 1984, another 27 million jobs were added.[36] With a bit of retraining and readjustment, most of those who had lost jobs in old, dying industries were able to find new jobs in emerging service and information fields.[37]

Most of them. But not all of them. Some like Mick Gallin never made the transition.

Between 1981 and 1984, there were almost 2.6 million people that joined Mick Gallin on the long list of former workers who had exhausted their unemployment benefits without finding replacement work.[38] 2.6 million people joined him in the long, frustrating search for jobs: scanning the want ads every day, making the rounds of employment services, union halls, trade schools, and government offices, pounding the pavement, sending out letters and resumes, and hoping against hope that something would break. Soon. Before *they* broke. Like Mick Gallin.

Housing and Unemployment

Sustained unemployment and major industrial transition are fuel for the consuming fires of homelessness. The link between joblessness and homelessness is obvious enough. With no money coming in, people can't afford to pay the rent. It's that simple. They are displaced.

Not all of these displaced workers finally wind up in the street or in the shelters or in tent cities. There are alternatives to homelessness for the displaced. But they are few and far between.

Many of the displaced unemployed "double up" with others: moving in with parents, sharing an apartment with siblings, or pooling resources with friends. The New York Housing Authority estimates that 17,000 families are "doubling up" in that city's public housing projects alone.[39] That amounts to one out of every ten households officially living in the projects.[40] Sociologist Henry Schechter estimates that nationwide "the number of families living with others as 'subfamilies' doubled, from a low of 1.3 million in 1978 to 2.6 million in 1983. Similarly, the number of unrelated individuals living with others went from 23.4 million in 1978 to 28.1 million in 1983."[41]

Many others of the displaced unemployed are able to avoid homelessness by securing public housing. In 1983, nearly 160,000 families applied for such assistance in New York alone.[42] Unfortunately, with a low 3.8% turn over rate nationwide, and with waiting lists as long as five to six years, the relief public housing can give is minimal.[43]

So where do the rest go? Where do the displaced unemployed go when they can't move in with family or friends, when they are unable to get public assistance?

Hundreds of articles and feature stories in chronicles as varied as *The Wall Street Journal*[44] and *People Magazine*,[45] *The New York Times*[46] and *Rolling Stone*,[47] *Newsweek Magazine*[48] and *The Humble Echo*,[49] *The Christian Herald*[50] and *The U.N. Habitat News*,[51] have documented their flight to the streets, their flight into homelessness. Invariably the chronicles sample the heart-wrenching riches to rags stories that abound in times like these.

Stories of people like Mick Gallin.

For fourteen years, Mick worked hard. He was one of 3,500 steel workers in the U.S. Steel mill in Youngstown, Ohio. He'd always been thankful for his job — all the more so when in 1977 he saw 4,100 of his friends and neighbors lose theirs when the Campbell Works of the Youngstown Sheet and Tube Company closed its gates for good. He had read in the papers how as many as 35% of those former workers were forced into early retirement — at less than half of their previous salary.[52] Another 15% were still looking for work a year later.[53] About 40% had been able to find other work, but most had taken huge wage cuts.[54] The remaining 10% were forced to take to the streets.[55] So, Mick was thankful and "counted his blessings." He redoubled his efforts to make himself indispensible to his employers.

All to no avail.

On Thanksgiving Day, 1979, in a message that certainly brought no holiday cheer to Mick's celebration, U.S. Steel made a dramatic announcement in *The New York Times*:

"The United States Steel Corporation has announced that it will close fourteen plants and mills in eight cities. About 13,000 production and white-collar workers will lose their jobs. The cutback represents about 8% of the company's work force. The retrenchment is one of the most sweeping in the industry's history . . . in spite of high demand for steel in the last two years."[56]

Needless to say, Mick was stunned.

He quickly moved to put his financial house in order. He cashed some bonds, liquidated a retirement fund, cancelled two insurance policies, and consolidated his credit union accounts. He was single with no dependents, so with all his savings, he figured he had enough to live on for eight months, if need be. Add to that six months of unemployment, and he could survive for more than a year. He knew a lot of his friends and co-workers would have a hard time just trying to make it a week. He'd never believed in living "hand to mouth."

Circumstances would soon *make* him a believer.

He just could *not* find a job. And he tried everything. Even McDonalds.

Weeks went by. And then months. Finally, the months turned to years.

All the careful planning in the world could never have prepared Mick for the kind of calamity he faced. In the twenty-six months that elapsed following the closing of the Youngstown mill, Mick only worked seventy-two days. Mostly odd jobs.

When at last he was evicted from his apartment, he made a last ditch, desperation visit to the state employment office. When that too ended in frustration, he took his life rather than face the future homeless as well as jobless.

Job Creation

Recognizing the dire effect joblessness has had on their communities, and its close correspondence to homelessness, a large number of congressional leaders have made "job creation" a top priority in domestic legislation. Since 1981, more than seventy-two "job stimulation," or "job preservation," or "job creation" riders have been attached to bills as wide-ranging as gasoline tax increases to road repair legislation.[57] House Speaker Tip O'Neill argued in 1983 that "one way or another, we are going to have to step in and get our people back to work."[58] Unfortunately, sixty-nine of the seventy-two riders called for federal tax dollars to provide the necessary job openings.[59] Instead of stimulating the economy from the bottom up by removing disincentives, regulatory restrictions, developmental controls, and windfall profits taxes—the things that forced U.S. Steel to close Mick Gallin's plant—the legislation simply inflicted more hardships on business by imposing top down controls through subsidies, limitations, interventions, and restrictions—the very kinds of tactics that caused the economic transitions of the 70s and 80s to sour in the first place.

The legislative initiative to generate jobs was well intended —jobs obviously must be generated—but fatally flawed, for two basic reasons.

First, real job creation can only occur through economic growth. Prosperity or wealth is not a stable commodity that can simply be managed and redistributed in order to achieve equality or justice. It is rather the result of productivity. It is the fruit of work.[60] Thus in the long run, spreading existing wealth around doesn't help anyone, in fact it only hurts everyone.[61] Only by work, by the sweat of our brows, can our fields of thorns and thistles yield a bounteous harvest.[62] The flaw of the legislative initiative has been that it focuses almost exclusively on the distribution of wealth (more salaries dispensed), ignoring the need to stimulate production (economic growth).[63]

Second, the job creation initiative is based upon the idea that "society owes people a living." America was founded as "the land of opportunity." The rights guaranteed by our society have always been "life, liberty, and the pursuit of happiness." But entitlement to a particular standard of living, or to a particular level of economically defined social guarantees, has never been a part of our system.[64] Always generous and always charitable, Americans have nevertheless maintained a bootstrap ethic: Hard work, diligence, and productivity are the only means to improve the lot of the poor. Thus, until the "war on poverty" was initiated in the mid-60s, virtually all charitable efforts in this country were aimed at expanding the opportunities afforded the poor by expanding the economy in general. Entitlement was never an issue. Opportunity was.

The U.N.'s Answer

Like the congressional leaders who have pushed through job creation bills in the legislature, the officials in charge of the U.N.'s International Year of the Homeless comprehend the close correspondence of joblessness to homelessness. And like those legislative leaders, U.N. spokesmen see the state as "the necessary facilitator of job creation and equitable job distribution."[65]

So, though most of the International Year concern has been focused on "the development of sheltering options, and the removal of socio, ethno, and legal obstacles to advancement,"[66] the idea of "governmentally subsidized development programming" takes a high profile as well.[67]

Unfortunately, the same two fatal flaws that have crippled the job creation initiative in the U.S. have also infected the U.N.'s agenda. Several brochures and monographs produced by the UNCHS allude to the "just redistribution" of earth's "fixed resources."[68] They speak of man's "right to work"[69] and his "right to employment."[70] They even castigate free market economies for "raising living standards before affording full and equitable employ."[71]

The solution? More "governmental control,"[72] more "centralized regularization,"[73] and more "state supervision"[74] of "hiring practices, and income distribution."[75]

Gleaning

Clearly, the legislative leaders and the U.N. officials are correct in their assertion that the homeless must find employment. But how should that employment be supplied?

According to the Bible, work is the means by which the poor advance their lot. God awards power, wealth, blessing, and dominion to those who labor diligently (Deuteronomy 8:18; Proverbs 10:4). Far from being a part of the fall's curse, work is a vital aspect of God's eternal purpose for man (Genesis 1:28). In fact, "a man can do nothing better than find satisfaction in his work" (Ecclesiastes 2:24; 3:22). That is why God built work opportunities for the poor into the fabric of the Old Testament society.[76]

But instead of making a continual redistribution of wealth

the basis of job creation, God made new production the stimulus. His laws are explicit.

> Now when you reap the harvest of your land, you shall not reap to the very corners of your field, neither shall you gather the gleanings of your harvest. Nor shall you glean your vineyard, nor shall you gather the fallen fruit of your vineyard; you shall leave them for the needy and for the stranger. I am the Lord your God (Leviticus 19:9-10).

> When you reap your harvest in your field and have forgotten a sheaf in the field, you shall not go back to get it; it shall be for the alien, for the orphan, and for the widow, in order that the Lord your God may bless you in all the work of your hands. When you beat your olive tree, you shall not go over the boughs again; it shall be for the alien, for the orphan, and for the widow. When you gather the grapes of your vineyard, you shall not go over it again; it shall be for the alien, for the orphan, and for the widow (Deuteronomy 24:19-21).

Landowners in Israel were not to be saddled with the added burden of *subsidizing* the living of the poor, but they *were* to provide them with the means, the opportunity to *make* their living themselves. The poor were not to bleed off the profits of landowners, stealing from them the fruit of their labors. Instead, the poor were to engage in *production* themselves, living off the fruit of *their* labors.

Thus, ancient Israel was a *true* "land of opportunity." God's laws expanded opportunity by expanding the economy in general.

Instead of straining the economy with top down controls and mandates for redistribution, God's law stimulated the economy with bottom up incentives and opportunities.

The poor were enabled, not just appeased. And the wealthy were not penalized in the process. It was a system in which the rich could get richer (if they contrived to work hard and obey God's laws) but then so could the poor (if *they* worked hard and obeyed God's laws). It was a system that broke the connection between joblessness and homelessness by giving the dispossessed *opportunities* within the growing economy.

Progressivism

Biblical faith is progressive. Humanism is conservative, whether left or right, whether liberal or traditional.[77] The Biblical faith constantly presses for advance. It breaks old wineskins (Luke 5:37-38). Humanism constantly presses for stabilization. It relies on old broken cisterns (Jeremiah 2:13).

The reason is simple. Biblical faith is innately optimistic.[78] Humanism is innately pessimistic.[79]

The Bible shows the righteous man starting with a corrupted earth: thorns and thistles (Genesis 3:18). Through diligent labor, obedience, thrift, and righteousness, man shapes and tills and rules over the earth. Under the guidance of the Holy Spirit, he takes it from chaos to order. By the power of the Holy Spirit, he takes it from a wilderness into a garden (Isaiah 51:3; Isaiah 58:10-12; Ezekiel 36:33-36). The Bible is the story of Paradise Restored.[80]

Humanism on the other hand, looks at history quite oppositely. The story of man for the humanist begins east of Eden in pristine beauty.[81] But with civilization comes pollution, ecological imbalance, shortages, and chaos. The best man can hope for is to stall the inevitable: utter desolation. The sun is burning out. The atmosphere is disintegrating. The ecosystem is collapsing. Man holds a very delicate balance. According to the humanist, life on earth is the story of Paradise Lost.[82]

Thus in times of tension, in times of change, Christians look forward with anticipation, with hope, and with faith. While humanists tremble, fret, and fear, Christians move ahead, challenging the obstacles, utilizing opportunities, and posing solutions. Humanists are forced to fight to maintain, to conserve the status quo, and to resist the future.

Conclusion

Long term sustained unemployment leads inexorably to homelessness. Much of the reason for the sudden epidemic proportions of dispossession in the U.S. is the transitional nature of our economy and the incumbent rise in joblessness.

It only stands to reason then, that a major factor in combatting homelessness should be job creation.

Many leading figures in both the U.S. Congress and the United Nations argue that Government must create those jobs through various legislative means, subsidizing the economy with tax dollars when necessary. But legislative controls, subsidies, and regulation are a large part of the problem in the first place. Those are the kind of change-resistant pessimistic measures that compounded unemployment, slowed economic transition, and stymied entrepreneurial activity. You can't treat a disease with ever-increasing doses of the disease. Even immunization doesn't work that way.

In contrast to that kind of top down imposition on the economy, God's plan for Israel involved an optimistic, bottom up stimulation of the economy, expanding job opportunities through economic growth.

If homelessness is to be solved in any measure, jobs will have to be created. And job creation can only occur when the economy is freed for growth.

It has often been said that the Bible is more up to date than tomorrow's newspaper. In this case, we can congruently assert without hesitation that the Bible is more up to date than tomorrow's legislative proposals.

Though the many lights dwindle to one light,
There is help if the heavens have one;
Though the skies be discrowned of the sunlight
    And the earth dispossessed of the sun,
They have moonlight and sleep for repayment,
When, refreshed as a bride and set free,
With stars and sea-winds in her raiment,
    Night sinks on the sea.

A. C. Swinburne

THE SKIES DISCROWNED: THE FARM CRISIS

The American farmer is in trouble. And as a consequence, America is in trouble.

You probably don't need to be told. That message has been emblazoned across the pages of every major newspaper and magazine in the land.

But if you ever meet up with Gerry Everman, he'll probably tell you anyway. He wants to make certain that the message gets through. Telling folks has become his consuming passion, his main aim and ambition in life. A kind of personal jihad. If you get within a hundred yards of him, he'll tell you: "The American farmer is in trouble. And as a consequence, America is in trouble."

Gerry knows from personal experience. He works the register at a small building supply and hardware store in Queens today. But just two years ago, he was the proud proprietor of a small truck farm in central Missouri. Like his father before him, and his grandfather before that, Gerry grew several small cash crops, kept a few dairy cows, experimented with a fledgling vineyard, and leased out portions of his modest property to some local grazers. Nothing spectacular, but it was a living. It was, in fact, a good living.

In 1977 the local agricultural agent convinced Gerry to expand and update his equipment and facilities. Land values were soaring, crop prices were keeping pace with inflation, and banks were actively loaning, so with only a little hesitation, he took the plunge. He bought new tractors and harvesters and rebuilt barns. He raised the standard of the small operation to the point that it matched the best of the best — it rivaled the automation of many "corporate farms."

But then the bottom fell out. In November 1983, Gerry went to see his banker in order to get a loan for seed and fertilizer, his perennial post-harvest, pre-tilling chore. To his utter astonishment, the banker turned him away. It seems that because of the now-plummeting values on prime Missouri cropland, Gerry's equity had been more than cut in two. His debt service was triple "what it should have been." So, even though he had never been delinquent on his payments — not once in the thirteen years he'd done business with the bank — he was no longer considered a "good credit risk."

Without credit, Gerry was unable to put in a crop that year. And despite the fact that he still had income from his dairy cows and rental properties, without a crop he was unable to keep up with his bills.

Eighteen months later, Gerry's farm was sold at an auction. He was lucky. The auction brought forty-five cents on the dollar. Most auctions do well to get half that. Even so, the creditors got everything and suddenly Gerry was without a job, without a home, without anything.

"Thirteen years of work and what have I got? . . . Nothin' at all," he said. "Nothin' at all . . . an' I'm tellin' ya' what. If it can happen to me, it can happen to anyone. The American farmer is in trouble. An' if he's in trouble, the rest of the country is in double trouble."

Double Trouble

According to the Census Bureau, only 14% of this nation's poor live in the decaying inner cities.[1] Another 47% live in the large metropolitan areas or urban suburbs.[2] But all the rest, a full 39% of the total poor population, live in rural regions.[3] Of the more than 34.6 million poor Americans, 13.5 million live in the country.[4] They are farmers, ranchers, loggers, hired hands, or migrant harvesters. They are people that supply our grocery shelves, stock our markets, and produce the raw materials on which our industry depends. And many are now homeless as well as poor. As many as one-third of our nation's homeless are from rural areas.[5]

And it doesn't look to get better in the near future.

All across the vast farm belt there is mounting alarm that the grim harvest of failures and foreclosures that has marked the agricultural economy for the last five years will continue on indefinitely.[6] The fact is, the American farmer is facing the biggest farm depression in fifty years — since the Great Depression.[7] More than 400,000 farms are currently threatened with bankruptcy and foreclosure.[8]

With farm debt approaching the $200 billion mark, banks are beginning to get nervous.[9] "When a farmer's debt-to-asset ratio climbs above 26% or so," says banker Mal McCabe, "financial institutions are forced — by market necessities — to call their loans due."[10] That hard economic reality has been especially bitter in states like Iowa where in 1986 the *average* debt-to-asset ratio is 36.9%, and North Dakota where the average is 34.7%, and Nebraska: 34.3%, and Kansas: 31.8%, and Illinois: 30.8%, and Michigan: 28.6%, and Wisconsin: 26.2%.[11] It is really no wonder then that in 1984 the Farmers Home Administration (FHA) reported a delinquency rate of more than 25%,[12] and most experts were estimating that another 30-40% escaped insolvency only by temporarily refinancing debt.[13] "Most farmers are just buying time now. Waiting for the inevitable," said McCabe.[14]

Over the last decade, farmers have had good harvests.[15] Their efficiency has improved dramatically due to the "green revolution" and other technological advances.[16] The weather has not been terribly adverse.[17] Rainfall has been generally good.[18] Demand for food products is up.[19] Marketing, processing, and distribution are no problem whatsoever.[20] So why are we in the midst of a terrible farm crisis?

"The fact is that the 'farm crisis' is not a 'farm crisis' at all," says Vern Oglethorpe, an Iowa farmer. "It is a political crisis."

Farm Debt

In many ways, farmers have no one but themselves to blame for the massive debt load they suffer under. They, after all were the ones to sign the contracts, buy the machinery, and expand the operations. This is the position Budget Director David Stockman took when he opposed farm bailouts in 1984.[21] But in many other ways, Vern Oglethorpe is right and David Stockman is wrong: The farm crisis has been precipitated by a number of ill-advised political moves.

In the seventies, land values steadily increased to alarming highs due to a heavy handed expansion of the money supply by the Federal Reserve and the incumbent double-digit price inflation.[22] At the same time, government supports for farm commodities cut overhead and increased equity for many farmers by as much as 70%.[23] Federal Land Bank personnel notified their loan offices throughout the country to "get ready for $5000 per acre land."[24] Based on that kind of enthusiastic projection, most rural bankers accelerated their easy loan programs, accepting the overpriced land as collateral. Even farmers who had no need for investment or expansion capital were advised by government farm agents and by their bankers to take advantage of the situation. Everyone was betting that both the land value escalation and the general price inflation would continue far into the foreseeable future.[25]

They bet wrong. By the summer of 1986 more than 10% of the farmers in the corn belt owed more than 70% of their entire net worth.[26] Elsewhere the situation was little better. Interest payments drained away their life blood while their incomes — set by government decreed prices — sharply declined.[27] Their land value plummeted — acreage selling at prices 60% below 1980 levels.[28] And an overvalued dollar priced them out of most foreign markets, making them the supplier of last resort.[29]

So perhaps Vern Oglethorpe is right: The farm crisis is, at the bottom line, a political crisis.

Foreign Policy

But it wasn't just the government's monetary and farm administration policies that precipitated the current crisis. Foreign policy foibles also contributed to the American farmer's demise.

Several times in the eighties Washington propped up communist dictatorships threatened with collapse due to food shortages. Instead of benevolently allowing those governments to fall and channeling aid directly to the people and to resistance groups, the State Department supported the Marxists, and at a price American farmers could ill afford. Scripture commands us to feed even our enemies when they are hungry and to give them drink when they are thirsty, for in so doing we heap burning coals upon their heads (Romans 12:20). But Scripture also commands us not to be overcome by evil but rather to overcome evil with good (Romans 12:21). The tough question we have to ask is, "Has our aid to communist regimes actually fed the hungry, or has it only solidified the death grip control of their evil empires?"

In 1983, the USDA provided the faltering government of communist Poland with $51.2 million worth of cheese, butter, and dried milk.[30] In 1984, the U.S. provided $22.7 million worth of food to communist Ethiopia and in 1985 sent an additional $127.6 million.[31] Still another $100 million in aid was slated for 1986, despite the fact that it had become widely known that the Ethiopian regime was deliberately fabricating famine conditions in order to subjugate a strong rebel opposition movement in the northern provinces, and was withholding food aid from the most hard hit famine area.[32]

Similar arrangements have enabled the communist dictatorships of Zimbabwe, Mozambique, Tanzania, Somalia, and Nicaragua to establish and consolidate control during times of instability.[33]

And what does the farmer at home have to show for all this benevolence?

Looming foreclosure. Their produce, bought at below market prices, is charged back against their accounts through taxes in order to fund the giveaways. And then they are charged back again through Defense Department expenditures. It's no wonder then, that many farmers are protesting that they've got "the best enemies that money can buy . . . twice!"[34]

In addition, every time agricultural experts have made advances that might give farmers at home a competitive edge in the intensely emulative world market, the State Department has given them away as well.

"If a country wanted to increase yields," says Bob Meyer, former Assistant Secretary of Agriculture, "it was given our new seed varieties. The United States sent teams abroad to teach the modern miracles of fertilizers and then helped finance foreign building of fertilizer plants. We sent teams to teach about erosion. When foreign farmers had bugs, we sent insecticides. If there were weeds, we sent herbicides. We taught foreigners how to plant, grow, combine, mill, gin, package, can, and sell. We even helped them build dams, irrigation systems and sold them tractors at subsidized rates. And when our agricultural competitors wanted to see how the American farmer operated, we took them into our homes, fed them, gave them gifts, and showed them demonstrations of our techniques, complete with pictures. And all this was going on at a time when the cost of our land, labor, and water was slowly rising. Eventually, the cost of growing our crops became much higher than that of our students — or more precisely, our competitor nations. We had educated them and given them all of our scientific advances. Today, that makes about as much sense as IBM giving free use of its patents to its competitors."[35]

Using American techniques, and American dollars, and American machinery, the rest of the world can now produce the major crops for less than we can. Thus, our exports in 1985 were down 17% due to the high cost of our goods.[36] Argentina can sell wheat in the U.S. at a cheaper price than Kansas farmers can sell it — that's why in 1985, 46.2 million tons were brought in.[37] Canada can sell beef in the U.S. far cheaper than Texas cattle ranchers can — that's why 1.3 million head of cattle were imported in 1985.[38] Western Europe can sell pork in the U.S. at a lower price than Tennessee hog farmers can — that's why 126 million pounds of pork were imported in 1985.[39]

American farmers have always been generous. In times of genuine need they have always responded with selfless honor, and rightly so. But the State Department has adopted a policy that utilizes food as a political bargaining chip.[40] "When the government intervenes in any industry," says political analyst Joel Scheibla, "with the intention of buying political favor or gaining political advantage, the scheme always fails. Always. In the case of the politicization of farming, the scheme has been disastrous."[41] According to Scheibla we've been terribly cavalier in "wielding food as the ultimate political weapon, but we've ended up clumsily hurting all the wrong people . . . we've bankrupted the bread basket."[42]

Perhaps Vern Oglethorpe is right. The farm crisis is indeed a political crisis.

Farm Subsidies

In his now famous book *A Time for Truth*, former Secretary of the Treasury William Simon asserted: "More than sixty million Americans now get some kind of check from the government! They gather beneath the federal faucet. They agree that it pours forth a torrent, and that the handle appears to be missing. But rather than summon a plumber, they jockey for position beneath the stream with buckets, pans, and cups."[43] Among those millions now jockeying for positions are America's farmers. Taking advantage of the various farm subsidy programs as many as 72% of all those occupied with full time agriculture have resorted to the federal dole.[44] They say they can't make it any other way.

In 1985, the government provided $18.7 billion to farmers to produce, or not to produce certain commodities.[45] In 1986, $20.4 billion was set aside, nearly a tenfold increase since the beginning of the decade.[46] That makes farming the most heavily subsidized industry in America.

Thomas Jefferson once asserted, "Were we directed from Washington when to sow and when to reap, we should soon want for bread."[47] Apparently Washington never got the message.

And it still hasn't.

The result has been that agriculture in the U.S. has been reduced to a welfare client, more dependent on the winds and whims of Washington than the rains and vanes of Kansas. As Assistant Secretary Meyer has said, the farmer has "become dependent on the government for a quick fix for all his problems. If prices get too low, the government is expected to bail the farmer out. If a storm tears up his crops, the government gives him low interest loans. If there is a drought, the government lends him money. It's the same for a flood, a freeze, a fire. If the farmer wants to make improvements to his land, the government will help him irrigate, drain or put up windbreaks. Dream it up and Uncle Sam will finance it, including even taking the land out of production . . . Why? To assure a plentiful supply of cheap food — enough to feed half the world. The only problem is that the bottom has fallen out. Half the world doesn't need our food, or can't pay for it. As that credit so lavished on our farmers comes due, foreclosures result."[48]

Getting On With Life

After Gerry Everman lost his farm, he moved in with his sister and brother-in-law. "For a couple a' weeks. Just t' get things sorted out." But there wasn't much left to sort. "I knew I would have to move on . . . I couldn't stand the sight a' somebody else workin' my place." So one afternoon he just loaded up what was left of his earthly belongings in the back of an old Ford pickup and bid the only home he'd ever known farewell.

He drove to St. Louis. "I spent about four days there lookin' for work. Put in applications at lots a' places. But nothin' turned up, so I figured I'd try Chicago. My money wasn't gonna last too much longer I knew, so I was kinda itchy t' get settled." Chicago wasn't much better. "Not hiring" signs were posted everywhere it seemed. It was the same in Detroit, Toledo, Cleveland, Akron, Pittsburgh, Philadelphia, Trenton, and Newark. By the time he arrived in New York City he was almost out of gas, almost out of money, and almost out of hope. "My third day here, I found this job. Workin' the register at a hardware store in Queens is not really my idea of a solid career move . . . but it's somethin'. At least I'm workin'. In a couple a' more weeks I'll have enough saved up to get me an apartment. Then I can stop sleepin' in the truck at night. Then I can maybe . . . get on with life."

Most farmers are survivors. Like Gerry Everman, they will make their way. They will find a way. They will somehow or another "get on with life." But with the farm crisis escalating with every passing day, and homelessness claiming more and more of their number, that task is becoming ever more formidable.

The U.N.'s Answer

The focus of the U.N.'s International Year of the Homeless has been almost exclusively on urban overcrowding and urban development. The question of what to do with the millions upon millions of rural refugees once they reach the cities has outstripped all other considerations. The U.N.'s concern is more with what to do with the water flooding in, than with how to plug the dike. Its concern is to treat symptoms, not to find cures.

What little the U.N. International Year officials have said concerning the farm crisis has carefully repeated the tired old clichés of government control and centralization; again advocating *more* of what got farmer in this mess in the first place. In one seminar, they spoke of the necessity to "collectivize the means of agricultural production," and to "regularize and regulate the ownership apparatus of key agricultural regions."[49] In another seminar, they spoke of the "essential role of pre- and post-production subsidy supports in arresting the tyrannical forces of the marketplace."[50] In other words, the same old cant.

One constantly recurring phrase in all these International Year seminar transcripts is "the security afforded by government planning and involvement." At a conference in Calcutta, one U.N. official asserted that "the free market, left entirely to itself, involves urban populations in a dangerous game of survival. The security afforded by government planning and involvement in agriculture is very simply indispensible, a modern necessity provocated by a burgeoning world population explosion."[51] At another conference in Nairobi, a U.N. spokesman keynoted with this: "Security is the issue at hand in agricultural policies today. Global security and the availability and accessibility of cheap food for the vast urban populations are inextricably linked. Thus, the security afforded by government planning and involvement must be guarded at all costs."[52] At still another conference in Stockholm a U.N. staffer waxed eloquent saying, "The modern mind must be reoriented to the realities of the modern world. By habit we've come to think of security in terms of military forces and capabilities. The traditional symbol of a security threat has been massed weapons of mass destruction. We must dash these illusions. We must see security in terms of independence and food stockpiles, not in terms of independence and defensive arsenals. We must comprehend that the security afforded by government planning and involvement in food production and distribution is the greatest security of all."[53]

Clearly then, to the U.N., collectivization, regulation, subsidization, and regularization are matters of security. Farmers must submit themselves to the state for the good of all, for the common security.

The Quest for Security

Baal was the great lord over the pantheon of gods worshipped by the Canaanites when Joshua led Israel into the Promised Land. The god was thought to control fertility in agriculture, and since the land had very few natural streams or springs and an abominably uncertain rainfall, the Canaanites placed tremendous emphasis on obtaining his favor. It was a critical matter of security, more important even than appeasing the god of war. This led them to extreme practices like ritual prostitution (John 2:17; Jeremiah 7:9; Amos 2:7), self abuse (1 Kings 18:28), and even child-sacrifice (Jeremiah 19:5).

When the Israelites failed to drive the Canaanites out of the land, but instead intermarried with them, the problem of the relationship between Yahweh and Baal was raised. According to Biblical scholar Arthur Cundall, "Yahweh had given Israel a considerable victory over the Canaanites and thus His supremacy was unquestioned." Unfortunately though, "The average Israelite associated Him with the wilderness in which they had spent the major portion of their lives. In Canaan they were dependent upon the fertility of the land, which, in popular thought, was controlled by Baal. Many, therefore, conceived it wise to pay a deference to the pagan god."[54] This tendency to follow the course of expediency was aggravated by the sensuality and materialism of the Canaanite cultus. Baalism was not only expedient, it was fashionable and fun! So, the Israelites struck a devil's bargain. They continued to honor Yahweh, but no longer as the one, true God. Instead, in the interests of security — agricultural security — they placed another god before Him.

According to John Whitehead, "Humanism can be defined as the fundamental idea that people can begin from human reason without reference to any divine revelation or absolute truth, and by reasoning outward, derive the standards to judge all matters. For such people, there is no absolute or fixed standard of behavior. They are quite literally autonomous . . . a law unto themselves. As such, there are no rights given by God; no standards that cannot be eroded or replaced by what seems necessary, expedient, or even fashionable at the time. Man, it is presumed, is his own authority, his own god in his own universe."[55] That being the case, Israel's quest for security — their Baalism — was blatantly and classically humanistic.

The Israelites either forgot about or ignored the revelation of God concerning their security (Deuteronomy 28) and reasoned for themselves. They determined on their own authority to follow the "necessary," "expedient," and "fashionable" course to security. Many understood the nature of their devil's bargain but proceeded to capitulate to the passion and pragmatism of the moment anyway (2 Kings 15:34-35). The lesser of two evils, don't you know? The price you have to pay, don't you see?

In time, Baal worship became public policy, enforced by the government (1 Kings 8:4). This too was a matter of security. You can almost hear Jezebel or Ahab saying, "The security afforded by government planning and involvement in agriculture — Baal worship — is very simply indispensible, a modern necessity." Like the U.N. officials in our own day they began from "human reason without reference to any divine revelation." Like the U.N. officials in our own day, they sought a security of their own devising, apart from the sovereign hand of God.

But they were soon disappointed.

Instead of bountiful harvests, their allegiance to their humanistic Baals wrought only famine, drought, locust plagues, sirocco winds, and judgment. Just as in our day, allegiance to humanistic Baals has wrought only bankruptcy, foreclosure, and homelessness.

Israel had only one hope to reverse their fortunes. They had to renounce their false security — their Baals — and repent. They had to turn back to the Word of God as their only authority. They had to acknowledge Yahweh as the *one* true God, their hope and their salvation.

Similarly, there is but one hope for us to reverse the terrible traumas facing America's farmers. We must let go of the securities afforded by worldly reason and repent. We must renounce the manipulation, the deception, the price fixing, the tariffs, the artificial subsidy arrangements, and the outright theft that U.N. advocates and U.S. government officials have dabbled at over the last forty years. We must let go of our Baals and rely on the promise of God that if we do things His way, then and only then will He bless us with bounty. Then and only then will the flight from farming to homelessness be arrested.

Conclusion

Was Vern Oglethorpe right? Is the farm crisis in America a political crisis? Were hard working men like Gerry Everman ripped from the soil and thrust into dispossession by political forces well beyond their control?

Clearly, the agricultural system in America has become dependent upon the flux and anchor of a political system that jockeys markets with debt manipulation, price controls, land regulations, and crop subsidies. So, much of the farm crisis today, which has resulted in epidemic foreclosures and homelessness, has been precipitated by an obstinate adherence to long-discredited political maneuvers and machinations.

But there may be a deeper cause. The political insanity that has led farmers down a primrose path to ruin is rooted in a spiritual commitment to Baalistic humanism. In short, a return to fiscal conservatism is not the only thing that needs to happen to turn the farm crisis around, though that certainly wouldn't hurt. What American farmers need more than anything else is not another advocate in Washington, but an Advocate in Heaven. They need not so much a repeal of trade restrictions and tariffs as they do repentance of tawdry recalcitrance and treason.

The Baals must be thrown down.

Then the people can take Refuge. Then they can find Habitation, for the Lord God on High Himself will provide.

No refuge could save
    the bondsman, the hireling, the slave
    from terrors of the flight,
    from gloom of the grave,
When forced
    by 'ere wits to take
    the leave by the Dogtown Gate.

            Lawrence Dwight Appleby

TEN

LEAVE BY THE DOGTOWN GATE: TRANSIENCY

She was a child. Just fourteen. And in some ways, she looked it. Her petite hands were smooth and uncalloused. Her slender frame was lithe and supple. Her face, unlined and unblemished despite a layer of grime, was pert and perky — as only a fourteen-year-old's could be.

Thus, you might have believed her age — but for her eyes. Her eyes were hard, steely. They bespoke a hidden life of long days and even longer nights. They didn't sparkle like the eyes of a child. They were dull, mean-edged, and wary. Their patina was colored by experience. Apparently, the wrong kind of experience. It was as if all that sorrowful ill-experience had found commodious cellarage in two sad, dark caves. Unfathomable. Impenetrable.

"Had me a Disneyland life. Before." Her voice was as hard as her eyes. It too belied her age. "Had me a fine life."

"Yea, tell 'm 'bout the house. The bike an' all." Her elderly companion too, was an oddity, a bevy of contradictions. In a Shakespearean troupe, she'd have played a hag. But this was no theatrical masque she wore. Her bedraggled yellowing hair, her drooping eyes, her open, untended ulcerations, they were all too real. "Yeah, hon, tell 'm."

"Well, y'know it was pretty reg'lar."

"Yeah, reg'lar high life."

"No, no. Come on, Elz. Weren't no high life. Just reg'lar, y'know, American. Daddy, he worked real hard. Momma, she took care a' things. Had a house. Y'know, with sidewalks, an'

flowers roun' the edges. Had me a bike. A shiny red one. Rode it
to school an' roun'. Never were no worries ' bout food an' such.
Just never were. But then, that was before."

"Yeah, hon. Before."

That was before Anya Schiller had taken to the road. That
was before she'd met up with her down and out guardian angel,
Elz Weltzberg. That was before her eyes had gone hard. That
was before.

"That was before, an' this is now."

"Yeah, an' ne're the twain shall meet. Right, hon?"

"I guess."

Before, was when Anya was twelve. Before was two years
ago.

"Go on, hon, tell 'm."

"Well . . ." there was a long, choked pause. The prodding
had apparently touched a raw nerve. The cold, dark wells that
were her eyes suddenly filled to overflowing. Tiny rivulets cut
through sooty layers to pale skin.

Elz saw it coming. She wrapped her atrophied arms around
Anya and patted her lovingly, comfortingly with a filthy maw. "It
ain't been easy for her," she explained. "Huh! Understatement!"

At that, head hung, Anya moved away. She walked across
the stretch of gravel and sand that separated us from her make-
shift shelter. Elz, without averting her eyes from the pitiful sight
that the young girl made, took the cue and picked up the story
almost whispering.

"See, her Daddy'd been strugglin' some time. Layoffs an' all.
But 'cuz he'd work, he'd always seem to make ends meet. Odd
jobs, y'know. Things was tight, but they'd make it, he always
told 'm."

Her voice was cracked and harsh. Too much time. And too
many bottles of rye.

"Then tho', they lost their place. Foreclosed on." She spat the
sentence out with disgust. Or was it disdain? Who knows?

Anya was puttering. Perched on an old discarded barrel, she
kicked at a pile of skree and rubbish. She toyed with the shabby
edges of her jeans. She ran her fingers through grimy strands of
hair. Anything to keep from hearing our conversation. Anything
to keep from reliving her nightmare past.

I was beginning to see that remembering was anathema on

the streets. Remembering was taboo. Remembering was painful.

"At first, they didn' know what to do. They could a' moved in with the grandparents. But they was already puttin' up a couple a' other a' the kids. I think that was it. I don't know. Yeah, I think that was it . . . Whatever. They figured with Anya and the two babies — three kids an' all — it'd be just too much. Anya's daddy, he was proud. Didn' like charity, y'know. Never even collected on unemployment."

Anya was up now, walking toward us again. She couldn't stand to be a part of our conversation. She couldn't stand not to be. Her eyes were hard again. Like before. Haunting.

Elz looked her way and began again. This time more carefully. "So, they just up and moved. Weren't no jobs there in Baltimore. Was Baltimore, wasn't it, hon?"

"Yeah, Baltimore." Anya's terseness matched her mood. Elz didn't seem to notice.

"There was s'posed t' be work to be found in Florida, tho'. They figured, why not give it a shot. Packed up everything they could. Piled into the ol' car. An' left. Just left cold. Drove off into the sunset."

"That was the end of the good times." Anya said it with all the finality and solemnity of a eulogy. "That was the end of it all. Oh, I mean we was still together an' all for a while. But once we'd left home — Baltimore — that was the end."

The story came out like that. In fits and starts. Anya would tell a bit of it, then fall into a silent gloom. Elz would pick it up and carry it for a while. Then it would go back to Anya. Back and forth. Back and forth. For nearly four hours we talked. Or really, they talked. I mostly listened.

There were no jobs in Florida. At least not for someone with few skills and no contacts, someone like Anya's father. So they moved on. West to New Orleans. North to Little Rock. Backtracking to Atlanta. More desperate with each passing moment. Tensions rising. Tempers flaring. Life crumbling. Hope dissipating.

"The movement changed them," wrote John Steinbeck of another time, another place, yet oh so familiar. "The highways, the camps along the road, the fear of hunger and the hunger itself changed them. The children without dinner changed them, the endless moving changed them."[1]

By the time they had reached Atlanta, Anya's family too had changed. Her mother had changed. Her father had changed. The other two kids had changed. "An' I guess I was changed most of all."

After two weeks in the city, the family simply split up. "Mamma took the two little ones back to Baltimore . . . I think. Daddy, he just disappeared one night. One day he was there. The next, he was gone. Just like that. An' me . . . well, I'd met Elz here at a KOA Campground. We kinda decided to make a go of it, just the two of us."

A bit of wandering had ended them up here, in an abandoned gravel beach site along the Hudson River. A bit more could lead them — Lord knows where.

I looked at them both with wonderment.

"A lotta miles. We done a lotta miles together."

"And miles to go before we sleep, hon. Miles to go before we sleep."

Transiency and Homelessness

Wandering is a way of life for most homeless. For some, it is the beginning of the end. For some it is a means to an end. And for some, it is simply an end in itself. According to demographer Alton Ford, "migratory patterns increase significantly during times of economic duress. People start searching for greener pastures."[2] Unfortunately during times of economic duress, there may not be any greener pastures. In that case, those who had left hearth and home behind may find themselves stranded — strangers in a strange land, like Anya and Elz. New Oakies pursuing new grapes of wrath.

In 1981 and '82, cities like Detroit and Lansing were suffering terribly under the burdens of double digit inflation and double digit unemployment due to state interference in the marketplace.[3] Meanwhile, cities like Dallas and Houston boasted the lowest unemployment and cost of living figures in the nation.[4] It wasn't long before word spread. By late winter, nearly 2000 new families a week were arriving in Houston.[5] Michigan license plates became so common that native Texans bemoaned "the invasion of the black platers."[6] U-Haul dealers in Dallas were having to pay drivers to transport their glutted overstock back north.[7]

Thousands were in search of the good life.

They came to the Sunbelt because it was being touted as the nation's "job mecca." *The Houston Chronicle* had the largest "Help Wanted" section in the U.S.[8] Copies of the Sunday edition sold for as much as $20 in Detroit unemployment lines. It was a boomtown, and it drew economic refugees from the north like moths to a candle flame.

According to the U.S. Department of Commerce, almost seven million people moved to the Sunbelt from the northeast and the midwest.[9] Another 4.7 million moved to the West.[10] "This stream of migrants is so vast," said one study, "that if they all had come from the six New England states, this entire region would have been left without a single man, woman, or child."[11]

In 1979, 8%, or almost one in every twelve Americans sixteen years of age and older, were living in a state different from the one they had lived in just five years earlier. By 1984, that percentage had jumped to 12%.[12]

Unfortunately, the economic promise of the Sunbelt was illusory. Though certainly healthier than the postindustrial Midwest and Northeast, the job market simply could not absorb the thousands of new workers.[13] The housing industry was unprepared for the sudden influx.[14] The schools, already struggling to keep up, were strained to the breaking point.[15] Social service agencies were buried beneath an avalanche of need.[16] Thus, those who followed their hopes and dreams south all too often were sorely disappointed. They could see evidence of boomtown's boom all about them, but were unable to tap into its riches themselves.[17]

Having sacrificed everything to make the move, in most cases, the migrants could ill afford long, protracted searches for jobs or apartments. As hours stretched into days, days into weeks, and weeks into months and still no jobs were to be found, many of them wound up homeless. Living out of the back of their cars, in public campgrounds, under bridges, and in abandoned warehouses, they were caught between the allure of promise and the din of reality. They wound up like Anya and Elz, living by their wits, wandering from place to place, and hoping against hope.

The incidence of homelessness during this most recent migratory surge, says Alton Ford, "is certainly the highest since the earliest days of the Oakie exodus during the Great Depression. Perhaps it's the highest ever."[18]

A Nation of Migrants

Though it may have been new to Anya and Elz, migration is nothing new to most Americans. After all, America is a nation of immigrants and settlers. Our history is punctuated with the bold pioneering bursts that sent opportunity seekers through the Cumberland Gap, down the Mississippi, across the Great Plains, and up the Oregon Trail. In 1849 thousands left their homes in a gold rush to California. In 1854, 1871, 1906, and 1932, depressions sent thousands more scrambling across the nation in search of opportunity — in search of a place they could call "home."

Between 1820 and 1978, almost fifty million people emigrated to the United States[19] — displaced, uprooted, looking for the green pastures and still waters of home. In the first decade of this century alone, 8.8 million people arrived at Ellis Island[20] to gaze upon Liberty who beckoned: "Give me your tired, your poor, your huddled masses yearning to breathe free, the wretched refuse of your teeming shore."[21] During that single decade, the nation's population swelled by over 11% simply as a consequence of this deluge.[22]

And though they entered at the gates of Liberty in New York, they certainly didn't stay put. They migrated to every corner of this vast new land. Thousands of Scandinavians took to the rich hills of Minnesota and Wisconsin. Germans moved about, finally settling in Missouri, Texas, and Nebraska. Basques spread into Nevada, Utah, and Idaho. Poles settled in Michigan, Illinois, and Colorado. Italians staked out Pennsylvania, Ohio, and Indiana. Chinese migrated throughout California, Texas, and Massachusetts. Caribbean Islanders moved into Louisiana, Florida, and Georgia. The entire nation was abuz with movement.

This nation was built by newcomers, outsiders, aliens, and sojourners. It was built by people who left all that was near and dear to follow a dream to a better place.

Transience has always been an aspect of our national profile.

Settlement and Resettlement Laws

The free acceptance, and even encouragement of transience in early America is an aberration in Western history. Aliens and sojourners, far from being treated as a national resource, as an impetus for the fulfillment of a "Manifest Destiny," have been more often regarded as threats to the security and stability of the social and economic order.[23]

In 1662, during the fourteen year reign of Charles II, England passed the Law of Settlement.[24] An amendment to the Elizabethan Poor Laws, this statute was designed to empower local justices, churchwardens, and overseers to expel outsiders from settling in a particular parish or county. If the magistrates, by whatever objective or subjective measure they chose, determined that the settler was undesirable, or incapable of supporting himself without resorting to relief, then he could be sent back to the place from which he had come.

The statute was an act of parochial caution. Since relief was a local responsibility, the magistrates wanted to make certain that they only had to care for their *own* poor. They wanted nothing to do with someone else's poor, someone else's problem. "Keep the outsiders out," they cried. The king answered with the Settlement Law, thus establishing residency requirements for the poor, restricting their travel, limiting their labor options, and narrowing the focus of relief.

The effect of the law was to keep people where they were. It stymied opportunity. It discouraged initiative. It created labor imbalances. And it turned some counties into virtual prisons of deprivation. Forced ghettoization. The great economist Adam Smith thought the situation abominable enough to devote a section of his *Wealth of Nations* to a critique of it. He argued not only that the law was a tyrannical infringement of citizens' liberties, but also that it restricted the "free circulation of labor" so essential for growing economies.[25]

In 1795, after more than a century and a quarter of protest, and owing greatly to Smith's concerns, the Settlement Law was superceded by a series of new statutes variously called the "Relocation Laws,"[26] the "Colonial Laws,"[27] and the "Resettlement Laws."[28] The pendulum had swung to the opposite extreme. These laws, rather than coercively containing the poor, required the forceful eviction and conveyance of the poor. The relief rolls, the workhouses, the debtors' prisons, and the destitute counties, it was thought, could be emptied by moving the poor and homeless to the colonies or to developing regions where labor shortages prevailed. Forced migration.

Parliament went from one extreme to another. When at times English social welfare policies seemed a bit schizophrenic —unabashed enclosure during the Great Depression of 1854: settlement; and unremitting triage during the Irish Potato Famine of 1846: resettlement—it was due to these two dramatically divergent traditions.

Without the clear direction of Scripture, it seems, men left to their own devices are tempest tost to and fro on the waves of doubt, dashed from dire to drastic with no in between.

Carrying on the Traditions

Interestingly, both extremes—settlement or containment and resettlement or consignment—are still well represented in modern social welfare policies. Even in the U.N.'s recommendations for the International Year of the Homeless, the two traditions are readily apparent.

"In order to stabilize migratory movements and transitional panics," says one U.N. publication, "residency requirements, density level enforcements, and decentralization effectualization will be essential. Homelessness cannot hope to be addressed until sample populations are fixed."[29] This containment ideal is best exemplified by the efforts of the Communist governments in Guyana, Angola, and Nicaragua. The UNCHS looks admiringly at Nicaragua's settlement program, calling it "an ambitious plan to the year 2000" which aims at "the decentralized distribution of population from one national center—Managua—through nine regional centers, with 20,000 to 100,000 inhabitants and a catchment area of 50,000 to 500,000, to nineteen secondary centers . . . and fifty-two service centers."[30]

The idea of all this is, very simply, to *keep the poor in their place*. Stop migration. Inhibit transiency. Hold homelessness at bay by ghettoizing the poor.

Though certainly in the U.S. such repressive measures are not allowed, containment sentiments can still be discerned in rent control,[31] industrial regulation,[32] and farm subsidy measures.[33] In addition, 46 of the 50 states have residency requirements for relief applicants that also effectively enforce the settlement mindset.[34] Each of those policies serve in one way or another to stifle opportunity and stymie change.

Simultaneously and quite schizophrenically, modern social

welfare policies have promoted resettlement as well. So, not only have they attempted to *keep* the poor in their place, they have at the same time attempted to *put* the poor in their place.

"Controlled and directed population transfers," says a U.N. newsletter, "often is the only possible solution . . . the last governmental resort . . . to encroaching homelessness."[35] This resettlement ideal too is best exemplified by the efforts of the communist governments in Surinam, Ethiopia, and Afghanistan. Especially admired by the U.N. in this regard is Afghanistan's conveyance program. Once the home of over 200,000 Afghans and the agricultural center of the nation, the Panjier Valley was systematically depopulated and denuded through chemical dusting and soil salting.[36] But while most advocates of freedom throughout the world were decrying the tactic as a tyrannical maneuver to quell the rising tides of Mushadine resistance to communism, the U.N. heralded Kabul's move, saying that the government had taken "judicious steps to relocate and disperse dense concentrations of vagrants and bedouins into developed regions."[37]

The idea of all this is, very simply, to deny the poor the opportunity to make their own way by controlling their movements. Uproot them. Displace them. Whatever. Just control them.

In the U.S., though forced resettlement is certainly illegal, its presuppositions are nonetheless evident in our social welfare fabric. The Farmers Home Administration (FHA), which has a part in 42% of all U.S. home and farm mortgages, began its life during FDR's New Deal as the Resettlement Administration (RA).[38] Under the leadership of Rexford G. Tugwell, the RA not only absorbed the rural relief and rehabilitation programs of the old Federal Emergency Relief Administration and the Division of Subsistence Homesteads, it also initiated several innovative consignment projects. Tugwell worked to resettle urban slum dwellers and the depression homeless in "autonomous garden cities" and submarginal farmers in "new, productive farm villages."[39] Following the pattern of Mussolini's collectivization in Italy, he developed three "suburban greenbelt cities," a few dozen "new farm communities," and laid the groundwork for the "federal housing" and "urban renewal" master plans.[40] During WWII, the RA was gleefully dismantled and replaced by the attenuated FHA, but many of its aims lived on. To this day, the

Federal Housing and Urban Renewal programs serve to uproot and transplant the poor, often into terribly alien circumstances and situations.[41]

The Compulsion to Control

How can the humanists who formulate the social welfare policies of the U.N. and the U.S. Government hold to two contradictory approaches to solving the problems of homeless migration? How can they endorse policies of containment and resettlement simultaneously? The answer is two fold.

First, without the solid guidance afforded by God's Word, the humanists are forced to grasp at straws. They willingly try anything that looks as if it might work. They perpetuate old myths and traditions. All this because they have no other answer. As Gary North has asserted, "there is no other sure foundation of true knowledge except the Bible. The only firmly grounded economics is Christian economics. All non-Christian approaches are simply crude imitations of the truth—imitations that cannot be logically supported, given their own first principles concerning God, man, law, and knowledge."[42]

Second, humanism assumes that since there is no God above, since we are left with "cosmic purposelessness," man must assume a place of sovereignty.[43] According to Joseph Fletcher, famed for his development of "situational" ethics, "To be men, we must be in control. That is the first and last ethical word."[44] And how do we obtain that control? Through an overarching central government.

Is there a problem? Homelessness? Desperate transiency? Mass migration? The only answer the humanist knows is *control*. Control the poor by *keeping* them in their place. Control the poor by *putting* them in their place. It's six of one, a half dozen of the other. The bottom line is *control*.

To the Uttermost

The Biblical faith in contrast to humanism has freedom as its bottom line. Jesus came to open prison doors and to "set the captives free" (Luke 4:18-19). He bought us back from the slave market of sin, broke our shackles, undid our yokes, and afforded us liberty (Galatians 5:1; John 8:36). This does not mean that we can do whatever we wish, indulging in libertinism and rebellious anarchy (1 Corinthians 6:20; Titus 2:14). No, we have been set free to follow the true course of liberty: obedience to God's Law. But it does mean that we no longer need to resort to the coercive and repressive tactics of containment and resettlement in order to solve the dilemma of homelessness.

The freedoms established and enforced by God's Law encouraged expansion, provided real options, guaranteed justice, and eased transitions. Instead of sequestering the poor in ghettos, or by uprooting the poor and scattering them to the four winds, Biblical Law urged mobility through opportunity. Aliens and sojourners were to be treated with respect and compassion (Exodus 23:9). Strangers were allowed to participate in the life of the community (Exodus 20:10; Leviticus 16:29; Exodus 12:19). Relief was afforded to all equally (Deuteronomy 24:17-22). Inheritance laws mitigated against stasis and concentration and encouraged moving out to the uttermost parts of the earth to take dominion for Christ (Leviticus 25:8-55).

The difference then between Biblical faith and humanism is, as Gary North has asserted, the difference between "Dominion Religion" and "Power Religion."[45]

And that makes all the difference.

Conclusion

In times of economic distress, people very often pull up their stakes and move on. That's a distinctly American legacy.

Sometimes migration is caused by homelessness, as in the case of Elz Weltzberg. Sometimes it causes homelessness, as in the case of Anya Schiller. Either way, it causes upheaval, disruption, and disorientation. On the other hand, it allows people to adapt to changing conditions and to pursue opportunity wherever it may lead.

For this reason, Biblical Law buffers the disadvantages and highlights the advantages of migration rather than clamping down on the situation with heavy handed controls. Humanism doesn't have that option, so it resorts to either containment or resettlement, coercively *keeping* the poor in their place in the former, coercively *putting* the poor in their place in the latter. So instead of alleviating the anguish of homelessness, the humanist proposals only aggravate it.

In order to overcome homelessness, the migrant poor need

the liberty to pursue opportunity. Thus what they need are the open arms of the Biblical system, not the cold steel trap of the humanist system.

In the U.S. this Biblical freedom does exist at least in part. Thus, unlike the third world squatter camps and the refugee hovels in the U.N.'s model nations, the tent cities in Houston, Phoenix, Los Angeles, etc. were only temporary. Dislocation and homelessness gave way to new starts, new opportunities, new homes — for most, anyway.

"The truth shall make you free . . . and you shall be free indeed" (John 8:32, 36).

Amidst the flash and the hype,
Matrix folding round like an origami trick,
   a raw metal sound,
    and smells of burning circuitry
You have to wonder if it's all
   only apparently real.
Still the cry arises
Wafting sweet in the night
   Mama don't take
   my Kodachrome away.

                       Tristram Gylberd

MAMA DON'T TAKE MY KODACHROME AWAY: THE MEDIA

Broad brush strokes of orange frame the impressive skyline and reflect in the gentle ripples of the river. A perfect backdrop. Poignant.

A camera pans, left to right, finally fixing on a small, droopy canvas tent. Panoramic contrast: The glitter and glitz of the cityscape is still in the corner of the pose; the tent is staked alone in a sea of mud.

A zoom-in shows a tired and bedraggled Mom tucking in her little ones for the night, a sputtering campfire slowly dying a few feet away. A close-up to the sad eyes, a tilt to her chest, grimy hands clasped, clutched in prayer. She is a modern media icon, a portrait of the dispossessed.

Audio voice-over: "It is inevitable. Somewhere along the way, the ordeal that robs the jobless migrants of their money, pride, and hope, finally begins gnawing at the bonds of faith and family too."

Tiny voices rise above the din of crickets, the rustling of wind in the trees, and the lapping water on the bank: "Now I lay me down to sleep . . ."—a slow pan to the childrens' faces, then a tight-pull with full contrast: It casts deep shadows across their eyes, sunset glinting orange on their bright complexions—". . . pray the Lord my soul to keep. . . ."

Cut-back to the mother shows a solitary tear welling; she turns quickly away.

Audio voice-over: "For the homeless . . ."—pan-right reveals a single man holding a microphone, a reporter—". . . the

153

heart wrenching moments of daily life . . ."—casually dressed, strong features highlighted by the slowly extinguishing sunset behind—". . . cut deep troughs of remembrance in the hearts and minds of all who have ears to hear, to all who have eyes to see."

Close-in, tight on the reporter's stern, yet compassionate expression. Crusty, but benign. Pathos. After an appropriately reflective pause—twelve seconds: "This is Ben Thompson, on the banks of the San Jacinto River. Channel Four Action Alert News."

"Cut . . . that's a wrap."

"Okay. Let's hit it. We gotta get this in and edited for the broadcast at ten."

"Pulitzer material, Ben. Great stuff."

"Well thanks, Maggie. Let's hope so."

"Hustle, hustle guys. Get a move on."

The mom, object of so much attention just moments ago, looks past the tent flap as the crew loads mini-cams, lighting towers, monitors, audio mixers, and other assorted video gadgetries into two vans. The hustle and bustle sweep right by her and her small family. Like life.

The reporter, noticing her at last, walks toward the tent, awkward and sheepish now. Not at all the image of sophistication he casts on camera. "Mrs. Tolbert, I, uh . . . I want to thank you for your cooperation on this piece."

"No problem," she replies as she steps from the tent.

"I'd like to help . . . if there's. . . ."

"No. We'll be fine."

He pulls a twenty out of his wallet and thrusts it toward her. "I'd like to at least pay you for your trouble . . . for your time."

"Thanks." She takes the money and turns back toward the tent.

He stands there for a moment, uncertain about what to say or do, and then he too turns to go.

"It's too bad it won't make a difference," she says as she slips past the flaps.

He stops in his tracks. A furrow of determination gouges his Adonisian good looks. A challenge. "I'll make it make a difference," he promises.

The stunning and innovative piece that night, Thanksgiving Eve, received such widespread acclaim that Ben Thompson was given the go-ahead to film an entire series on the subject to air Christmas week.

The series was equally provocative and powerful. It was disturbing and influential. Its staccato images of dispossession were etched indelibly in the impressionable minds of the viewers. Awards were in the offing. Key political figures began to call with regularity to offer their remarks, their impressions. Alternating waves of guilt and pity provoked a widespread public debate.

"It *has* made a difference," Ben told himself after an especially tiring afternoon. "I *made* it make a difference. The *truth* about homelessness is out. And I did it."

The Newsmakers

More than sixty years ago, Walter Lippman made a painful distinction between "news" and "truth." He said, "The function of news is to signalize an event; the function of truth is to bring to light the hidden facts, to set them into relation with each other, and make a picture of reality on which men can act."[1] According to Lippman, the differences between "news" and "truth" stemmed not so much from the inadequacies of journalists, but "from the exigencies of the news business, which limits the time, space, and resources that can be allotted to any single story."[2] He concluded that if the public required "a more truthful interpretation of the world they lived in, they would have to depend on institutions other than the press."[3]

Unfortunately, most journalists today are entirely unable to see the distinction between "news" and "truth" that their mentor Lippman made.

Ben Thompson can't.

In fact, as Edward Jay Epstein has observed, "Newsmen now almost invariably depict themselves not merely as reporters of the fragments of information that come their way, but as active pursuers of the truth."[4] Invariably they have, like Ben Thompson, taken up the challenge to "make a *difference*," to get "the *truth* out."

According to the current vein of thought among journalists, anyone who merely "reports the news," or "repeats the facts," has simply not done his job. He has merely played the part of a stenographer. A reporter must "investigate." He must ferret out "hidden truths," the "realities" that underlie the "naked facts." In the post-Watergate era, even the severest critics of the press attribute to it "powers of discovery that go well beyond reporting new developments."[5]

To modern newsmen, there is no distinction between "news" and "truth."

Sadly, there is no distinction between "news" and "truth" to modern viewers either.

And that makes for a terribly volatile situation. For as Francis Schaeffer asserted in his watershed work, *How Should We Then Live*, "There are certain news organizations, newspapers, news magazines, wire services, and news broadcasts which have the ability to *generate* news. They are the news*makers*, and when an item appears in them it *becomes* the news."[6]

If there is no distinction between "news" and "truth" in the minds of either journalists or consumers, and the "news" is "created" by the journalists, then they have actually "created" the "truth" as well. The newsmakers have become the truth-makers. Having eaten from the forbidden tree, they have become like gods in their own sight, knowing good and evil.

The opportunity for, and in fact the inevitability of manipulation in such a situation is frightening. Schaeffer has argued that modern media, especially television, manipulate viewers just by their normal ways of operating. "Many viewers," he says, "seem to assume that when they have seen something on TV, they have seen it with their own eyes. It makes the viewer think he has actually been on the scene. He *knows*, because his own eyes have seen. He has the impression of greater direct objective knowledge than ever before. For many, what they see on television becomes more true than what they see with their eyes in the external world. But this is not so, for one must never forget that every television minute has been edited. The viewer does not see the event. He sees an edited form of the event. It is not the event which is seen, but an *edited symbol* or an *edited image* of the event. An aura and illusion of objectivity and truth is built up, which could not be totally the case even if the people shooting the film were completely neutral. The physical limitations of the camera dictate that only one aspect of the total situation is given. If the camera were aimed ten feet to the left or ten feet on the right, an entirely different 'objective story' might come across. And, on top of that, the people taking the film and those editing it often do have a subjective viewpoint that enters in. When we see a political figure on TV, we are not seeing the person as he necessarily is; we are seeing, rather, the image someone has decided we should see."[7]

In his scathing critique of ethics in journalism, *The News at Any Cost*, Tom Goldstein suggest that not only are reporters the "kingmakers" and "kingbreakers" of our day, they are the "unacknowledged legislators" of our none too pluralistic society.[8] They shape cultural mores, he says, affect the outcome of political contests, create the parameters of public issues, unveil hidden truths — whether true or not, and dictate the social agenda, all on a two-hour deadline! They function not only as the judge, jury, and executioner in the courtroom drama of life, but also as both public defender and criminal prosecutor.

Such power should not be taken lightly. It colors everything it touches.

And very clearly, it touches the issue of homelessness, coloring more than a little.

Prime Time Guilt and Pity

Ever since the progressivist movement at the turn of the century, muckraking journalists have plied guilt and pity as their stock and trade in reporting social issues. Notice how many stories of disparate poverty and homelessness suddenly appear each year during the holiday season, between Thanksgiving and Christmas. That's no accident. Breast beating doesn't sell well in July. But it's a hot item during the holidays when people's heartstrings are easily tugged upon. So since they only have about a month to beat their breasts, they beat them loud and fast.

For example, in November 1982 *The Wall Street Journal* broke a story about homeless and jobless exiles from the north crowded into "tent towns and cardboard camps scavenging for survival."[9] The story focused primarily on a small encampment along the San Jacinto River near Houston. The story struck a nerve. The media saw an opportunity and quickly rushed in to capitalize.

Within two weeks, more than 350 newsmen descended on the encampment just in time for Thanksgiving copy deadlines.[10] They came from nearly every corner of the world including South America, Germany, England, and Japan.[11] The three national television networks sent crews to cover the story as did *Newsweek*, *Time*, *The New York Times*, *Rolling Stone*, and (predictably) *The National Enquirer*.[12] Book publishers swooped in as did movie producers and talk show hosts as widely ranging as Phil Donahue and Alan King.[13]

The result?

"This place has turned into a crummy soap opera," said one tent city resident at the time, "and we're the cast of characters."[14]

Another resident complained, "the media have been tripping all over each other on this story. You see cameramen filming photographers shooting reporters interviewing tent people. It's a damn media circus."[15]

The situation raged so far out of control that the tent city residents met together and appointed a "press relations representative." Can you imagine?! His job entailed arranging interviews, suggesting story ideas, and even providing photographs to the press. "I sort of direct the script," the PR man asserted without a bit of chagrin.[16] And why not? "I've discovered that poverty is really whatever the media wants to make it," he said. So, he simply set out to be a kind of "product quality control supervisor."

Later however he would lament, "Let me tell you, the media has created a monster. A real monster." They changed the story by becoming the story. And the worst of it was, they passed it all off as "truth." So the newsmakers had indeed become the truthmakers.

As soon as the holidays were past, the story was dropped, forgotten. A tent city had been transformed overnight from a Hooverville into a Hollywood movie set. But now it no longer had a reason for existence, and within a few weeks was disbanded.

It would be another year before homelessness would again invade the public consciousness. The American public would have to wait until the guilt and pity season rolled around once again to hear from ABC, NBC, CBS, *Time*, and *Newsweek*.[17] And so the old song and dance goes, season after season. Of the 210 stories written about homelessness in *The New York Times*, *The Washington Post*, and *The Los Angeles Times* in 1985, 156 of them, or about 75%, were written in or around the holidays. " 'Tis the season to feel guilty, fa la la la la la la la la."

Clearly something manipulative is going on here. The press has wielded its power to make news and make truth, thus dictating the parameters of this public issue and dictating its social agenda. Homelessness, as it is perceived by most Americans, is almost entirely an invention of the media moguls, a product of guilt and pity holiday machinations.

Sadly, most educated people know full well what the press is doing on these occasions, and as a result are skeptical, become hardened, and pass the matter off.

Cashing In

Recognizing the central role the media plays in defining and directing the homelessness issue, the United Nations has planned a massive media blitz to promote the ways and means of the International Year of the Homeless.[18] And recognizing the critical importance of the holiday season for the success of any such media campaign, the U.N. has geared up for an unprecedented Thanksgiving to Christmas publicity burst.[19] After their spectacular successes with previous International Years, agency officials have been confident from the start that their efforts will pay off and pay off big.[20]

Utilizing USA for Africa, Band Aid, Comic Relief, Live Aid, and Hands Across America as a spring board, various advocacy groups and U.N. agency heads together were able to finalize plans for six major TV news documentaries, three movie length features, a multimedia exhibition sponsored by HUD, seventeen corporate sponsors for TV ads and billboards, as well as innumerable magazine and newspaper spreads — all to be unleashed on the public during 1986 and 1987 holidays.[21]

The newsmakers and truthmakers intend to create a great deal of "news" and a great deal of "truth" in a hurry. They intend to cash in. They intend to be the lever and fulcrum to effect a social *welfare* revolution if not a *social* revolution. They intend to steal the hearts of the people under the cover of philanthropic concern, thereby establishing their rule in name as well as in fact. They intend to "make a difference."

Like Ben Thompson, they will use their video images. They will wield their tools of electronic alchemy to turn anecdotes into "news," "news" into "truth," and "truth" into "power." Conspiracy buffs, alert! This one's for real.[22]

The Conspiracy

Absalom was the passionate third son of David, King of Israel. His personal comeliness and charisma was matched in greatness only by his undisciplined ego and ambition. Thus, he was forever getting himself into trouble and embroiling the palace in controversy and scandal (2 Samuel 13:38-39; 14:28). When finally his father received him back into favor, the old king was repaid by a plot against his throne.

> And Absalom used to rise early and stand beside the way to the gate; and it happened that when any man had a suit to come to the king for judgment, Absalom would call to him and say, "From what city are you?" And he would say, "Your servant is from one of the tribes of Israel." Then Absalom would say to him, "See, your claims are good and right, but no man listens to you on the part of the king." Moreover, Absalom would say, "Oh, that one would appoint me judge in the land, then every man who has any suit or cause could come to me, and I would give him justice." And it happened that when a man came near to prostrate himself before him, he would put out his hand and take hold of him and kiss him. And in this manner Absalom dealt with all Israel who came to the king for judgment; so Absalom stole away the hearts of the men of Israel (2 Samuel 15:2-6).

Playing the part of the people's advocate, Absalom stole away their hearts. With delicious whisperings and twisted murmurings he plied circumstances in his favor. With great skill and evident adroitness he slanted the facts, edited the truth, and filtered the news always with an eye toward the ratings.

Then, at the peak of the game, he upped the ante.

> Now it came about at the end of forty years that Absalom said to the king, "Please let me go and pay my vow which I have vowed to the Lord, in Hebron. For your servant vowed a vow while I was living at Geshur in Aram, saying, 'If the Lord shall indeed bring me back to Jerusalem, then I will serve the Lord.'" And the king said to him, "Go in peace." So he arose and went to

Hebron. But Absalom sent spies throughout all the tribes of Israel, saying, "As soon as you hear the sound of the trumpet, then you shall say, 'Absalom is king in Hebron.'" Then a messenger came to David, saying, "The hearts of the men of Israel are with Absalom" (2 Samuel 15:7-10, 13).

Absalom covered his conspiracy with a cloak of righteousness. His conniving, malignant intentions were obscured by a thoroughly benevolent, pious exterior.

And the king, taken as he was by that exterior, didn't know what was happening until it was too late. By then he was too compromised to arrest the crisis. He was forced to flee (2 Samuel 15:14). He had to learn the hard way, as Eve had before him, that just because someone or something looks "good," "desirable," or even "delightful," is assurance of precious little (Genesis 3:6). He had to learn the hard way, as Paul would after him, that just because someone or something comes disguised as an "angel of light" or a "servant of righteousness," is no guarantee of anything (2 Corinthians 11:14-15).

What Absalom did was to take very real concerns and issues and blow them out of proportion, twisting the situation to serve his own ends: the overthrow of the reigning administration. He took facts, figures, and anecdotes and molded them and shaped them to fit his own predisposition. He called on all his skill, all his charisma, all his personal attractiveness and all his inside contacts. He played on the emotions of the people. He showed an impeccable sense of timing. In short, he manipulated the situation masterfully. He exploited an aged king, a complacent administration, and latent discontent, making "news" and making "truth" by the sheer force of his proficient willfulness — not at all unlike the modern news media and their masterful manipulation of social issues like homelessness to give credence to *their* particular socio-political cause.

Absalom wreaked a lot of havoc. So has the news media. But there is one thing that neither of them counted on: The good guys always win in the end. There may be defeats along the way. There may be major set backs from time to time. Tranquility may be dashed. The faithful may be sent into flight. But only for a time. In the end, the cause of the righteous will be upheld (Job

27:16-17). The true truth will come out (Ezekiel 36:33-36). God's people will prevail (Matthew 6:10; Matthew 16:8). If—and that is a big "if"—if they will only do right, cling to the blessed hope, and stand steadfast on the very great and precious promises of God (Joshua 1:7-9).

Absalom wanted to make a difference. He used the issue of justice as his foil. Similarly, the news media is out to make a difference. The U.N. is out to make a difference. They use the issue of justice, of homelessness as their foil. As a result, the *real* issues are lost in the scramble for control, for power. In the end, the poor—the ones with the least to lose—lose the most.

Conclusion

Homelessness is a very real problem. There can be absolutely no doubt about that. The news media has not fabricated the crisis, but what they have done is to color the crisis to their own advantage. They have masterfully wielded guilt and pity as weapons turned against the current social welfare system, perhaps the entire social system.

Thus they have manipulated the dispossessed, turning them into symbols, as prods to the consciences of the American populace. Like the Bolshevik revolutionaries who claimed to be the benevolent liberators of the people, these benefactors have only *used* the poor and the homeless for their own ends, oppressing even more than the previous "masters."

Their crusade has only *apparently* been real. In truth, it has been but a lie.

It has been a hurtful lie.

Meanwhile, back on the streets, Ben Thompson drives his Porsche 924 to his lush suburban home, and a mom beds down her little ones inside a small droopy canvas tent—both glance toward the impressive skyline, lost in the shadows . . . in the shadows of plenty.

After many an hour of hard drinking
the survivor's answer was still the same:
Golden the Ship was—Oh! Oh! Oh!

Cordwainer Smith

THE GOLDEN SHIP:
THE SECULAR DRIFT

Jimmy stood out in the hallway fidgeting. Tears streaked his cheeks. His head reeled. Not believing the task before him, he reached for the door handle again—the tenth time in as many minutes. He took a deep breath and entered the busy office.

The room had classic corporation lines. Clean. Efficient. Modern.

"Well hello there, Jimmy. What can we do for you today?" The sleek secretary was genuinely friendly. Her smile comforted him a bit, and at the same time saddened him all the more.

"Uh . . . is Mr. Greenspan in his office? Do you think I can see him for a minute?"

"He sure is. Let me buzz him. See if he's got some time."

Jimmy swallowed hard. What would he say? How would he react?

Greenspan appeared at his office door and beckoned to the tall, lanky youth. "Come on in, Jimmy, how are things?"

Jimmy wanted to turn and run. He hated this. *Hated* it. Tears welled up in his eyes again. His throat tightened. He fought for control, taking a seat in front of the man's comfortable and commodious desk. Looking around, a flood of memories cluttered his consciousness. Just three months ago sitting here, in this very room, in this very chair, he'd been given the chance of his life. His dream come true. Now he had to throw it all away.

"Mr. Greenspan, I have to . . . I uh, I have to . . ."

"What is it, Jimmy? Trouble?"

"I'm gonna have to . . . quit." There. He'd said it.

"Do what?" The man was obviously taken aback. Flabbergasted.

"I have to quit. I don't want to. I have to. The government's making me."

"I . . . I don't understand, Jimmy. What on earth is going on? Everything was just beginning to work out."

Quietly, between sobs, the youth related the tragic story. His family — Mom and Dad, and five younger sisters — lived in a rat infested Harlem tenement building, and had for all of Jimmy's nineteen years. About eight years ago they applied for subsidized housing in a new city project. For eight years they had fought off the rats, endured the slum-like conditions, evaded the street gangs, and lived on the edge, waiting desperately for the day when their approval came through. Finally, that day had come.

But the good news was bad news.

For the last three months, Jimmy had been in training at Greenspan's Manhattan communications company. In another month, he would become a full-fledged computer technician. Greenspan had taken a risk, and on the advice of a counselor at New York's State Employment Service had hired Jimmy Washington — a bright and determined high school dropout from a poor black family in the slums. Jimmy had done well. Too well.

It seems that with Jimmy's salary, the family was thrown into an income bracket too high to qualify for subsidized housing. But since no one else in the family could get a job, no matter how hard he or she tried, there wasn't enough coming in to get them out of the slums. In order to remain eligible for the housing program, Jimmy would have to quit. He would have to throw away his one chance to build a future. He would have to give up his job so that the family could escape the slums.

Greenspan's hands were as bound as Jimmy's. He couldn't cut the youth's salary because of Government mandated minimums. "I'm damned if I do, and I'm damned if I don't," he flustered.

"Me too," said Jimmy. "Me too."

"Sometimes I get the feeling that maybe . . . that well, maybe the government's 'war on poverty' has become more like a . . . well, a war on the poor."

"Tell me about it."

Two weeks later, Jimmy stopped by Greenspan's office one last time, to pick up his final paycheck, and to say goodbye. "I really do appreciate all you tried to do for me," he said. "I guess it was just never meant to be."

"No Jimmy," Greenspan replied bitterly. "It *was* meant to be. What's going on here is wrong. All wrong."

Amiss and Remiss

What's going on here is wrong, all right!

The "war on poverty" was supposed to end hunger and homelessness. Its programs were supposed to equip the young, protect the old, and provide opportunity for everyone in between.

But after billions upon billions upon billions of dollars spent in the effort, the poor are worse off than before.

"The time has come," say Congressman Newt Gingrich and legislative assistant Ralph Hellman, "to recognize that the problems of the welfare state are fundamental. No amount of minor change will cure the disease of poverty. We have developed a liberal welfare state with values and institutions that are destructive, one that actually creates more misery and more poverty. To offer the able-bodied a life on welfare takes away hope for being productive while offering a ghetto of the mind. To offer shelter without opportunity is to create a prison of the spirit."[1]

The litany of failure is astounding. It is not merely anecdotal, marring the lives of a few like Jimmy Washington. It has cut a wide swath of devastation through the hopes and dreams of millions.

In 1950, one out of every twelve Americans or about 21 million lived below the official poverty line.[2] In 1979, that figure had risen to one out of every nine, or about 26 million.[3] Today, one out of every seven, or about 34 million, fall below the line.[4]

More than 25% of all American children live in poverty — up from 9.3% in 1950 and 14.9% in 1970.[5] And for black children under age six, the figures are even more dismal, if you can imagine: an astounding 51.2%.[6]

Today, as many as 81% of elderly women living alone live in poverty — all too often in shameful, abject poverty — up from a mere 37% in 1954.

And of course, as many as three million Americans are homeless, living out of the backs of their cars, under bridges, in abandoned warehouses, atop streetside heating grates, or in lice-infested public shelters.

So, what has the war on poverty done to stem this rising tide of desperation?

Virtually nothing. At least, nothing positive. Nothing constructive.

"The welfare system is a disaster," say Gingrich and Hellman. "Since it doesn't treat people as human beings, it corrodes the spirit. Because it doesn't approach the future in a positive way, it dilutes the hope of the poor. Since it serves the welfare bureaucracy at the neglect of the welfare recipient, it preserves the past at the expense of the future. It makes welfare clients of the poor, who are overseen by bureaucrats who think they know how to make decisions for their clients' lives."[7]

In every way, shape, and form imaginable, the "war on poverty" has eroded the core values of the American system. Again, according to Gingrich and Hellman, "It has shifted from free enterprise toward government bureaucracies. It has replaced an opportunity-focused development of technology with a 'limits to growth' psychology and a latent fear of the future. It has moved power from individual citizens to powerful, centralized and professional bureaucracies. And it has replaced a nation of people and institutions clearly built on the Judeo-Christian tradition with an intolerant secular state."[8]

And as if all that weren't enough, the "war on poverty" has squandered vast amounts of time, money, and resources as well.

In 1951, spending for all the government's social welfare programs only amounted to $4 billion a year.[9] By 1976, the "Great Society" voted in by the "Silent Majority," was spending $34.6 billion a year.[10] In 1981, welfare advocates bemoaned the fact that social welfare spending was "limited" to a "miserly" $316.6 billion![11]

Food stamp spending rose from $577 million in 1970 to an almost unfathomable high of $10.9 billion in 1984.[12]

In the two-and-a-half decades since the "war on poverty" was initiated, health and medical expenditures have increased *sixfold* (inflation adjusted, in constant dollars); public assistance costs have risen *thirteenfold* (again in constant dollars); education expenditures outstripped pre-reform levels *twenty-four times*; social insurance costs rose *twenty-seven times*; and housing costs inflated a whopping *129 times*.[13]

By 1984, welfare spending of every sort — including social

security, Aid for Families with Dependent Children (AFDC), Unemployment Insurance, Supplemental Security Income (SSI), Workman's Compensation, Food Stamps, and the federal housing projects—claimed 63.4% of the federal budget.[14]

But instead of making things better, this extremely costly, ever-escalating "war on poverty" only made things *worse*.[15] As Gingrich and Hellman have argued, and as Charles Murray,[16] Walter Williams,[17] Thomas Sowell,[18] Henry Hazlitt,[19] George Gilder,[20] Lawrence Mead,[21] Clarence Carson,[22] David Chilton,[23] and a whole host of others have shown, the very policies that were intended to *help* the poor only *aggravated* their plight. Welfare policies undermined their families, encouraged promiscuity, promoted dependence, provided disincentives to work and industry, and contributed to epidemic homelessness.

The "war on poverty" was idealistically fought with righteous verve and passionate zeal.[24] But what have been the spoils of this "war"?

There is more misery than ever before.

There is more poverty than ever before.

There is more homelessness and hopelessness than ever before.

What went wrong? How did we get so far off the track?

Well, it's a long, long story.

Before Luther

In 1528, Martin Luther, father of the Reformation and a great man of letters, edited and published a curious little book entitled *Liber Vagatorum*—"The Book of Vagabonds and Beggars." Arguing that there was a direct relationship between religious reform and the elimination of homelessness, he offered the book as a practical manual for poverty relief, "the next and most important item on the agenda of revival."[25] It marked a major turning point in Western thought.

The book urged the abolition of begging and vagrancy by the establishment of a social welfare system coordinated by the civil magistrates. Until that time, the approach of government to the problem of poverty and homelessness had been simply to absolve itself of any responsibility whatsoever. Until Luther quite persuasively argued otherwise, most people felt that ample facilities existed for meeting economic distress without the interference or regulation of princes, lords, and counselors of state.

What were these facilities?

There was, first of all, the widespread, *unorganized* relief that the poor obtained for themselves through begging. This was an accepted and acceptable method of help (Luke 16:19-22; Matthew 15:22-28). The asking and giving of charity was, in fact, an integral part of medieval life and the wandering beggar was one of the characteristic figures of the age. He had received a dramatic place and honorable endorsement from Francis of Assissi and many other religious leaders. The mendicant friar, the pilgrim to the Holy Land, the scholar at the university, the wandering minstrel or juggler or jester—they all had social approval when they sought for alms. They gave to homeless begging a kind of honor, a status, an ethical currency that made governmental involvement not only unnecessary, but undesired as well.

In addition to mendicancy, before Luther there were three avenues of *organized* help available to the needy that served to keep the magistrates from considering social welfare initiatives. One of these was the ancient and long-established institution of the guilds. Whether they were social, craft, or merchant guilds, all of them emphasized cooperative self-help, brotherhood, and mutual benefit. Thus in times of privation or calamity, they took care of their own. In addition, most of the guilds maintained "works of charity" for the indigent in their communities. This involved such things as feeding the needy on feast days, stocking a common pantry with corn and barley for emergency relief, the maintenance of hostels for destitute travellers, and other kinds of intermittent and incidental help.

Besides the guilds, there were numerous private foundations established throughout Christendom designed specifically to meet the needs of the homeless and poor. It is quite evident from records of the day that bequests and large gifts by individual benefactors were as much a part of the medieval culture as they are of our own.[26] At the time of the Reformation there were in England no fewer than 460 charitable foundations.[27] Money was not only willed for the establishment of almshouses, hospitals, orphanages, hostels, schools, asylums, poor farms, and granaries, but also was designated to cover funeral costs, widows' pensions, tenement improvement, and other philanthropic enterprises on behalf of the poor.

Finally, and most importantly, there was the Church. Before

Luther, virtually no one would have or could have imagined that the magistrates could match the efficiency and efficacy of the prelates in caring for the poor. The Church's system was comprehensive, being divided into two spheres: parish relief, and monastic hospitality.

From the earliest days, local Churches gave charity central prominence in their ministries.[28] Much of the structure even of parish life was determined by the exigencies of relief.[29] The combined effect of the teaching of the Apostle Paul,[30] Clement of Alexandria, Athanasius, Augustine, Chrysostom, Cyril of Jerusalem, and virtually all the other early Church fathers[31] however much they may have differed in other matters, was to make almsgiving an indispensable aspect of Church life. Charity became a symbol of faithfulness. It was looked for as a sign of spiritual vitality. It was commonly accepted as a way of grace, a mark of sainthood, and a surety of eternal reward.

Local Churches generally interpreted the Bible as teaching that the tithe was to be divided into thirds.[32] One part for the maintenance of the Church, an equal part for the support of God's servants, and the final portion for those local poor bound in thraldom. This system was continually upheld as God's plan for caring for the needy, both by ecclesiastical authorities like Boniface in 752, Nynniaw in 810, Gregory VII in 1075, and Savonarola in 1494,[33] and by civil authorities like King Ethelred in 1014, King Cnut in 1035, King Edward II in 1349, and King Henry VII in 1488.[34]

Utilizing the Poor Tithe, the local parishes set up hostels, established hospitals, organized emergency volunteers, coordinated health and hygiene efforts, stockpiled food stuffs, and superintended work crews. The charity was personal, flexible, and accessible, but perhaps more importantly, it was *pastoral*. Because of this pastoral element, parish relief far, far surpassed the guilds and the private charities in its effect. This was due to three important factors.

First, the Church was able to renew and refresh the minds of the poor through the teaching of the Word. Right doctrine gave them comfort, established real hope, challenged old habits, and revitalized faithfulness and responsibility. That was a factor the private initiative philanthropies, no matter how efficient, could not hope to match.[35]

Second, the Church was able to readjust the poor both to God's society and to the world in worship through the sacraments. Weekly communion enabled the poor to participate in a tangible offering *to* God, a consecration *before* God, a communion *with* God, and a transformation *in* God. They were thus able to reorient themselves to *reality* in a fashion that would be utterly impossible any other way through any other agency.[36]

Third, the Church was able to disciple the poor. It was able to retrain them, to reform their lifestyles, and to re-orient them, affording them opportunities for service. It gave them a purpose, a place of importance in parish life. The rituals of worship and consistent discipleship repatterned them in humility, joy, and accountability. The rituals of parish reparation and diaconal care repatterned them in diligence, responsibility, and perseverance.

Thus parish relief was a comprehensive program of charity that generally was able to meet the needs of all local poor and homeless.

But what of the wandering poor, the pilgrim, and the migrant worker? What of the exile, the alien, and the sojourner? What provision could the Church make for them?

According to Thomas Fuller's *Church History*, published in 1655, the great monasteries that dotted the European Continent, and in fact all of Christendom, served to care "for all the non-localized poor." And says Fuller, "Their hospitality was beyond compare . . . they kept most bountiful houses. Whosoever brought the face of a man, brought with him patent for his free welcome to sup, to work, to worship, to convene, to refresh his bowels by the bowels of mercy, til pleased he to depart."[37]

Thus the monastery was an oasis of compassion amidst the desert of the world. And though not as comprehensive nor as accountable as in the local parish, relief in the monastery was accompanied by many of the same pastoral benefits that so distinguished congregational charities.

There were times and places where the Church's program of charity fell into decrepitude due to graft, corruption, apostasy, or calamity so that the poor and homeless were utterly neglected. And those times and places occurred with greater frequency and intensity as the medieval period drew to a close.[38] The Roman Church had drifted far from its Biblical moorings. Apostasy affected every aspect of the Church's mission, including its mission to the dispossessed.

Even so, before Luther, virtually no magistrate sought to contravene the complete separation of government and charity. Even monarchs like Scotland's Queen Margaret, who had great concerns for the poor, channeled their energies on their behalf through the Church, not through the court.[39]

After Luther

But all that changed with the Reformation and the influence of Martin Luther.

The Reformation affected virtually every aspect of life in Christendom.[40] Mostly, for the good. The Bible was reestablished as the sole rule for life and godliness. Orthodoxy was reaffirmed. Apostasy was condemned. Corruption was exposed. Revival was sparked. Commerce was invigorated. Culture was spawned. Constitutional liberty was institutionalized. Souls were saved, captives were set free, and life abundant was granted to millions.

The Reformation caused a great deal of social upheaval, needless to say. Again, mostly for the good. Still, there were some adverse effects, especially for the poorest of the poor.

Local parishes all too often were thrown into an uproar, a political brouhaha, that disrupted whatever was left of their relief efforts. Instead of discipling the needy, ministers and deacons wrestled over doctrinal concerns and struggled over the reins of power. The poor were left out.

Monasteries, already waning in number and influence due to corruption, were often forcibly closed down, thus eliminating that outlet of service to the destitute and homeless. In 1536 and 1539 Henry VIII expropriated all the monasteries within his domain and divided their properties among his loyal followers.[41] Similar measures in Germany and Switzerland substantially diminished the availability of aid to the needy. And though Bucer, Knox, Zwingli, and other reformers valiantly worked to restore charity on a city by city and parish by parish basis, the numbers of homeless and destitute only increased all the more.[42] In fact, of all the reformers, only Calvin was able to make significant inroads in and around his city of Geneva.[43]

Luther, knowing that the abominable situation of homelessness and dispossession had to be tended to if Christendom were to further advance and if the Reformation were to survive, published *Liber Vagatorum* and promoted its innovative notions.

Luther's plan called for the establishment of a "common chest." He recommended that "there shall be ordered for the burghers and kept in place for all times, two casks or council chests in which bread, cheese, eggs, meat, and other foods and provisions shall be placed; and there shall also be a box or two wherein money may be put for the upkeep of the common chest."[44]

In addition to voluntary contributions from various sources there was to be a "tax requirement" committing each inheritor, merchant, craftsman, and peasant to contribute to the chest each year.[45] Servants and young laborers who did not own property but had "burgher and parish rights" would have their portion deducted by their employers. All this was to be above and beyond the tithe and would finance all relief as well as cover the costs of public education and pay the salaries of the clergy. The fund was to be expended by ten supervisors or overseers, independent of the Church but "chosen in an open burgher's meeting in the parish hall."[46]

Almost immediately, the citizens of Leisnig in Saxony and Ypres in France made Luther's plan public policy.[47] In less than a year, Germany's Emperor Charles V, England's Queen Anne Boleyn (and thus King Henry VIII), France's Francis I, and Scotland's James V accepted and implemented the plan in some way, shape, or form, or another.[48] A social welfare revolution occurred almost overnight. Like the Reformation itself, it swept across the continent, leaving it forever altered. The effect was threefold.

First, Luther's plan shifted responsibility for the poor *from the Church to the state*. This jurisdictional turnaround was based upon his conviction that the Church was "an institution of grace," while the state was an "institution of works."[49] He wanted a wall of separation between the two.[50] He wanted to limit the Church to "spiritual authority" and the state to "cultural authority," having suffered long under the corrupted medieval Church bureaucracy. Every change in the social welfare system in the West since 1600 has simply been a development of this "Luther-esque" presupposition: Relief is the state's responsibility, *not* the Church's.

Second, though Luther's plan maintained distinctions between the "deserving" and the "undeserving" poor, the secularization of relief necessitated a redefinition of those terms. No longer were the poor categorized by their relationship to the church. Instead, they were identified by their trade,[51] their property,[52] their heritage,[53] their education,[54] or their proclivity to work.[55]

The Biblical notion of the covenant was of necessity ignored.[56] Again, every change in the social welfare system in the West since 1600 has simply been a development of this "Luther-esque" presupposition: The prerequisites for relief eligibility are to be secular, *not* covenantal.

Third, though Luther himself never intended his plan to be anything but compassionate, most of the magistrates who implemented it made certain that public relief was thoroughly stigmatized. In most instances, it was punitive and repressive, acting more as a deterrence to the dole than anything. Since relief had become a benefit of citizenship dispensed bureaucratically like any other governmental service, it was no longer necessarily hedged from harshness by compassion and grace as charity had been. It was susceptible to every wind of doctrine that blew across the political landscape. Again, every change in the social welfare system in the West since 1600 has simply been a development of this "Luther-esque" presupposition: relief entitlement is *not* charity.

Martin Luther was, of course, a great hero of the faith in many, many ways. But in the area of poverty relief he introduced a bane that the Church still labors under today.

The Long Term and the Short Term

James B. Jordan has written that "the three faces of Protestantism were, and are, the imperial or nationalistic face, the sectarian or drop-out face, and the catholic face. The Reformers can fairly easily, though roughly, be divided into these three groups. There were drop-out anabaptists; there were those who looked to the state for reformation; and there were those who sought to reform the Church in a catholic manner, apart from the state. In brief, the Lutherans and the Anglicans tended to be magisterial in their approach, setting the prince or the king over against the Pope of Rome. Calvin and Bucer, along with some of the other Swiss Reformers, focussed more on a reformation of the catholic Church, and avoided nationalism."[57]

He continues, asserting that "Luther provided a convenient way for the princes of Germany to do what they had always wanted to do: take over the visible power of the Church. Luther so stressed the personal and charismatic aspect of the Gospel, over against the institutional side, that his movement fitted nicely with the designs of the princes. At the same time, from a political point of view, Luther and his followers needed the help of 'godly princes' in order to protect them from Papal threats.

"Conflicts in Germany over the Reformation eventually led to the formulation *cuius regio, eius religio*: whoever reigns, his religion. The faith of a given region would be determined by the religion of the ruling prince. At this point, Lutheranism in Germany had become pretty much wholly statist in character, in terms of any real independent power for the Church. Lutheran acquiescence in the power of the state has continued to be a problem for Christianity in Germany down to the present day, and accounts for the passivity of the Lutheran Churches in the face of Nazism."[58]

And of the other great magisterial reformation that took place in England, Jordan writes, "Everybody knows that Henry VIII had less than pure motives in 'reforming' the English Church. It is noteworthy that the first 'reforming' act of the new Church was the elimination of two feast days from the medieval calendar: the feast of the martyrdom of Thomas Becket, and the day observed to memorialize the public penance performed by Henry II, who had been responsible for Becket's death. Becket had stood against the power of the state, and for the integrity of Church government. The magisterial reformation in England clearly set its face against any true Church government."[59]

Thus while the anabaptists were dropping out of sight altogether, scuttling themselves into a cultural backwater and an evangelical ghetto, and while the Swiss Reformers were striving to cleanse and reform the "one, holy, catholic Church," Luther and his followers in Germany and England were falling into the trap of statism.

Because the Roman system was so terribly and malignantly corrupt, this centralization of power was actually an improvement over the short run. The poor who were once wards of the Church and who were now wards of the state certainly saw some short term benefits. But in the long run, because the Scriptural pattern had been abandoned, they suffered more than ever under the collapsing rot of the late medieval Romanist system. Two wrongs never make a right.

Unfortunately, the pattern was set. The dye was cast. Luther's three magisterial presuppositions became the fount from which Western social policy would flow ever after.

Reform Movements

The three presuppositions that were Luther's bequest on Western social policy — that relief was the state's responsibility, that its eligibility requirements must be secular, and that it was a citizen entitlement — have *rarely* been seriously challenged by liberals *or* Protestant conservatives. Even amidst periods of serious, comprehensive reform, the presuppositions have remained intact.

The renowned reform prompted by the Elizabethan Poor Laws, passed beginning in 1563, actually did precious little to alter relief policies. If anything, the Poor Laws entrenched those policies even more. Their "reform" focused only on *how* the policies were to be implemented, not *if* or *why*.[60] Though they introduced a number of innovations — clear prescriptions for distinguishing between the "vagrant" and the "helpless and halt," for creating employment, for implementing programs of deterrence, and for registering the indigent — none of those innovations challenged the three basic presuppositions.[61]

Similarly, the reforms of George I in 1722 introduced several progressive programs — the establishment of workhouses, of welfare case workers, and public almshouses.[62] But relief was still unquestionably the state's responsibility: secular in orientation, and a citizen's entitlement.[63]

Unfortunately, the system wasn't working. As good as it all looked on paper, somehow human nature made a mess of it in practice.

It was agreed that relief was the government's responsibility and not the Church's. But *who* in the government? What branch? What department? Which agency? Local or national? And who would pay? When the task of relief rested on the shoulders of the Church, everyone knew who, what, when, where, how, and why because it was all outlined in Scripture. But as for the government, that was another matter. The poor began to suffer immensely as various magistrates tried to pass the buck.[64]

It was agreed that relief was to be hedged against graft and corruption by certain prerequisites, by certain eligibility requirements. But what should they be? As long as relief was in the hands of the Church that issue was clear enough: Scripture set the guidelines. But the secularizing process moved the screening of applicants into a hazy realm of uncertainty. As a result, discrimination, subjectivity, and bias crept into the process.[65] The poor suffered all the more.

It was agreed that relief was a right of citizenship. But before long, the upper and middle classes began to grow resentful. They wearied of meeting this entitled obligation.[66] When relief was a function of the Church and its ministry, it was dispensed with charity, but now animosity and vindictiveness crept in. Relief programs became punitive. And again the poor suffered.

Before long, the situation was utterly abominable.[67]

The horrid conditions imposed upon the poor by the maladministration of the various social welfare programs brought a storm of protest and spawned a vast number of private alternative programs. Inspired by the writings of Adam Smith in the 1770s,[68] of Joseph Townsend in the 1780s,[69] of T. R. Malthus in the 1790s,[70] and perhaps most especially of Thomas Chalmers in the 1830s,[71] a number of dedicated and compassionate social activists entered onto the relief scene. In 1860, John Richard Green founded the London Society for the Relief of Distress.[72] In 1862, Frederick Denison Maurice established the Society of Christian Socialism, attracting the avid support of John Ruskin, Thomas Huxley, and Charles Dickens.[73] In 1869, Octavia Hill launched the work of the remarkably influential Charity Organization Society.[74] And contemporaneously the charitable enterprises of Charles Haddon Spurgeon,[75] Florence Nightingale,[76] and Langdon Lowe[77] shaped the nature of compassionate ministry well into the twentieth century.

Even so, after all was said and done, these private initiative alternatives were widely regarded as supplements to, but never as replacements for, the government's system. As historian Charles Kingsley reported, "The societies for relief and the christian charities had then, as now, an honored place in the social welfare structure but only in a subsidiary manner. Magistratal oversight is an unquestioned reality. What with their parochial and pastoral intents and purposes, the private works cannot hope to claim wide public appeal beyond their present narrow contribution."[78] In short, the three basic presuppositions first proposed by Luther remained unchallenged despite a vigorous reform movement.

Into the Modern Era

Shortly after the onslaught of the Great Depression, both the British and American governments initiated a number of new reforms to combat hunger and homelessness. In England the

Beveridge Report, and in the U.S. the New Deal, ushered in hundreds of new programs, projects, and administrations to care for the swelling ranks of the destitute. Vast changes were in the offing.

By the spring of 1933, when Franklin Delano Roosevelt assumed the office of President, almost one-third of the American labor force was unemployed.[79] Wages had plummeted to an average of $17 a week.[80] Immediately the President signed the Emergency Relief Act, thus centralizing the apparatus of welfare and vastly expanding its spectrum. By the following spring, nearly twenty million people had gone on the dole for the first time. They received food, lodging, and cash. They received medical care and vendor goods. They received rehabilitative training and public works employment. They received the most comprehensive package of social benefits since the golden age of the Roman and Incan Empires.[81] Under the Determination of Needs Act of 1941 a similar transformation shook the social service apparatus in England. But notice, though the programs had grown, developed, multiplied, and expanded, the basic presuppositions upon which these programs had been built remained unaltered. As Charles Murray has commented, "Conservative mythology notwithstanding," none of the 30's reforms "had much to do with the purposes of welfare." They merely "changed the locus of the institutions that provided the welfare."[82] The presuppositions remained intact.

In 1964, President Lyndon B. Johnson ushered in another social welfare revolution by declaring an "unconditional war on poverty."[83] His reforms picked up where his hero Roosevelt's left off. Billions of dollars were poured into thousands of projects administered by hundreds of agencies.

The "war on poverty" was driven by a passionate and idealistic philosophy that offered a dramatic departure from previous social welfare thought in a number of areas.

Roosevelt had argued that "continued dependence upon relief induces a spiritual and moral disintegration fundamentally destructive to the national fiber. To dole out relief in this way is to administer a narcotic, a subtle destroyer of the human spirit. It is inimical to the dictates of sound policy. It is in violation of the traditions of America."[84]

His successor Harry Truman often quipped, "No more soup

lines, no more dole, and no more battlefields; that's what I want to see."[85]

But President Johnson wanted to "de-stigmatize relief."[86] He wanted to "remove the shame and the deterrence."[87] He wanted to "banish forever the notion that public assistance is somehow morally tainted."[88]

With this new philosophy in tow, Johnson initiated housing programs to shelter the homeless, training programs to employ the jobless, feeding programs to satisfy the hungry, and entitlement programs to pay the destitute. The undertaking was monumental.

But even though eligibility requirements were looser than ever before, and costs were higher than ever before, and ambitions were greater than ever before, the philosophy that gave rise to the "war on poverty," as unique and innovative as it was, still did not vary an iota from the three basic presuppositions Martin Luther had established half a millennium earlier. It was still assumed that relief was the responsibility of the state, not the Church. It was still assumed that eligibility for relief was to be determined by secular means, *not* covenantal means. And it was still assumed that relief was a citizenship privilege, *not* charity.

So it is to this day.

Now clearly, vast, vast changes have taken place in the social welfare system in the West over the last 500 years. Pragmatically and ideologically, the differences between the modest proposals in *Liber Vagatorum* and the radical programs in the "war on poverty" or the U.N.'s International Year of the Homeless are immense. But *presuppositionally*, the differences are incidental.

Liberals and conservatives stand on the same side of the fence when it comes to those presuppositions. Their quibble is over the *shape* that those presuppositions take in public policy, or over the *scale* of involvement, but never over the presuppositions themselves. As economist Lawrence Mead asserts, "Most prescriptions for American social policy say that Washington is doing either *too much* or *too little* for the poor."[89] But that Washington should be doing anything at all is seldom questioned. Liberals don't question it. Obviously, the U.N. doesn't. And few conservatives question it any longer.

Conservatives who have argued against state involvement in charity have at the same time failed to break with Luther's presuppositions. Some conservatives want *local* government to bear sole responsibility for relief. Others want all relief to be done by private charities, but private charities are not the same thing as the Church. Private charities share Luther's presuppositions that (1) charity is the work of society in general, not of the institutional Church; (2) eligibility for relief is based on secular criteria, not on the covenant; and (3) relief is a privilege of citizenship, not charity — though not all private charities hold this third view.

You have to search pretty hard to find anyone who breaks with this basic model.

The Failure

Yes, it is true that since the "war on poverty," matters have gotten out of hand entirely. Yes, cash entitlement programs serve as disincentives to work and family.[90] Yes, welfare housing only immobilizes the poor in an environment of crime, despair, and destruction.[91] Yes, minimum wage laws breed discrimination and eliminate opportunity.[92] Yes, occupational licensing pushes the poor out of the assembly lines and into the bread lines.[93] But all of these ills are but symptoms of a larger disease with which both liberals and conservatives have been afflicted.

The reason the conservatives have had no better luck in developing a workable social welfare policy than the liberals is that both sides have approached the issue from the *same* side. Conservative humanism is no better than liberal humanism.

And the fact is, the presuppositions that the liberals and conservatives share, the presuppositions that have guided social welfare policy determinations for the last 500 years, are humanistic.

Neither the liberals nor the conservatives who have tried to hammer out solutions to the problems of hunger and homelessness can be faulted for their concern (Psalm 41:1). Where they went wrong was in taking matters into their *own* hands. Instead of "searching the Scriptures to see whether these things were true" (Acts 17:11), they "did what was right in their own eyes" (Judges 21:25). For all their good intentions, their programs were blatantly man centered, because their presuppositions were man centered.

According to the Bible, the first presupposition is dead wrong. Relief is *not* the responsibility of the state. God did not tell the government to feed the hungry, clothe the naked, and shelter the homeless. God told us to. He told the Church. Any other perspective is humanistic.

According to the Bible, the second presupposition is dead wrong. Relief is *not* secular, so its prerequisites cannot be secular. Relief is sacred. It is covenantal. It cannot be understood or undertaken apart from the covenant community. Any other view is humanistic.

According to the Bible, the third presupposition is dead wrong. Relief is *not* an entitlement. It is charity. It is a grace gift. It is the manifestation of compassion and love, not obligation and right. Any other view is humanistic.

Why was Jimmy Washington more hurt than helped by the government housing program?

Why has the "war on poverty" failed so miserably?

The answer is simple. American social welfare policy has been meticulously built on a presuppositional foundation that is innately humanistic. And humanism always falters and fails, ignoring as it does the only reliable guide to truth and life: the Word of God.

So, the soup lines grow. The flop houses fill to overflowing. The dole expands far beyond the bounds of sanity. And young men like Jimmy Washington watch as their dreams are trounced, as their fears are confirmed, and as their lives waste away.

Conclusion

The most important shift in Western social welfare policy did not occur when President Roosevelt introduced the New Deal. Nor did it come when President Johnson declared the "war on poverty." It had occurred long, long before, during the Reformation. That secularizing shift argued that relief was the government's responsibility. It argued that the requirements for relief had to be neutral, non-parochial in nature. And it argued that relief was an entitlement, not charity.

Every social welfare development from that time forward, whether liberal or conservative, whether compassionate or malevolent, has simply perpetuated these assumptions and their root humanism.

That is why the programs, the projects, and the postures of Western social welfare have so often failed. That is why when these presuppositions are pushed into prominence, as they have been with the "war on poverty," the failure is even more prominent. More often than not, the programs intended to help the poor and homeless only hurt them more than before.

Chaos and ruin are the natural fruits of humanism. They always have been. They always will be.

PART THREE

BREAKING THE CASTE

Behold, how fitly are the stages set
For their relief that pilgrims are become,
And how they us receive without one let
That make the other life our mark and home.

What novel ties they have, to us they give,
That we, though pilgrims, joyful lives may live,
They do upon us too such things bestow,
That show we pilgrims are, where 'ere we go.

John Bunyan

He liked being a rich, wild young man on Earth ever so much better than being a respectable spinster under the grey skies of Old North Australia. When he dreamed, he was sometimes Eleanor again, and he sometimes had long morbid periods in which he was neither Eleanor nor Rod, but a nameless being cast out from some world or time of irrecoverable enchantments. In these gloomy periods, which were few but very intense, and usually cured by getting drunk and staying drunk for a few days, he found himself wondering who he was. What could he be?

Cordwainer Smith

RECOVERABLE ENCHANTMENTS: A BIBLICAL PERSPECTIVE

Ever since the Fall, homelessness has been an endemic problem in human society. Rebellion against God always results in dispossession.

Adam and Eve had a magnificent mountain home in Eden and the outlying lands (Genesis 2:8-15; Ezekiel 28:13-14). It was a home lush with vegetation and rich with wealth (Genesis 2:8-9; 11-12). It was well watered, lavishly stocked, gloriously adorned, and fabulously furnished (Genesis 2:10-14). It was teeming with exotic animals, fruit bearing trees, and crystalline rivers (Genesis 2:8-17, 19-20). It was laden high with precious stones, jewels, and minerals (Ezekiel 28:13). It was nothing short of *Paradise.*[1]

But Adam and Eve lost possession of their inheritance. Because of their rebellion against God they were driven out of their garden home (Genesis 3:23-24). The Curse was placed upon the land, gradually transforming it into a howling wilderness of thorns and thistles (Genesis 3:17-19). For the rest of their days they were homeless squatters, making do as best they could east of Eden (Genesis 3:23-24, 4:16).[2]

Such has been the lot of disobedient men ever since. Not only are they cut off from God, corrupted by depravity, and blinded by debauchery, but the rebellious are also uprooted from the land, evicted from their homes, and cast into the wilderness (Deuteronomy 29:28). Homelessness is a natural consequence of the Fall, a Curse borne by all the sons of Adam.

When Cain rebelled, God poured out the full measure of that Curse upon him.

> Then the Lord said to Cain, "Where is Abel your brother?" And he said, "I do not know. Am I my brother's keeper?" And He said, "What have you done? The voice of your brother's blood is crying to Me from the ground. And now you are cursed from the ground, which has opened up its mouth to receive your brother's blood from your hand. When you cultivate the ground, it shall no longer yield its strength to you; you shall be a vagrant and a wanderer on the earth." And Cain said to the Lord, "My punishment is too great to bear! Behold, Thou hast driven me this day from the face of the ground; and from Thy face I shall be hidden, and I shall be a vagrant and a wanderer on the earth . . ." (Genesis 4:9-14).

He became homeless. Indeed later when he finally tried to settle down, he went to the land of Nod (Genesis 4:16). "Nod" means "wandering." Cain became a nomad, a man without a home, a man marked by dispossession.

Again, when the world turned from God in wicked rebellion, He cursed it, blotting out all mankind, save Noah and his family (Genesis 6:5-8, 7:23). The ungodly were driven from their homes and dispossessed to the uttermost.

When the wicked tried to reverse the consequences of the Fall by their own efforts, by building a tower into the heavens, God again uprooted them. They wanted to prevent themselves from being scattered from the land (Genesis 11:4). They wanted to establish a new Eden, a New Age, by the strength of their own hands, and by the cunning of their own minds. But the great experiment at Babel failed and the rebellious were scattered out of the land away from their homes (Genesis 11:8).

The region of Sodom and Gomorrah, once a lush and abundant land not at all unlike Eden (Genesis 13:10), and home to a rich and proud people (Genesis 14:1-24), was judged when those people turned to harlotries and abominations. It became a land of "brimstone and salt, a burning waste, unsown and unproductive" (Deuteronomy 29:23). Its only surviving inhabitants were cast out of their homes to take refuge in the hills and caves (Genesis 19:30).

When the Israelites rebelled stubbornly at Kadesh-Barnea, just as they were about to take possession of the Promised Land, God focused the brunt of the Curse on them. Thus they wandered in the wilderness for an entire generation, homeless and dispossessed (Numbers 14:26-35).

Later when they had finally obtained their home in Canaan, they again rebelled and again fell under the Curse. First, the Northern Kingdom was exiled in 722 B.C. by the Assyrians (2 Kings 17). Next, the Southern Kingdom was exiled in 586 B.C. by the Babylonians (2 Kings 24). Finally, *all* the Jews were cut off from their homes and forced into dispossession in 70 A.D. by the Romans (Matthew 24).

All throughout the Bible, the pattern is clear: God punishes the rebellious, making them a scattered, homeless people. God's Word is sure and unwavering: If we continue in our sin and refuse to heed His statutes and commands, He will make us wandering vagabonds, weak, weary, worn, and dispossessed.

If you are not careful to observe all the Words of this Law which are written in this Book, to fear this honored and awesome Name, the Lord your God, then the Lord will bring extraordinary plagues on you and your descendants, even severe and lasting plagues, and miserable and chronic sicknesses. And He will bring back on you all the diseases of Egypt of which you were afraid, and they shall cling to you. Also every sickness and every plague which, not written in the Book of this Law, the Lord will bring on you until you are destroyed. Then you shall be left few in number, whereas you were as the stars of heaven for multitude, because you did not obey the Lord your God. And it shall come about that as the Lord delighted over you to prosper you, and multiply you, so the Lord will delight over you to make you perish and destroy you; and you shall be torn from the land where you are entering to possess it. Moreover, the Lord will scatter you among all peoples, from one end of the earth to the other end of the earth; and there you shall serve other gods, wood and stone, which you or your fathers have not known. And among those nations you shall find no rest, and there shall be no resting place for the sole of your foot; but there the Lord will give you a trembling heart, failing of eyes, and despair of soul. So your life shall hang in doubt before you; and you shall be in dread night and day, and shall have no assurance of your life (Deuteronomy 28:58-66).

Since all men are sinners (Romans 3:23), we all fall under the Curse. We are all *naturally* inclined to nomadism and dispossession.

That's the bad news.

The New Home

But thanks be to God, He has not left us in that helpless estate. He has offered us a glorious Hope by grace. He has offered us Salvation from the Curse (Romans 8:1-2), Redemption from the wilderness (Ephesians 2:4-7), and Restoration to a New Home in a New Eden (Romans 8:18-22).

That's the good news.

Thus says the Lord God, "On the day that I cleanse you from all your iniquities, I will cause the cities to be inhabited, and the waste places will be rebuilt. And the desolate land will be cultivated instead of being a desolation in the sight of everyone who passed by. And they will say, 'This desolate land has become like the Garden of Eden; and the waste, desolate, and ruined cities are fortified and inhabited.' Then the nations that are left round about you will know that I, the Lord, have rebuilt the ruined places and planted that which was desolate; I, the Lord, have spoken and will do it" (Ezekiel 36:33-36).

Thus, while godless men continue to reap the bitter harvest of homelessness, God gives His faithful people Rest by grace. He restores us to our original purpose. He brings us into His Household (Ephesians 2:12-22).

And the Home He gives us, the Restoration and Rest He offers us, is not merely spiritual, to be realized only when we attain to the by and by. He gives us a Home here and now. He plants us in the land (Exodus 15:17). He blesses us in the land (Deuteronomy 28:2-6). He establishes our future in the land (Luke 19:13).

"Land is basic to dominion," says theologian David Chilton, "therefore, Salvation involves a Restoration to land and property. In announcing His covenant to Abram, the very first sentence God spoke was a promise of land (Genesis 12:1), and He completely fulfilled that promise when He saved Israel (Joshua 21:43-45). This is why Biblical Law is filled with references to property, law, and economics; and this is why the Reformation laid such stress on *this* world, as well as the next. Man is not saved by being delivered out of his environment. Salvation does not rescue us from the material world, but from *sin*, and from the effects of the Curse. The Biblical ideal is for every man to own property, a place where he can have dominion and rule under God."[3]

God promised Abram a Home. He promised him eternal Salvation *and* a habitation on earth. When Abram was nothing but a wandering shepherd, God offered him Shelter by grace.

> To your descendants I have given this land, from the river of Egypt as far as the great river Euphrates: The Kenite and the Kenizzite and the Kadomite and the Hittite and the Perizzite and the Rephaim and the Amorite and the Canaanite and the Girgashite and the Jebusite (Genesis 15:18-21).

When Abram's descendants were driven from their homes by famine, God moved the heart of Pharaoh in Egypt to open his land—a land like the Garden of the Lord (Genesis 13:10)—to them saying,

> Now you are ordered, "Do this: Take wagons from the land of Egypt for your little ones and for your wives, and bring your father and come. And do not concern yourselves with your goods, for the best of all the land of Egypt is yours" (Genesis 45:19-20).

Later, when conditions in Egypt made life unbearable for the people, God promised them a New Home, a land flowing with milk and honey, a land where much of the Curse had been reversed, a land "like the Garden of Eden" (Joel 2:3).

> And the Lord said, "I have surely seen the affliction of My people who are in Egypt, and have given heed to

their cry because of their taskmasters, for I am aware of their sufferings. So I have come down to deliver them from the power of the Egyptians, and to bring them up from that land to a good and spacious land, to a land flowing with milk and honey, to the place of the Canaanite and the Hittite and the Amorite and the Perizzite and the Hivite and the Jebusite. And now, behold, the cry of the sons of Israel has come to Me; furthermore, I have seen the oppression with which the Egyptians are oppressing them. Therefore, come now, and I will send you to Pharaoh, so that you may bring My people, the sons of Israel, out of Egypt" (Exodus 3:7-10).

Whenever righteous people have been exiled, alone, in a dry and weary wasteland, God has come to their rescue and given them Shelter. He has given them a Home.

A father of the fatherless and a judge for the widows, is God in His holy habitation. God makes a Home for the lonely; He leads out the prisoners into prosperity. Only the rebellious dwell in a parched land (Psalm 68:5-6).

That is why throughout the ages, His people have cried out in praise, saying,

I love Thee, O Lord, my strength. The Lord is my rock and my fortress and my deliverer, My God, my rock, in whom I take refuge; my shield and the horn of my salvation, my stronghold. I call upon the Lord, who is worthy to be praised, and I am saved from my enemies (Psalm 18:1-3).

In Salvation God not only washes away our sins (1 Corinthians 6:11) and Restores us to fellowship (1 Corinthians 1:9), he also Redeems us from our wanderings, and gives us a Home (Psalm 107:1-9).

This great privilege comes to us "by grace through faith, and this not of ourselves, it is the gift of God" (Ephesians 2:8-9). There is absolutely nothing that we can do to earn it, merit it, or deserve it.

Of course, with great privilege comes great responsibility. "To whom much is given, much is required" (Luke 12:48).

At the exodus, Israel was called out of homeless bondage, and promised a New Home. But at Kadesh-Barnea they refused to receive it (Numbers 14). Thus, they remained in the wilderness, wandering and dispossessed.

When they finally returned to Kadesh-Barnea after a generation, Moses warned them that if they rebelled, they would suffer expulsion just like their parents, just like Adam and Eve (Deuteronomy 28:2-68). He warned them that their New Home was *received* by grace, but *kept* by faithfulness.

This message was reiterated by all the prophets from Isaiah to Amos, from Jeremiah to Zephaniah, from John the Forerunner to Paul the Apostle. With a single voice they exhorted the people to remain faithful ("faith-full" or "faith that is full" of righteous good deeds; see Philippians 2:12-16; James 2:14-26). Otherwise, they would lose their promised dominion, their Home.

Our Heavenly Home

In the New Covenant our promises are better, our hope is better, and our Home is better than that of the sons of Sinai and Moriah. For by Christ, "the Apostle and High Priest of our Confession" (Hebrews 3:1), we have become partakers of a Heavenly calling and entered into Zion.

> For you have not come to a mountain that may be touched and to a blazing fire, and to darkness and gloom and whirlwind, and to the blast of a trumpet and the sound of Words which sound was such that those who heard begged that no further Word should be spoken to them. For they could not bear the command, "If even a beast touches the mountain, it will be stoned." And so terrible was the sight, that Moses said, "I am full of fear and trembling." But you have come to Mount Zion and to the city of the living God, the heavenly Jerusalem, and to myriads of angels, to the general assembly and Church of the first-born who are enrolled in heaven, and to God, the Judge of all, and to the spirits of righteous men made perfect, and to Jesus, the mediator of a New

Covenant, and to the sprinkled blood, which speaks better than the blood of Abel (Hebrews 12:18-24).

We have a Home. We have been made heirs to a Kingdom (Romans 8:17) and citizens of a Holy Nation (Philippians 3:20). Christ has prepared mansions for us (John 14:1-3) in a magnificent city (Revelation 21:1-27). We have been enthroned (Ephesians 1:3, 2:6).

But again, this New Home is not simply pie in the sky for the sweet by and by. Our New Home is real here and now as well, for *God has given us a taste of Heaven on earth in the Church.*

The Church gives us contact with our Heavenly Home in worship.[4] During worship we *actually* climb up the Mountain of God and gather around His Throne (Hebrews 4:16). We *actually* ascend into the Heavenlies (Ephesians 2:6). We *actually* join in the Heavenly Throng singing praises unto our King (Hebrews 12:1-2). We *actually* sample the wonder of Heavenly Fellowship in our fellowship with one another (1 John 1:3). We *actually* eat Heavenly Food when we take the Lord's Supper (John 6:32-58). God *actually* inhabits our praise (Psalm 85:14), comforts our woes (John 14:16-18; 2 Corinthians 1:3-5), fills up our lack (Matthew 6:25-34), and empowers our work (1 Thessalonians 1:5; 2 Timothy 1:7). In the Church we are afforded Sanctuary and Refuge. We are given our Home.

> When we were overwhelmed by sins, you atoned for our transgressions. Blessed is the man you choose and bring near to live in your Courts! We are filled with the good things of your House, of your Holy Temple. You answer us with awesome deeds of righteousness, O God our Savior, the hope of all the ends of the earth and of the farthest seas, who formed the mountains by your power, having armed yourself with strength, who stilled the roaring of the seas, the roaring of their waves, and the turmoil of the nations (Psalm 65:3-7).

As in the days of the Old Covenant, life under the Shelter of the Church is a gracious provision of Almighty God. There is nothing we can do ourselves to earn it, deserve it, or merit it. It is the gift of God.

Even so, with privilege comes responsibility. We who reap the benefits of life in the Sanctuary of the Church must remain faithful.

> Who may ascend the hill of the Lord? Who may stand in His holy place? He who has clean hands and a pure heart, who does not lift up his soul to an idol or swear by what is false. He will receive blessing from the Lord and vindication from God his Savior. Such is the generation of those who seek Him, who seek Your face, O God of Jacob (Psalm 24:3-6).

Every home has standards. To dwell in God's Home, the Church, we must abide by God's standards. To reap the benefits of His Sanctuary, the Church, we must uphold our responsibilities. God will not bless disobedience. God will not harbor wickedness. Thus those who will not work may not eat (2 Thessalonians 3:10); those who will not repent may not eat (1 Corinthians 5:1-13); and those who take it upon themselves to eat anyway are stricken or killed dispossessed (1 Corinthians 11:27-30).

Our New Home is received by grace, but kept by faithfulness.

The Biblical View of History

Jesus explained to His disciples just how the principles of the Curse, with its inherent homelessness, and grace, with its inherent dominion, are manifested throughout history. He said,

> The Kingdom of Heaven may be compared to a man who sowed good seed in his field. But while men were sleeping, his enemy came and sowed tares also among the wheat, and went away. But when the wheat sprang up and bore grain, then the tares became evident also. And the slaves of the landowner came and said to him, "Sir, did you not sow good seed in your field? How then does it have tares?" And he said to them, "An enemy has done this!" And the slaves said to him, "Do you want us, then, to go and gather them up?" But he said, "No, lest while you are gathering up the tares, you may root up the wheat with them. Allow both to grow together until the harvest; and in the time of the harvest I will say to

the reapers, 'First gather up the tares and bind them in bundles to burn them up; but gather the wheat into my barn'" (Matthew 13:24-30).

Explaining this parable later, He said,

> The one who sows the good seed is the Son of Man, and the field is the world; and as for the good seed, these are the sons of the Kingdom; and the tares are the sons of the evil one; and the enemy who sowed them is the devil, and the harvest is the end of the age; and the reapers are angels. Therefore just as the tares are gathered up and burned with fire, so shall it be at the end of the age. The Son of Man will send forth His angels, and they will gather out of His Kingdom all stumbling blocks, and those who commit lawlessness, and will cast them into the furnace of fire; in that place there shall be weeping and gnashing of teeth. Then the righteous will shine forth as the sun in the Kingdom of their Father. He who has ears, let him hear (Matthew 13:37-43).

Essentially what Jesus was saying was that as history moves along, the basic principles of wickedness and righteousness are worked out more and more consistently. Evil matures and becomes ever more evil, ever more distinctive. Likewise godliness matures and becomes ever more godly, ever more distinctive. Tare-maturation will evidence itself in horrid debauchery and unimaginable abomination: killing babies, cursing God, perverting the marriage bed, running after strange flesh, etc. Tare-maturation will also evidence itself in ever-increasing instances of homelessness. *Humanism breeds dispossession.* As time moves along and men become more and more self-consciously tare-like, more and more self-consciously anti-Christ, the Curse becomes more and more evident. They don't *want* God's New Home offered in the Church. They *prefer* their pitiful bivouac in the tombs. They persist in their rebellion to the end, gnawing their tongues, and calling for the rocks to fall on them (Revelation 6:16).

> But realize this, that in the last days difficult times will come. For men will be lovers of self, lovers of

money, boastful, arrogant, revilers, disobedient to parents, ungrateful, unholy, unloving, irreconcilable, malicious gossips, without self-control, brutal, haters of good, treacherous, reckless, conceited, lovers of pleasure rather than lovers of God; holding to a form of godliness, although they have denied its power; and avoid such men as these. For among them are those who enter into households and captivate weak women weighed down with sins, led on by various impulses, always learning and never able to come to the knowledge of the truth. And just as Jannes and Jambres opposed Moses, so these men also oppose the truth, men of depraved mind, rejected as regards the faith. But they will not make further progress; for their folly will be obvious to all, as also that of those two came to be (2 Timothy 3:1-9).

As history draws toward consummation, evil will become ever more consistently evil. The tares will mature.

But notice: "They will not make further progress" (2 Timothy 3:9). Why will they not make further progress? Because just as the tares continue to mature, so does the wheat. The Church becomes more and more powerful as history proceeds. She becomes more and more self-consciously Christ-like. The fact that Heaven and the Church are the *only* True Sanctuary becomes clearer and clearer as time goes on. The fact that the Church provides the only hope of Refuge from the howling wilderness becomes ever more evident.

Making a Home

To assume that international associations like the U.N., or national civil governments, or non-sectarian community groups, or even para-church organizations can make significant inroads into the problem of homelessness is to underestimate tragically the comprehensive scope of the Curse. To assume that *any* organization, association, or program aside from the Church can reverse the exile of man and bring him Home again is to be sorely deluded.

To secularize the apparatus of care to the dispossessed is to dismantle the apparatus of care. By making relief governmental, non-parochial, and non-beneficent, we have stolen from the dispossessed any and all hope. Regardless of how well intentioned and philanthropic our efforts may be, if they avoid offering the homeless True Sanctuary, then we only drive them deeper and further into the howling wilderness; we only highlight the Curse.

That is why the Church must offer the True Home to the homeless, not just at the theological or theoretical level, but by all kinds of practical good works.

In writing to Titus, the young pastor of Crete's pioneer Church, the Apostle Paul pressed home this fundamental truth with impressive persistence and urgency. The task before Titus was not an easy one. Cretan culture was terribly tare-ish. It was marked by deceit, ungodliness, sloth, and gluttony (Titus 1:12). And Titus was to provoke a total Christian reconstruction there! He was to offer those men of the Curse nothing less than Sanctuary in Christ and Christ's Household of faith. No simple chore! Thus, Paul's instructions were strategically precise and to the point. Titus was to preach the glories of grace, but he was also to make those good deeds evident. He was to offer Refuge *really*, not just theoretically. Charity was to be a central priority.

Paul wrote:

> For the grace of God has appeared, bringing salvation to all men, instructing us to deny ungodliness and worldly desires, and to live sensibly, righteously and godly in the present age, looking for the blessed hope and the appearing of the glory of our great God and Savior, Christ Jesus; who gave Himself for us, that He might redeem us from every lawless deed and purify for Himself a people for His own possession, zealous for good deeds (Titus 2:11-14).

This was a very familiar theme for Paul. He returned to it at every opportunity. Earlier, he had written to the Ephesian Church, saying,

> For by grace you have been saved through faith; and that not of yourselves, it is the gift of God; not as a result of works, that no one should boast. For we are His workmanship, created in Christ Jesus for good works, which God prepared beforehand, that we should walk in them (Ephesians 2:8-10).

God saves us by grace. There is nothing we can do to merit His favor. We stand condemned under His judgement. Salvation is completely unearned (except by Christ), and undeserved (except to Christ). But we are not saved capriciously, for no reason and no purpose. On the contrary, "we are His workmanship, created in Christ Jesus for good works." We are "His own possession," set apart and purified to be "zealous for good deeds." We are to *demonstrate* the reality of God's grace to the rootless and hopeless. We are to authenticate God's offer of a True Home with charity.

So, Paul tells Titus he must order his fledgling ministry among the Cretans accordingly. He himself was "to be an example of good deeds" (Titus 2:7). He was to teach the people "to be ready for every good deed" (Titus 3:1). The older women and the younger women were to be thus instructed, so "that the Word of God might not be dishonored" (Titus 2:5); and the bondslaves, "that they might adorn the doctrine of God our Savior in every respect" (Titus 2:10). They were all to "learn to engage in good deeds to meet pressing needs, that they might not be unfruitful" (Titus 3:14). There were those within the Church who professed "to know God, but by their deeds they deny Him, being detestable and disobedient, and worthless for any good deed" (Titus 1:16). These, Titus was to "reprove . . . severely that they might be sound in the faith" (Titus 1:13). He was to "speak confidently, so that those who had believed God might be careful to engage in good deeds" (Titus 3:8).

As a pastor, Titus had innumerable tasks that he was responsible to fulfill. He had administrative duties (Titus 1:5), doctrinal duties (Titus 2:1), discipling duties (Titus 2:2-10), preaching duties (Titus 2:15), counseling duties (Titus 3:1-2), and arbitrating duties (Titus 3:12-13). But intertwined with them all, fundamental to them all, were his *charitable* duties.

And what was true for Titus then, is true for us all today, for "these things are good and profitable for all men" (Titus 3:8).

The Bible tells us that if we will obey the command to be generous to the poor, we ourselves will be happy (Proverbs 14:21), God will preserve us (Psalm 41:1-2), we will never suffer need (Proverbs 28:27), we will prosper and be satisfied (Proverbs 11:25), and even be raised up from beds of affliction (Psalm 41:3). God will ordain peace for us (Isaiah 26:12), authenticate our faith (James 2:14-26), and bless our evangelistic message (Isaiah 58:6-12).

Therefore let us be "zealous for good deeds" (Titus 2:14). For we are the dispossessed's *only* hope. We are their only Refuge from the howling wilderness.

We must become more and more wheat-like as time goes by.

Conclusion

Homelessness is a natural consequence of the Fall. It is a part of the Curse. As a result, the more rebellious men get, the more homelessness there will be.

God offers a Refuge: the Church. He has in fact always offered Sanctuary to the faithful. Unfortunately some men, driven as they are by the Curse, refuse God's offer. They persist in their rebellion.

Still other men, though, yearn for the True Home that God offers. Thus, we must faithfully extend that offer to the dispossessed by our own good deeds.

We must offer them what the U.N. and the federal government can never hope to offer: escape from the Curse that *makes* them homeless.

How lovely are Thy Dwelling Places, O Lord of Hosts! My soul longed and even yearned for the Courts of the Lord; my heart and my flesh sing for joy to the living God. The bird also has found a house, and the swallow a nest for herself, where she may lay her young, even Thine Altars, O Lord of Hosts, My King and my God. How blessed are those who dwell in Thy House! They are ever praising Thee. How blessed is the man whose strength is in Thee; in whose heart are the highways to Zion! Passing through the valley of Baca, they make it a spring, the early rain also covers it with blessings. They go from strength to strength, every one of them appears before God in Zion. O Lord God of Hosts, hear my prayer; Give ear, O God of Jacob! Behold our shield, O God, and look upon the face of Thine anointed. For a day in Thy Courts is better than a thousand outside. I would rather stand at the threshold of the House of my God, than dwell in the tents of wickedness.

For the Lord God is a sun and shield; the Lord gives grace and glory; no good thing does He withhold from those who walk uprightly. O Lord of Hosts, how blessed is the man who trusts in Thee (Psalm 84:1-12).

They have looked each other between the eyes,
    and there they found no fault,
They have taken the Oath of the Brother-in-Blood
    on leavened bread and salt:
They have taken the Oath of the Brother-in-Blood
    on fire and fresh-cut sod,
On the hilt and the halt of the Khyber knife,
    and the Wondrous Names of God.

Rudyard Kipling

FOURTEEN

THE INSTRUMENTALITY OF MANKIND: A BIBLICAL PATTERN

God is just.

He works righteousness and justice for all (Psalm 33:5). Morning by morning, He dispenses His justice without fail (Zephaniah 3:5) and without partiality (Job 32:21). All his ways are just (Deuteronomy 32:4) so that injustice is actually an abomination to Him (Proverbs 11:1).

It is for this reason that Scripture continually emphasizes the fact that God Himself protects the weak, the oppressed, the orphan, the widow, and the homeless. God's justice demands that those who are most vulnerable, most susceptible, and most insecure be defended. So, He cares for them. He doesn't care for them any more than He cares for others, for He is no respecter of persons (Acts 10:34). But He *does* care for them. He most assuredly will not tolerate any injustice. Thus, He is especially adamant about ensuring the cause of the meek and the weak (Psalm 103:6).

Time after time, Scripture stresses this important attribute of God.

> But the Lord abides forever; He has established His Throne for judgment, and He will judge the world in righteousness; He will execute judgment for the peoples with equity. The Lord also will be a Stronghold for the oppressed, a Stronghold in times of trouble (Psalm 9:7-9).

"Because of the devastation of the afflicted, because of the groaning of the needy, now I will arise," says the Lord; "I will set him in the safety for which he longs" (Psalm 12:5).

And my soul shall rejoice in the Lord; it shall exult in His salvation. All my bones will say, "Lord, who is like Thee, who delivers the afflicted from him who is too strong for him, and the afflicted and the needy from him who robs him?" (Psalm 35:9-10).

A father of the fatherless and a judge for the widows, is God in His holy habitation. God makes a Home for the lonely; He leads out the prisoners into prosperity, only the rebellious dwell in a parched land (Psalm 68:5-6).

With my mouth I will give thanks abundantly to the Lord; and in the midst of many I will praise Him. For He stands at the right hand of the needy, to save him from those who judge his soul (Psalm 109:30-31).

I know that the Lord will maintain the cause of the afflicted, and justice for the poor (Psalm 140:12).

How blessed is he whose help is the God of Jacob, whose hope is in the Lord his God; who made heaven and earth, the sea and all that is in them; who keeps faith forever; who executes justice for the oppressed; who gives food to the hungry. The Lord sets the prisoners free. The Lord opens the eyes of the blind; the Lord raises up those who are bowed down; the Lord protects the strangers; He supports the fatherless and the widow; but He thwarts the way of the wicked (Psalm 146:5-9).

The afflicted and needy are seeking water, but there is none, and their tongue is parched with thirst; I, the Lord, will answer them Myself, as the God of Israel I will not forsake them. I will open rivers on the bare heights, and springs in the midst of the valleys; I will make the wilderness a pool of water. I will put the cedar in the wilderness, the acacia, and the myrtle, and the olive tree; I will place the juniper in the desert, together with the box tree and the cypress, that they may see and recognize, and consider and gain insight as well, that the hand of the Lord has done this, and the Holy One of Israel has created it (Isaiah 41:17-20).

God cares for the poor. He offers them Refuge from the Curse.

And His people are to do likewise. We too are to defend the cause of the meek and the weak. We are to offer them a Home. This in fact is a primary indication of the authenticity of our faith. "This is pure and undefiled religion in the sight of our God and Father, to visit the orphans and widows in their distress and to keep oneself unstained by the world" (James 1:27).

We are called to "do justice" and to "love kindness" (Micah 6:8). We are to be ministers of God's peace (Matthew 5:9), instruments of His love (John 13:35), and ambassadors of His Kingdom (2 Corinthians 5:20). We are to care for the helpless, feed the hungry (Ezekiel 18:7), clothe the naked (Luke 3:11), and shelter the homeless (Isaiah 16:3-4). We are to do as He does.

Doing Unto Others

God desires that we follow Him (Matthew 4:19). We are to emulate Him (1 Peter 1:16). We are to do as He does. In effect, we are to do unto others as He has done unto us.

That is the ethical principle that underlies the "Golden Rule" (Matthew 7:12; Luke 6:31).

God has comforted us, so we are to comfort others (2 Corinthians 1:4). God has forgiven us, so we are to forgive others (Ephesians 4:32). God has loved us, so we are to love others (1 John 4:11). He has taught us, so we are to teach others (Matthew 28:20). He has borne witness to us, so we are to bear witness to others (John 15:26-27). He laid down His life for us, so we are to lay down our lives for one another (1 John 3:16).

When we were needy, neglected, and naked, He cared for us. He attended to our sorrows, clothed us with glory and lavished riches upon us. When we were impoverished and imprisoned, He paid our debts and set us free. When we were lost in the darkness, afraid and forlorn, He came to guide us with Light and assure us with His Life. So now we are similarly to care for others (Luke 10:30-37). With great privilege comes great responsibility. We are to do unto others as He has done unto us.

Whenever God commanded Israel to imitate Him in ensuring justice for the wandering homeless, the alien, and the sojourner, He reminded them that *they* were once despised, rejected, and homeless themselves (Exodus 22:21-27; 23:9; Leviticus 19:33-34). It was only by the grace and mercy of God that they had been redeemed from that low estate (Deuteronomy 24:17-22). Thus they were to exercise compassion to the dispossessed. They were to give them Sanctuary.

Privilege brings responsibility. If Israel refused to take up that responsibility then God would revoke their privilege (Isaiah 1:11-17). If they refused to exercise reciprocal charity then God would rise up in His anger to visit the land with His wrath and displeasure, expelling them into the howling wilderness once again (Exodus 22:24).

The principle still holds true. This is the lesson Jesus was driving at in the parable of the unmerciful slave.

> For this reason the Kingdom of Heaven may be compared to a certain king who wished to settle accounts with his slaves. And when he had begun to settle them, there was brought to him one who owed him ten thousand talents. But since he did not have the means to repay, his lord commanded him to be sold, along with his wife and children and all that he had, and repayment to be made. The slave therefore falling down, prostrated himself before him, saying, "Have patience with me, and I will repay you everything." And the lord of that slave felt compassion and released him and forgave him the debt. But that slave went out and found one of his fellow slaves who owed him a hundred denarii; and he seized him and began to choke him, saying, "Pay back what you owe." So his fellow slave fell down and began to entreat him, saying, "Have patience with me and I will repay you." He was unwilling however, but went and threw him in prison until he should pay back what was owed. So when his fellow slaves saw what had happened, they were deeply grieved and came and reported to their

lord all that had happened. Then summoning him, his lord said to him, "You wicked slave, I forgave you all that debt because you entreated me. Should you not also have had mercy on your fellow slave, even as I had mercy on you?" And his lord, moved with anger, handed him over to the torturers until he should repay all that was owed him. So shall My heavenly Father also do to you, if each of you does not forgive his brother from your heart (Matthew 18:23-35).

In other words: Do unto others as God has done unto you. Privilege brings responsibility.

God has set the pattern by His gracious working in our lives. Now we are to follow that pattern by the power of the indwelling Spirit (John 14:15-26). We are to do as He has done.

The poor and homeless are living symbols of our former helplessness and privation. We are to be living symbols of God's justice, mercy, and compassion. We are to do as He has done (John 15:1-8).

But, just exactly *what* has He done? And how has He gone about doing it?

The Bible tells us that God has dispensed His justice and mercy among us through *service*, within the *covenant*, by *grace*.

Service

Jesus was a servant. He came to serve, not to be served (Matthew 20:28). And He called His disciples to do as He did. He called them to be servants (Matthew 19:30).

Sadly, servanthood is a much neglected, largely forgotten vocation in the modern Church. We're obsessed with leading, with headship, with prominence. We want dominion, not servitude.

That obsession though, as ironic as it may seem, has been, and continues to be, self defeating.

Jesus made it clear that if we want dominion, we must not grasp at the reigns of power and prominence. We must serve. It is only by service that we become fit for leadership. Jesus said, "Whoever wishes to be chief among you, let him be your servant" (Matthew 20:27). Our attitude "should be the same as Christs' who, being in very nature God, did not consider equality with God something to be grasped, but made Himself nothing, taking the very nature of a servant, being made in human likeness. And being found in appearance as a man, He humbled Himself and became obedient to death, even death on a cross. Therefore God exalted Him to the Highest Place and gave Him the Name that is above every Name" (Philippians 2:5-9, NIV).

This truth is reiterated throughout the Biblical narrative. The theme of the suffering servant who later triumphs, who *serves* faithfully and then succeeds, is in fact, the commonest of Scriptural themes.

Jacob *served*. He served his lawless uncle Laban under taxing circumstances for more than fourteen years, but then was exalted to high honor and position (Genesis 31:1, 36-42).

Joseph *served*. He served faithfully in Potiphar's house only to be falsely charged and imprisoned (Genesis 39:1, 7-20). But from the prison he rose meteorically to become Pharaoh's second in command (Genesis 41:38-43).

David *served*. He served in the court of King Saul as a musician (1 Samuel 16) and a warrior (1 Samuel 17). Envious, the king tried to kill him (1 Samuel 18, 19, 23), but David remained steadfast and his service ultimately won him the crown (1 Samuel 24:20).

Daniel *served*. He faithfully served Nebuchadnezzar and Darius, stirring the envy of the court's power-seekers. Their plotting landed him in the lion's den, but victory was snatched from the jaws of death (Daniel 6:3-28).

Similarly, Paul and Silas won Philippi from a dank, dark dungeon cell. Jeremiah won Judea cloaked in sackcloth and ashes. And Hosea won Israel from under the rubble of a broken home. They won because *service* leads to dominion. Humility leads to victory. Weakness is exalted from glory to glory, for "God resists the proud but gives grace to the humble" (1 Peter 5:5). "He scoffs at the scoffers but gives grace to the afflicted" (Proverbs 3:34).

Each one of these great heroes humbled himself under God's mighty hand (1 Peter 3:6). They submitted themselves. They served. They did as Jesus had done. And God honored that obedience with dominion.

It is no accident that those who are commissioned by the King of Kings to "take dominion over the earth" (Genesis 1:28), to "make disciples of all nations" (Matthew 28:19), to "be witnesses in Jerusalem, Judea, Samaria, and to the uttermost parts of the earth" (Acts 1:8), to do unto others as He has done unto us, administering *His* justice — these are commissioned as *servants*. Not overlords.

Paul called himself a *servant* (Galatians 1:10). That's all he ever aspired to be (Romans 1:1). Similarly, James (James 1:1), Peter (2 Peter 1:1), Epaphroditus (Colossians 4:12), Timothy (2 Timothy 2:24), Abraham (Psalm 105:42), Moses (Nehemiah 9:14), David (Psalm 89:3), Daniel (Romans 6:20), and all believers in general (1 Corinthians 7:22), are *all* called servants. They *all* did unto others as God had done unto them. They served.

Can we possibly aspire to anything more? Or anything less? Obviously, we have.

By spurning the work of charity and compassion to the homeless and helpless, by disdaining the dirty and laborious task of caring for the feebleminded wanderer, the filthy-fleshed alien, and the hapless, hopeless sojourner, by delegating our *service* to the government, we negate our dominion opportunity. By abrogating our place of service, feeding the hungry, clothing the naked, and giving a home to the homeless, we eliminate the possibility of reconstructing our culture, of rebuilding the ancient ruins, of raising up age-old foundations, of repairing the breach, and restoring the dwelling of righteousness (Isaiah 58:10-12). When we allow the state to take our place as "benefactors," not only are the poor oppressed all the more, but *we* lose *our* place of influence and effect (Luke 22:25-30).

God has called us to do unto others as He has done unto us. He served. We must serve. He bought our liberty through humble service, even death on the cross. We must buy back the captives of the land, loosening the bonds of wickedness, removing the yoke and setting the captives free (Isaiah 58:6).

The Covenant

We are to do unto others as God has done unto us.

And *what* is it that He has done? *How* has He done it?

He has dispensed His justice and mercy among us through *service*, within the *covenant*, by *grace*.

"The Biblical concept of the covenant," according to Gary North, "is the Bible's most important doctrine relating to the relationship between God and man."[1] If we do not understand the way the covenant works, then there is no way we can do unto others as God has done unto us. Even if we have servant's hearts, if we do not comprehend how service functions *within* the covenant, we will be unable to pattern our work in the world after God's work in us. Because the covenant *is* that pattern.

God's relationship with us is covenantal. He judges us covenantally. He comforts us covenantally. He fellowships with us covenantally. He disciplines us, rewards us, and cares for us covenantally.

Theologian James B. Jordan describes the covenant as "the personal, binding, structural relationship among the Persons of God and His people. The covenant, thus, is a social structure."[2] It is the divine-to-human/human-to-divine social structure. It is the legal means by which we approach, deal with, and know God. It is the pattern of our relationship.

According to Scripture, the covenant has five basic parts.[3] It begins with the establishment of God's nature and character: He is both transcendant and immanent, redeeming for Himself a people. Second, it proclaims God's sovereign authority over that people: They must obey Him. Third, the covenant outlines God's stipulations, His law: The people have clear cut responsibilities. Fourth, it establishes God's judicial see: He will evaluate His people's work. And finally, the covenant details God's very great and precious promises: The people have a future, an inheritance.

This outline of the covenant can be readily seen not only in God's dealings with Adam (Genesis 1:26-31; 2:16-25), Noah (Genesis 9:1-17), Abraham (Genesis 12:1-3; 15:1-21), Moses (Exodus 3:1-22), and the disciples of Christ (1 Corinthians 11:23-34), but also in the two tables of the Law, the Ten Commandments (two tables of five statutes)[4], the structure of the Pentateuch (five books), the Book of Psalms (five sections), the Book of Deuteronomy (five parts),[5] the Book of Revelation (five stages),[6] and many other passages of Scripture, both Old and New Testaments.[7] Again, this is because God deals with us covenantally. That is how He works in our midst.

The covenant is the *pattern* of our relationship with God. It is the *context* for His service.

Since we are to do unto others as He has done unto us, we obviously need to deal with one another in terms of the covenant. We need to build our human relationships around the five basic parts of the covenant. We need to do as He has done. We need to serve covenantally.

Covenantal Service

In practical terms, what that means is that we must not dispense mercy and care to the despised and homeless *promiscuously*. Neither may we *arbitrarily* determine the conditions, stipulations, and eligibility requirements according to our own whims, fancies, and prejudices. Our service must be covenantal. Our ministry must be in terms of a person's relation to the covenant.

As Herbert Schlossberg has argued, "Christians ought not to support any policy toward the poor that does not seek to have them occupy the same high plane of useful existence that all of us are to exemplify. 'Saving the poor' is a euphemism for destroying the poor unless it includes with it the intention of seeing the poor begin to serve others, and thereby validate the words of Jesus that it is better to give than to receive (Acts 20:35). Whereas humanitarian social policy keeps people hopelessly dependent, Christians should seek to remove them from that status and return them to productive capacity. Serving is a higher calling than being served."[8] We must lift the poor so that *they* can reciprocate, so that *they* can attain to a higher calling. That is at the heart of the covenantal pattern.

We must make absolutely certain that our helping really does help. A handout may meet an immediate need, but how does it contribute to the ultimate goal of setting the recipient aright? How does it prepare him for the job market? How does it equip him for the future?

These concerns are fully taken into account in God's provisions for aliens and sojourners in Israel. Because the Jews themselves were at one time sojourners in Egypt (Genesis 15:13; Exodus 22:21; Deuteronomy 10:19, 23:7), they were to treat the foreigners in their midst with respect and acceptance. Whether the sojourner was a part of an entire tribe, such as the Gibeonites (Joshua 9), or one of the remnant Canaanite people, or simply an individual settler, he was to receive full justice (Exodus 22:21, 23:9; Leviticus 19:33-34). He was to share in the inheritance of the Kingdom (Ezekiel 47:22-23). He was to be loved as a brother (Deuteronomy 10:19). He was included in the provision made for Cities of Refuge (Numbers 35:15; Joshua 20:9), in the charity network (Leviticus 19:10, 23:22; Deuteronomy 24:19-21), and equality under the Law (Leviticus 24:22). He was even ranked with the fatherless and the widow as being defenseless; and so the Lord Himself was his protection, judging all his oppressors (Psalm 94:6, 146:9; Jeremiah 7:6, 22:3; Ezekiel 22:7; Zechariah 7:10; Malachi 3:5).

But there were safeguards. The safeguards were partially designed to protect Israel from pagan pollution. But even more important than that, they protected the sojourners themselves from the ill effects of promiscuous entitlement. So for instance, there were ceremonial restrictions (Deuteronomy 7:1-6), and restrictions on cohabitation (Joshua 6:23). With special privilege came special responsibility. If the sojourner was to reap the rewards of Israel's Theocratic Republic, then he would have to function as a responsible, obedient citizen. Like any other member of the covenant he would have to honor the Sabbath (Exodus 20:10), the Day of Atonement (Leviticus 16:29), and the Feast of Unleavened Bread (Exodus 12:19). He shared the prohibitions on eating blood (Leviticus 17:10-13), immorality (Leviticus 18:26), idolatry (Leviticus 20:2), and blasphemy (Leviticus 24:16). He came under the Shelter of God's promises because he obeyed God's commands.

Nothing could stay God's hand from blessing those who honored Him, just as nothing could stay His hand from judging those who dishonored him. Thus, if the sojourner wished to share in the *privileges* of God's chosen people, *he would have to honor God by keeping His Word*. There was, and is, no other path to blessing.

Rahab the harlot, though she was not a member of God's covenant, came into the midst of it and submitted to God's rule, depending on His Word to live (Joshua 2:8-21). Though not of God's Household, she entered in, abiding by its standards, and thus obtained its securities. She turned her back on pagan Jericho and cast her lot with Almighty God and His people (Joshua 6:22-25). Her life and liberty could not have been had another way. Israel was an opportunity society, but only for those who observed the "rules."

Likewise, Ruth was not a member of God's covenant. She was a Moabitess (Ruth 1:4). A sojourner. But the charity of God's land of bounty and table of bounty was not closed to her (Ruth 2:2-23). She was given the opportunity to labor, to work, to glean, because she had committed herself to the terms of the covenant, the God of the covenant, and the people of the covenant (Ruth 1:16-17). The structures of charity in Israel expanded their reach to include her. Because the deeds of her mouth and works of her hands proved that she would depend on the Word of God to live, she was granted the privileges of the community of faith. She was brought into the circle of the covenant. She was given a Home.

This gracious provision of God is illustrated time after time throughout Scripture.

The Ethiopian eunuch obtained an entrance into the covenant (Acts 8:38) because he submitted himself to the terms of the covenant (Acts 8:36-37).

Cornelius the centurion obtained the promises of the covenant (Acts 10:44-48) because he trusted the Gospel of hope (Acts 10:22, 31, 44).

Similarly, when Jesus was in the district of Tyre and Sidon, a Canaanite woman received privileges of the covenant because of her great faith.

> And behold, a Canaanite woman came out from that region, and began to cry out, saying, "Have mercy on me, O Lord, Son of David; my daughter is cruelly demon-possessed." But He did not answer her a word. And His disciples came to Him and kept asking Him, saying, "Send her away, for she is shouting out after us." But He answered and said, "I was sent only to the lost sheep of the house of Israel." But she came and began to bow down before Him, saying, "Lord, help me!" And He answered and said, "It is not good to take the children's bread and throw it to the dogs." But she said, "Yes, Lord; but even the dogs feed on the crumbs which fall from their masters' table." Then Jesus answered and said to her, "O woman, your faith is great; be it done for you as you wish." And her daughter was healed at once (Matthew 15:22-28).

Just as the Gospel "is the power of God for salvation to everyone who believes, to the Jews first and also to the Greek" (Romans 1:16), so *the privileges of the covenant are available to everyone who submits to the terms of the covenant*, to the covenant member first and also to the sojourner.

But, privilege brings responsibility.

Jesus warned His disciples about sidestepping the boundaries of the covenant, saying,

Do not give what is holy to dogs, and do not throw
your pearls before swine, lest they trample them under
their feet, and turn and tear you to pieces (Matthew 7:6).

The Church is to be the Nursery of the Kingdom, nurturing
the nations on the goodness of God's bounty, but in order to taste
of that goodness, the nations must submit to God's rule (Matthew 28:19-20). To dispense the gifts of the Kingdom as an *entitlement* to any and all men without obligation — the ungrateful, the
slothful, the degenerate, the apostate, and the rebellious — is to
cast our pearls before swine!

Rahab had to demonstrate her faithfulness and her integrity.
She had to display fruits of repentance. Only then was she allowed
to taste the inheritance of the company of the faithful.

Ruth had to work. She had to glean. She had to show her dependence on the Word of God for her very life. Only then was
she allowed to reap the benefits of the opportunity society.

Similarly, the Ethiopian eunuch, Cornelius the centurion,
and the Canaanite woman all received special blessing from the
Lord because they demonstrated special dependence on the Lord.

In every case, all those who received the benefits of the covenant were either *in* the covenant (from the House of Israel), or
dependent *on* the covenant (the sojourner in the land).

Whenever anyone violates God's standards he loses his covenant privileges: Esau (Genesis 25:27-34), Korah (Numbers
16:1-35), Achan (Joshua 7:1-26), Saul (1 Samuel 13:5-14), Tobiah
(Nehemiah 4:10), Ananias and Sapphira (Acts 5:1-11), Demas
(2 Timothy 4:10), and Diotrephes (3 John 9). There is no entitlement. God does not promiscuously hand out the privileges of the
Kingdom.

God has exercised compassion, comfort, and charity on His
people. He has fed us from His rich estate! He has given us a
New Home. We then have been commissioned to nurse the
world with similar compassion, comfort, and charity. We are to
feed the world. We are to offer Sanctuary. We are to make certain
that righteousness is *done* as well as preached.

But charity is not to be dispensed as an *entitlement*, a *right*,
bearing with it no responsibilities or obligations.

Work is required because work is the means by which poverty
is transformed into productivity (2 Thessalonians 3:10).

Diligence is required because diligence is blessed with prosperity.

Family participation is required because families are the basic building blocks of society (1 Timothy 5:8).

Even more than these though, *obedience* is required. *Submission* to the standards of the Kingdom is required. In order to take advantage of the covenant privileges, a man must be *in* the covenant or dependent *on* the covenant. Even when the Church reaches out into the streets, and lanes, and hedgerows, drawing in the dispossessed, responsibility must be enforced.

Jesus said,

> When you give a luncheon or a dinner, do not invite your friends or your brothers or your relatives or rich neighbors, lest they also invite you in return, and repayment come to you. But when you give a reception, invite the poor, the crippled, the lame, the blind, and you will be blessed, since they do not have the means to repay you; for you will be repaid at the resurrection of the righteous. And then one of those who were reclining at the table with Him heard this, he said to Him, "Blessed is everyone who shall eat bread in the Kingdom of God!" But He said to him, "A certain man was giving a big dinner, and he invited many; and at the dinner hour he sent his slave to say to those who had been invited, 'Come, for everything is ready now.' But they all alike began to make excuses. The first one said to him, 'I have bought a piece of land and I need to go out and look at it; please consider me excused.' And another one said, 'I have bought five yoke of oxen, and I am going to try them out; please consider me excused.' And another one said, 'I have married a wife, and for that reason I cannot come.' And the slave came back and reported this to his master. Then the head of the household became angry and said to his slave, 'Go out at once into the streets and lanes of the city and bring in here the poor and crippled and blind and lame.' And the slave said, 'Master, what you commanded has been done, and still there is room.' And the master said to the slave, 'Go out into the highways and along the hedges, and compel them to come in,

that my house may be filled. For I tell you, none of those
men who were invited shall taste of my dinner'" (Luke
14:12-25).

The dispossessed are to be brought in. They are to take their
place around the table of the Lord. They are to be given a New
Home.

But as Matthew points out in a parallel passage, the dinner
and Home are not without obligation. *The covenant must be submitted to.*

> But when the king came in to look over the dinner
> guests, he saw there a man not dressed in wedding
> clothes, and he said to him, "Friend, how did you come
> in here without wedding clothes?" And he was speech-
> less. Then the king said to the servants, "Bind him hand
> and foot, and cast him into the outer darkness; in that
> place there shall be weeping and gnashing of teeth. For
> many are called, but few are chosen" (Matthew 22:11-14).

Pearls must not be cast before swine. Those who refuse to
come under the rule of God *can* not, *must* not come under the
protection and provision of God.

Biblical charity is gracious, but it is not promiscuous. Privilege brings responsibility.

And if blessing is possible only within the covenant, then the
poor must be brought into the covenant.

When we yield the apparatus of care to the state and the conditions of that care are secularized, the poor are more often than
not victimized: They wind up being buffeted either by miserly
discrimination or by smothering entitlements. But when we adhere to God's standards, then the poor are transformed from
poverty to productivity: They acknowledge the nature and character of God and thus are reoriented to reality (Psalm 73:16-20);
they submit to His authority and to His authority delegated in
the Church and thus are repatterned by worship, discipleship,
ritual, and fellowship for success and advance (Proverbs 2:6-22);
they obey His laws and thus inherit blessing (Deuteronomy
28:2); they yield to judgment and discipline and thus hedge in
destructive habits (Proverbs 1:8-19); and finally, they claim God's

promises and thus obtain *real* gains, *real* opportunities, and *real* advantages (Ruth 2-4). Only within the covenant can the destructive, suicidal, sluggardly, and debauched behavior of the hardcore homeless be cured. And only within the covenant can the oppressive, unjust, and discriminatory actions against the short term and deserving homeless be guarded against.

All throughout the cultural framework of ancient Israel, there were established structures for the people to serve the needy. There were provisions for free harvesting (Leviticus 19:9-10; Deuteronomy 24:19-22). There were alms feasts (Deuteronomy 14:22-29) and alms giving (Deuteronomy 26:12-13). There were debt cancellations (Deuteronomy 15:1-11) and special loans available (Leviticus 25:35-55). But notice: *None* of these structures was secular in orientation; *none* of them was placed under the auspices of the state; *none* of them was left to the discretions or discriminations of mere men. They were covenantal.

God serves us. So we are to serve others.

God serves us in the context of the covenant. So we are to serve others in the context of the covenant.

We are to do unto others as God has done unto us. We are to do as He does.

Grace

God has dispensed His justice and mercy among us through *service*, within the *covenant*, by *grace*.

Grace is the unearned, undeserved favor that God has poured out upon us on account of the sacrifice of Christ on our behalf (1 Peter 3:18). "We are saved by grace through faith," and this not of ourselves, "it is the gift of God" (Ephesians 2:8).

But again, with privilege comes responsibility.

> For the grace of God has appeared, bringing Salvation to all men, instructing us to deny ungodliness and worldly desires and to live sensibly, righteously and godly in the present age, looking for the blessed hope and the appearing of the glory of our great God and Savior, Christ Jesus; who gave Himself for us, that He might redeem us from every lawless deed and purify for Himself a people for His own possession, zealous for good deeds (Titus 2:11-14).

By grace we are "created in Christ Jesus for good works, which God prepared before hand, that we should walk in them (Ephesians 2:10).

In other words, God sheds His grace upon us, so we are to be gracious to others. We are to do unto others as God has done unto us. This truth is inherent even in the *word* "grace." The Greek is "charis," from which we get our word "charity." Grace and charity. They are inseparable concepts.

This principle is illustrated beautifully in Christ's parable of the Good Samaritan.

> "A certain man was going down from Jerusalem to Jericho; and he fell among robbers, and they stripped him and beat him, and went off leaving him half dead. And by chance a certain priest was going down on that road, and when he saw him, he passed by on the other side. And likewise a Levite also, when he came to the place and saw him, passed by on the other side. But a certain Samaritan, who was on a journey, came upon him; and when he saw him, he felt compassion, and came to him, and bandaged up his wounds, pouring oil and wine on them; and he put him on his own beast, and brought him to an inn, and took care of him. And on the next day he took out two denarii and gave them to the innkeeper and said, 'Take care of him; and whatever more you spend, when I return, I will repay you.' Which of these three do you think proved to be a neighbor to the man who fell into the robbers' hands?" And he said, "The one who showed mercy toward him." And Jesus said to him, "Go and do the same" (Luke 10:30-37).

In this story, Jesus uses an outcast, a Samaritan, as an example of perfect virtue. He strictly observed the Law, shaming the priest and Levite who "passed by on the other side" (Luke 10:31-32). He paid attention to the needs of others (Deuteronomy 22:4) and showed concern for the poor (Psalm 41:1). He showed pity toward the weak (Psalm 72:13) and rescued them from violence (Psalm 72:14). Knowing the case of the helpless (Proverbs 29:7), he gave of his wealth (Deuteronomy 26:12-13), and shared his food (Proverbs 22:9).

But his was not a dry, passionless obedience. He had "put on a heart of compassion, kindness, humility, gentleness, and patience" (Colossians 3:12). He "became a father to the needy, and took up the case of the stranger" (Job 29:16). He loved his neighbor as himself (Mark 12:31), thus fulfilling the Law (Romans 13:10).

The Samaritan fulfilled the demands of both Law and love! He demonstrated both obedience and compassion, holding to *both* the Spirit and the letter.

The priest and the Levite "did not remember to show loving-kindness" (Psalm 10:16), but the Samaritan rescued "the weak and needy to deliver them out of the hand of the wicked" (Psalm 82:4). Without hesitation. Without second thought. Without looking for excuses. He just did his job. He did what he *ought* to have done. He did what he *had* to do. Law *and* love in action.

The Samaritan is clearly a type, or a symbol, of Christ. Only *the* Good Samaritan (John 8:48), the Nazarene from "Galilee of the Gentiles" (Matthew 4:15) can do what the Law (the priest and the Levite) has failed to do. Only *He* has fulfilled the demands of perfect virtue (Matthew 5:17).

The victim on the roadside then is a type or a symbol of us, in our fallen, broken, and helpless destitution (Romans 7:18). Nothing can save us except the gracious succor of Christ (Romans 5:6-11).

The inn in the parable symbolizes the Church while the inn-keeper typifies her pastors (Acts 20:28).

All these details are extremely important because Jesus concludes the parable saying, "Go and do likewise" (Luke 10:37 KJV). In other words: "Do unto others as I have done unto you."

The parable establishes a *pattern* for caring for the needy. It is a simple pattern; do as Jesus did, *serving* with wine and oil, time and money, adhering to the *covenant*—spirit and letter, Church and pastors, and finally, ministering in *graciousness* and compassion.

Conclusion

Caring for the homeless and poor is a *sacred* duty. Only "a fool speaks nonsense and inclines his heart toward wickedness to practice ungodliness and to speak error against the Lord, to keep the hungry person unsatisfied and to withhold drink from the thirsty" (Isaiah 32:6). We are to care for the needy. And we are to care for them in the same manner that God has cared for us. We are to do unto others as He has done unto us. We are to dispense justice through *service*, within the *covenant*, by *grace*.

When we fail to *serve*, the state steps in and dominates, hurting the poor, setting them back. Farms are foreclosed on. Women are used and abused. The feebleminded are driven further and further away from reality. And the homeless are dispossessed all the more. They are left to fend for themselves, out in the howling wilderness.

When we fail to serve within the context of the *covenant*, again, the state steps in and tosses the poor between two extremes. Either they are smothered with promiscuous entitlements, stripping them of their dignity and their incentive, or they are penalized with discriminatory and arbitrary welfarism. Either way they lose. They are still left with no Home.

Finally, when we fail to serve within the context of the covenant *graciously*, the state steps in and imposes welfare as a citizenship benefit. Charity is lost. Compassion is lost. The personal care of the Scriptural Good Samaritan model is swallowed up by the bureaucratic care of the lords of the Gentiles model (Luke 22:25-30).

That is why *God didn't tell the government to feed the hungry, clothe the naked, and shelter the homeless*. He told us to. He told the Church.

Service. Covenant. Grace. Doing unto others as God has done unto us.

I see a Golden Age
dawning in the near future
. . . an Aubade
sweet and clear.

Erasmus

FIFTEEN

AUBADE:
A BIBLICAL HOPE

Over three hundred years ago, John Bunyan began his classic master-work, *Pilgrim's Progress*, with a desperate cry for direction:

> As I walked through the wilderness of this world, I lighted on a certain place where was a den, and I laid me down in that place to sleep, and as I slept I dreamed a dream. I dreamed, and behold I saw a man clothed with rags, standing in a certain place, with his face from his own house, a book in his hand, and a great burden upon his back. I looked, and saw him open the book, and read therein; and as he read he wept and trembled, and not being able longer to contain, he brake out with a lamentable cry, saying, "What shall I do?"[1]

Over three hundred years later, the cry still arises. The burden still exists.

Christian pilgrims still look out upon the wilderness of this world, seeing the calamities of the Curse: depravity, licentiousness, privation, debauchery, and blasphemy. They witness the tattered, ragged, and bedraggled humanistic culture gone awry: injustice, socialism, welfarism, abortion, media madness, and homelessness. Not surprisingly, they cry out with an almost desperate, despairing voice, "What shall I do? What *can* I do?" They yearn for direction.

Thankfully, throughout history there have always been stalwart pioneer pilgrims who have acted decisively on behalf of the poor and homeless. They have provided that direction. They have given True Sanctuary. They have forged ahead despite limited resources, despite outside animosity and opposition, and despite prevailing opinions and programs.

In fact, whenever true revival has broken out, God's faithful few, His remnant, have authenticated that revival with works of mercy. Hospitals are established. Orphanages are founded. Rescue missions are started. Almshouses are built. Soup kitchens are begun. Charitable societies are incorporated. The hungry are fed, the naked clothed, and the homeless sheltered.

Virtually all of the Church's greatest heroes are known for their compassionate care for the poor: Augustine and Athanasius, Bernard of Clairveaux and Francis of Assisi, John Wyclif and Jan Hus, John Calvin and George Whitefield, Charles Haddon Spurgeon and J. Hudson Taylor. On and on and on the litany of charity goes. From Francis of Sartoria to Francis Schaeffer, from Brother Lawrence to Mother Teresa, from Amy Carmichael to Ann Kiemel, obedient believers have always distinguished themselves by their selflessness and compassion.[2]

As their fellow travelers have cried out, "What shall I *do*? What *can* I do?", they provided direction. Some espoused *traditionalist* ministries focusing on service and covenant; others espoused *progressivist* ministries focusing on service and grace; still others espoused comprehensive *reconstructionist* ministries striving for a balance of service, covenant, *and* grace. These three "schools" of thought survive to this day, providing direction to our efforts on behalf of the homeless.

Traditionalist ministries represented by the old puritan philanthropies,[3] the Charity Organization Society,[4] and the Salvation Army,[5] have commonly provided food, clothing, and shelter for the destitute but have also hedged those provisions with careful restrictions and limitations. This is the kind of private charity paradigm that *conservatives* are most apt to memorialize, with its strong work ethic and its stipulations against indolence and vice.

Progressivist ministries represented by the social gospel movement,[6] the Franciscans,[7] and the Community for Creative Non-Violence,[8] also have commonly provided basic human services but with an activist bent. This is the kind of private charity paradigm that *liberals* are most apt to memorialize, with its strong demand for "rights" and its "anti-establishment" flavor.

Though traditionalists and progressivists have no doubt pursued their tasks with righteous zeal and passionate fervor, they often fall short of the ultimate goal of Scriptural poverty relief: getting the poor back on their own two feet, back to self-sufficiency. Though no one can doubt the tremendous impact that General William Booth and his Salvation Army or Mitch Snyder and his Community for Creative Non-Violence have had on the issue of homelessness, that lack is nonetheless glaringly evident.

Charity must be more than a reaction to governmental programs: a cry for tougher standards and fewer benefits from the conservative traditionalists; a cry for easier standards and more benefits from the liberal progressivists. Charity must reconstruct. It dare not simply be a social or political or economic tactic. Charity must offer a *real* hope in the face of a *real* Curse. As David Chilton has asserted, the "true Christian reconstruction of culture is far from being simply a matter of passing Law X and electing Congressman Y. Christianity is not a political cult. It is the divinely ordained worship of the Most High God." He goes on to argue that if our primary response to cultural problems is social or political action, "we are, in principle, atheists; we are confessing our faith in human action as the ultimate determiner of history."[9] Where traditionalist and progressivist ministries break down is the same place that Luther's secularization plan broke down: They fail to take into account the full and transforming *spiritual* dimension of relief.

Reconstructionist ministries represented by the Spurgeonic Charities,[10] Voice of Calvary Ministries,[11] and H.E.L.P. Services[12] have commonly tried to avoid the trap of either a conservative humanism on the one hand or a liberal humanism on the other. They have been Church oriented, sacramental, and integrationist. They have gone beyond soup kitchens, shelters, and self help enterprises, training the poor and homeless through godly discipline and discipleship to *make it* in the wilderness of this world.[13] They have included emergency relief in their repertoire of care,[14] but have incorporated job training,[15] spiritual counseling,[16] liturgical reorientation,[17] congregational fellowship,[18] and diaconal service as well.[19] They have sought to *transform* poverty into productivity. They have given the homeless True Sanctuary.

That is real charity!

As our pilgrims' cry arises, we should look to reconstructionist ministries for direction. Clearly, if homelessness is to be countermanded in any way, we are going to have to go beyond the old party lines of conservatism and liberalism. We are going to have to go beyond government welfarism. We are going to have to go beyond the U.N.'s socialist tinkering, and the media's guilt and pitying. We are going to have to bypass every program or plan tainted by humanism. We are going to have to buckle down, and get our hands dirty with the tough work of total reconstruction. We are going to have to provide answers, create alternatives, and develop models that truly work, that are genuinely Biblical. We are going to have to offer Refuge from the howling wilderness.

Reconstructionism is more costly than traditionalism. It is more comprehensive than progressivism. It is more difficult, more time consuming, and more life encompassing.

But then, it is also more Biblical.

And that makes all the difference.

Facing Goliath

It was more than a mismatch.

But the young shepherd boy fearlessly faced the gargantuan warrior before him with nothing but a sling, five smooth stones, and the assurance that God was sovereign.

The warrior stood head and shoulders above all the rest. Clad in armor, draped with the mantle of an awesome reputation, he struck an intimidating pose.

Still, the shepherd boy remained steadfast, unshaken.

> When the Philistine looked and saw David, he disdained him; for he was but a youth, and ruddy, with a handsome appearance, And the Philistine said to David, "Am I a dog, that you come to me with sticks?" And the Philistine cursed David by his gods. The Philistine also said to David, "Come to me, and I will give your flesh to the birds of the sky and the beasts of the field." Then David said to the Philistine, "You come to me with a sword, a spear, and a javelin, but I come to you in the name of the Lord of hosts, the God of the armies of Israel, whom you have taunted" (1 Samuel 17:42-45).

David was confident.

But it was an *impossible* situation. To say that the odds were against the brazen young Israelite is an understatement at the very best. It was suicidal.

Or, at least it looked that way. But then, looks can be deceiving. What *seems* to be, is all too often entirely out of line with the facts.

And what were the facts? What did David know that Goliath didn't?

David knew that the land belonged to God, not to the Philistines (Psalm 24:1). He knew that God had sovereignly entrusted the stewardship of the land to the chosen people (Joshua 1:2-6). He knew that if they would simply obey God's Word, heed His ordinances, keep His precepts, honor His statutes, adhere to His standards, and yield to his commands, then blessings would come upon them and overtake them (Deuteronomy 28:2; Psalm 19:7-11; Psalm 119:1-2). They would be blessed in the city and blessed in the country (Deuteronomy 28:3). They would be blessed with fruitfulness and blessed with bountifulness (Deuteronomy 28:4-5). They would be blessed coming in and blessed going out (Deuteronomy 28:6). Their enemies would be defeated and flee before them, in seven directions (Deuteronomy 28:7). They would abound in prosperity (Deuteronomy 28:11). For the Lord Himself would establish them as "a holy people to Himself" (Deuteronomy 28:9), and all the peoples of the earth would be sore afraid of them (Deuteronomy 28:10).

It *looked* like David didn't have a chance against Goliath.

But David knew better. He knew the facts.

He knew he wouldn't lose. He couldn't lose. As a faithful member of God's legion, he was *more* than a conqueror (Romans 8:37). He was an overcomer (1 John 5:4). He was victorious (1 Corinthians 15:57). Already. The battle had been won.

So he said as much.

"This day the Lord will deliver you up into my hands, and I will strike you down and remove your head from you. And I will give the dead bodies of the army of the Philistines this day to the birds of the sky and the wild beasts of the earth, that all the earth may know that there is a God in Israel, and that all this assembly may

know that the Lord does not deliver by sword or spear;
for the battle is the Lord's and He will give you into our
hands" (1 Samuel 17:46-47).

What bold faith! David had an "assurance of things hoped
for," a "conviction of things not seen" (Hebrews 11:1). He walked
by faith, not by sight (2 Corinthians 5:7). And thus he gained
God's favor, His approval (Hebrews 11:2). Against all odds,
against all reason, he snatched victory out of the snarling jaws of
defeat (Romans 8:28). He believed God for the impossible and
accomplished it (Philippians 4:13).

> Then it happened when the Philistine rose and came
> and drew near to meet David, that David ran quickly to-
> ward the battle line to meet the Philistine. And David
> put his hand into his bag and took from it a stone and
> slung it, and struck the Philistine on his forehead. And
> the stone sank into his forehead, so that he fell on his face
> to the ground. Thus David prevailed over the Philistine
> with a sling and a stone, and he struck the Philistine and
> killed him; but there was no sword in David's hand.
> Then David ran and stood over the Philistine and took
> his sword and drew it out of its sheath and killed him,
> and cut off his head with it. When the Philistines saw
> that their champion was dead, they fled. And the men of
> Israel and Judah arose and shouted and pursued the
> Philistines as far as the valley, and to the gates of Ekron.
> And the slain Philistines lay along the way to Shaaraim,
> even to Gath and Ekron (1 Samuel 17:48-52).

Just a few generations earlier, Israel had been willing to for-
feit their entire inheritance all for the sight of a few Goliath-like
warriors. "There are giants in the land," they said tremblingly
(Numbers 13:22).

"We are like grasshoppers in their sight" (Numbers 13:33).

"Perhaps, it would be best to return to Egypt," they muttered
in despair. "Perhaps slavery *was* better after all" (Numbers 14:3).

Given the choice of walking by faith or by sight, most of
those Israelites at Kadesh-barnea chose sight.

To be sure, they had witnessed God's miraculous interventions on their behalf. They had seen His very great and precious promises to them confirmed at every turn. There had been the ten plagues in Egypt. There had been the glorious exodus and the parting of the Red Sea. There had been the provision of manna from heaven. There had been the cloud by day, the fire by night, and the continual Presence at the Tabernacle. But now that they were on the threshold of the Promised Land; now that victory was imminent; now that they could consummate their covenant task they were nervous. They were full of doubt. They were hamstrung with faithlessness.

The land was flowing with milk and honey all right, just as God had promised (Numbers 13:27). It was rich with grapes, pomegranates, and figs (Numbers 13:23). It was all that they had hoped for, and more. But . . . it was filled with strong men and fortified cities (Numbers 13:28).

And . . . there were giants. Those indomitable giants.

Never mind that the land was already given into their hand (Numbers 13:30). Never mind that God was with them and had removed the protection of the enemy (Numbers 14:9).

Never mind all that! Look at those giants!

But notice, those giants never defeated Israel. They never had the chance, because Israel beat herself. With the bludgeon of pessimism. With the club of faithlessness.

And so the people retreated from their promises to wander in the wilderness for forty years (Numbers 14:32-35).

All because of the giants.

Unlike his forbears, David knew that he could "stand and not be shaken" (Hebrews 12:28). He knew that he could depend on God's Word. He knew that he did not have to yield before the utterly impossible circumstances that faced him. He knew that he could act decisively on the truth and reliability of God's testimony and that he would thus prevail. He even knew that he could make due without the entangling encumberments that the king had thrust upon him as a help, as added security (1 Samuel 17: 38-39).

Giants in the land?

So what! God raises up giant killers. In fact, He raises up whole armies of giant killers (2 Samuel 21:18-22).

As it was in the beginning, is now, and ever shall be.

There is a giant in the land.

Clearly homelessness is a complex problem of gargantuan proportions.

The odds are against us. It looks like an impossible task. Conquer homelessness? Yeah, sure! The Department of Health, Education, and Welfare has failed. The Department of Housing and Urban Development has failed. The United Nations has failed. The giant has thus far been invincible. Indeed, the odds are against us. How can we possibly win?

We can win because God has given us His promises.

> However, there shall be no poor among you, since the Lord will surely bless you in the land which the Lord your God is giving you as an inheritance to possess, if only you listen obediently to the voice of the Lord your God, to observe carefully all this commandment which I am commanding you today. For the Lord your God shall bless you as He has promised you, and you will lend to many nations, but you will not borrow; and you will rule over many nations, but they will not rule over you (Deuteronomy 15:4-6).

God has given us His promises. And His Word cannot fail. Thus, we cannot fail.

Time to Go to Work

David faced the giant. He took God at His Word. He went to work, and emerged victorious.

But he wasn't alone. Scripture is filled to overflowing with similar stories, similar heroes.

Against all odds, Caleb faced giants, and won (Joshua 14)!

Against all odds, Ehud faced the power of Moab, and won (Judges 3:12-30)!

Against all odds, Shamgar faced the power of the Philistines, and won (Judges 3:31)!

Against all odds, Deborah faced the power of Canaan, and won (Judges 4-5)!

Against all odds, Gideon faced the power of Midian, and won (Judges 6-8)!

Against all odds, the apostles faced the power of the Roman empire and won (Acts 8-28)!

Isn't it about time for us to demonstrate to an unbelieving world, that God can still beat the odds? Isn't it about time for us to prove to a fallen and depraved generation that God can raise up a weak and unesteemed people against all odds, and win? Isn't it?

> For though we walk in the flesh, we do not war according to the flesh, for the weapons of our warfare are not of the flesh, but divinely powerful for the destruction of fortresses. We are destroying speculations and every lofty thing raised up against the knowledge of God, and we are taking every thought captive to the obedience of Christ (2 Corinthians 10:3-5).

We are invincible (Ephesians 6:10-18; Romans 8:37-39). Even the gates of hell shall not prevail against us (Matthew 16:8). If, that is, we would only do our job. If we would only take the Gospel hope beyond, to "the uttermost parts of the earth" (Acts 1:8), if we would only "make disciples of all nations" (Matthew 28:19), if we would only "rebuild the ancient ruins . . . raise up the age old foundations . . . and repair the breach" (Isaiah 58:12) by caring for the poor, the afflicted, and the dispossessed (Isaiah 58:10).

It is time to go to work.

We may have to go it alone for a time. That didn't stop David (1 Samuel 17:40), so it shouldn't stop us.

We may have to work with few, or even no resources. That didn't stop Jonathan (1 Samuel 14:6), so it shouldn't stop us.

We may have to improvise, utilizing less than perfect conditions and less than qualified workers and less than adequate facilities. That didn't stop Peter, James, and John (Acts 4:20), so it shouldn't stop us.

We may have to go with what we've got, with no support, no notoriety, and no cooperation. That didn't stop Jeremiah (Jeremiah 1:4-10), so it shouldn't stop us.

We may have to start "in weakness and in fear and in much trembling" (1 Corinthians 2:3), without "persuasive words of wisdom" (1 Corinthians 2:4). That didn't stop the Apostle Paul (1 Corinthians 2:1) so it shouldn't stop us.

It is time to go to work.

Dominion doesn't happen overnight. Victory doesn't come in a day. So the sooner we get started, the better off we'll be. The sooner we get started, the quicker the victory will come. In order to get from here to there, we need to set out upon the road. At the very least.

There will never be an ideal time to *begin* the work of reconstruction, of charity. Money is *always* short. Volunteers are *always* at a premium. Facilities are always either too small, or too inflexible, or in the wrong location, or too expensive. There is *never* enough time, *never* enough energy, and *never* enough resources.

So what?

Our commission is not dependent upon conditions and restrictions. Our commission is dependent only upon the unconditional promises of God's Word.

So, we should just go. Do what we ought to. Starting *now*.

Conclusion

The work of Biblical charity must be undertaken *now*. We must rid our land of the spectre of homelessness. The only way to do that is to get started. Ourselves. Without the entangling encumbrances of the government or the U.N. or anything else that might compromise our efforts. Even if the odds are against us.

David knew the odds were against him, lopsidedly so, when he faced Goliath single handedly. But he also knew that God blessed obedience. He knew that God blessed valor. He knew that God's work done in God's way would never lack for God's provision and protection. So, he set out. And he won!

We are called to "walk by faith and not by sight" (2 Corinthians 5:7). We are to walk in the supernatural anointing of Almighty God, casting down strongholds, taking every thought, every word, every deed, every man, woman, and child captive for Christ (2 Corinthians 10:3-5).

We are not to tremble at the "giants in the land." For we are the giant killers, come at last!

And the sound of the ocean
   still rings in my ear
And the beckoning question:
   Why am I here?

Someday I know
   I'll find my way home.
Until then I'll walk these
   Crowded streets alone.
I'll sleep with the sidewalk
   Under my head.
While somewhere my children
   are fast in their bed.

But someday I know
   I'll find my way home.

                    Dennis Welch

SIXTEEN

PROOF IN THE PUDDING: A BIBLICAL REALITY

It can be done.

Homelessness can be conquered.[1] Biblically. One person at a time. One day at a time.

"I s'pose the proof's in the puddin'. An' I s'pose I'm the puddin'. I s'pose."

"Yeah, I think you're right, Earl. You're the pudding. You're the proof."

He smiled. His dark eyes danced gaily with the kind of sheer joy that comes with a hard fought, hard won victory.

I returned the smile. The victory was indeed sweet.

Earl had been homeless. But no more. He had been unemployed for nearly three years—since his Navy discharge. But no more. He had devolved into heavy drinking, careless carousing, and aimless wandering. But no more. He had begun drifting further and further from reality, out of touch, out of sight, out of mind. Literally. But no more.

"Ain't no magic wands. Ain't no easy ways out. It's been tough, I admit. But it's been worth it. Ever' bit."

I just smiled again.

He visited the Church first. He zipped in and out of the Sunday service so quickly that I missed him the first two times he came. I made a special effort to catch him the third Sunday, and I did, out in the parking lot. He didn't tell me then that he was homeless. But I could tell. Not that he was particularly unkempt or seedy. He just had that hollow look of sadness. There was that barrier, that wall that almost all homeless erect between themselves and the rest of the world.

We chatted. I broached the subject of the Gospel and he responded with genuine openness — tentative and cautious, but open. We parted cordially and I knew that God was not yet finished with Earl's life.

The next morning he showed up at my office. "I been thinkin' 'bout what we was talkin' 'bout after Church yesterday. I been thinkin' maybe it's time for me t' clean up my act."

We talked for two hours.

He told me where he'd come from. How he'd fallen into hard times. Why he'd degenerated so.

I told him about our ministry to the homeless. What all was involved. What it entailed.

He was game.

So was I.

And that was the beginning.

There were a number of physical matters to attend to at first: health, hygiene, habits, and housing. We secured the necessities, networking with a few other local agencies and Churches. A physician donated his services. A clothes closet donated a few new shirts and jeans. A Church opened up a small unused room in the Sunday School building as a temporary shelter.

A job was the next concern. Again, a bit of networking and cooperation turned up a convenience store opening within just a few hours. Earl could start training in two days.

He began intensive discipleship training, one on one counseling, and group Bible study. He submitted himself to the elders. Everything seemed to be going perfectly. Storybook perfection.

And then he blew it. He went on a weekend drunk. He frittered his first paycheck away on two evenings' debauchery.

I didn't know what to do.

Should I kick him out? Let him go? Show him that I really mean business?

I was never forced to make a decision. Earl disappeared. He took off. What had looked like a glorious victory had suddenly soured into a dismal and disappointing failure. Two steps forward, three steps back.

If that were the end of the story, then it would be an all too typical story. The kind of song and dance that homeless ministries must endure a thousand times every year.

But thankfully the story doesn't end there. Earl came back.

Like the returning prodigal, he was sheepish and uncertain. But I could see fires of determination in his eyes. Now he really was ready to make a go of it.

"I' m tired a' th' games. I'm tired a' messin' around. I'm tired a' sleepin' with th' sidewalk under my head."

He began a job training program. He went to work evenings and saved enough to move into a garage apartment. He resubmitted himself to the Church. And this time, he really meant it.

Now, obviously a lot of time and energy and effort went into Earl's rehabilitation. The broad brush strokes here don't even begin to detail the breadth and depth of effort required to help him. Hundreds of hours of counseling, tutoring, training, discipling, and exhorting were invested in just one homeless man. But that is the only way that rehabilitation can be effected. The hard way. The long, hard way. The long, hard, Biblical way.

There are no magic wands.

"If th' government had a' got a' hold a' me, they'd 'a prob'ly put me up in one a' them projects, like a rat in a cage. An' if a reg'lar charity had a' got hold a' me, they'd a' prob'ly just thrown food at me, like a beast in a zoo. Either way I'd been like a blamed animal, hemmed in. But doin' it God's way I been free t' be human and free."

"God's way is always the best way," I said.

"Ain't that the truth!" he laughed. "Here I am, same job a year later. Really makin' it now. I ain't exactly gettin' rich. But then again, at least I'm outta the ditch."

"At least."

"It can be done."

"Yeah, I think you're right, Earl. You're the pudding. You're the proof."

DO'S AND DON'T'S

First there was Band Aid. Then there was Live Aid, U.S.A. for Africa, Sport Aid, Comic Relief, and Hands Across America. Charity extravaganzas have been all the rage of late. But how much good have these glitzy efforts actually done? What have the millions upon millions of dollars raised actually accomplished?

According to *Spin*, a rock music magazine, "Live Aid raised the consciousness of the planet, the hopes of the starving in Africa, and $100 million. It almost raised Bob Geldof to a saint. But drenched in their own glory, the organizers of Live Aid made a fatal mistake: They completely misunderstood what was really happening in Ethiopia. Today, Live Aid may be helping to kill far more people than it ever had a hope of saving."[1]

What is true of the celebrity relief efforts in Ethiopia is equally true of most efforts to aid the homeless: What was begun as a mission of mercy has become an instrument of wrath in the greatest of the dispossessed's many tragedies. Our "helping" has actually been harmful. In order to avoid the pitfalls of such "harmful" helping in the future, *we must carefully adhere to the Biblical pattern*. And we must stridently shun all other plans, programs, and proposals. If we really want to help the homeless, then we must pay heed to a number of do's and don't's:

1. *Do* get involved with the poor and dispossessed. It is, after all, our Christian obligation. Whenever and wherever possible, the local Church should initiate a food relief program, a job placement service, and a counseling outreach for the needy. In addition, she should erect shelter for the homeless as God provides, or at the very least provide sheltering options. If every Church in America just got involved in a Biblical fashion, homelessness would be almost entirely eradicated overnight.[2]

2. *Don't* simply set out blindly to "help the poor." That was the mistake of Live Aid, Hands Across America, and the other

charity extravaganzas. First, find out what the *needs* are in your community. If there is already adequate emergency shelter but no food program or job placement service or trade school outreach, then obviously you don't want to start off building almshouses. Do a demographic study. Find out what services already exist. Talk to social service workers, police, community associations, hospital administrators, school teachers, and of course other pastors. Bring focus and purpose to your work.[3]

3. *Do* work in concert with others. Learn from existing programs. Supplement, don't supplant. We must begin to coordinate our efforts with existing programs in other Churches. We must network, perhaps even set up a computer link between ministries to share information, resources, and ideas. Our ultimate aim must be to do the work of the Kingdom, not to advance our own individual causes or reputations.[4]

4. *Don't* compromise Scriptural concerns just for the sake of harmony. Coordination and cooperation *are* important and it is doubtful that Christians will ever be able to make a significant dent in the monolithic culture of humanism until and unless we comprehend the necessity of catholicity, but we must never yield to the heresy of "peace and cooperation at any price." The principles of service, covenant, and grace must be enforced. On this, there can be no compromise. Scripture cannot be broken.[5]

5. *Do* make certain that the charity offered by your Church is distinctively ecclesiastical and not simply a conservative private initiative program along the lines of the "Luther-esque" charities, as we discussed in chapter 12. Make certain you offer the homeless True Refuge. Make certain that the very best of the historic Christian models, pastoral and monastic, are woven into the ministry: The homeless should be nurtured daily on the Word revealed, the Word made manifest, and the Word incarnate.

The Word *renews the minds* of the poor. Through the teaching of Scripture, the way and will of God is revealed. Right doctrine shatters old habits, explodes bad thoughts, and establishes *real* hope. The Gospel *changes* people. Thus, our charity agenda must not simply be one more conservative, deregulated, family-centered, work-oriented, and decentralized program. It must be forthrightly evangelistic. The poor need good news. They need *the* Good News.

The Word readjusts the poor both to God's society and to the world in worship, through the Lord's Supper. To take the Lord's Supper is not to indulge in an abstract theological ritual. It is a tangible offering *to* God, a consecration *before* God, a communion *with* God, and a transformation *in* God. It is thus a conscious drive at the heart of reality. It is the Word made manifest. In this simple yet profound act of worship, the meaning and value of all life is revealed and fulfilled. The poor, like all men, need a double dose of reality. And only the Church can serve up that reality as she gathers around the sacramental altar.

The Word reforms the lifestyles of the poor. The discipling and disciplining process of life in the local Church repatterns a man's ways according to the ways of the Lord, confronting him with the Word incarnate.

Like all the rest of us, the homeless desperately need the lifestyle adjustments that only life in the Body can effect. The *ritual* of worship and consistent discipleship trains them in humility, joy, perseverance, diligence, responsibility, and gives them a "new song." It instills in them Godly habits. It *repatterns* them according to the ways of God. Through constant fellowship within the community of faith, the homeless have these new habits reinforced. Their expectations and desires are slowly brought into conformity with the expectations and desires of the righteous. They are *reformed*. And the "boundary of fear" restrains the homeless from old patterns of sloth and self-destruction. Through work requirements, moral expectations, and community obligations, all enforced by Church discipline (Matthew 18; 1 Corinthians 5), they are encouraged to grow in grace and maturity. They learn that their attitudes, actions, and inactions have very real consequences (Galatians 6:7). They who are "weary and heavy laden" are *liberated* from the slave market shackles of the world and are yoked with the "gentle" and "easy" discipline of Christ instead (Matthew 11:28-30). They are able to come Home.

Thus, only a *distinctly* ecclesiastical outreach to the homeless — one that emphasizes the Word revealed, the Word made manifest, and the Word incarnate — can genuinely and effectively rehabilitate the homeless. Only the Church can offer Refuge from the howling Wilderness.[6]

6. *Don't* violate your own rules. If you've established a Scriptural standard for your ministry, don't abandon that standard whenever you run into an exceptional case. We can be flexible

without contravening the Bible's gracious program for relief. If
you have established a rule that the homeless must attend morning and evening prayer and Lord's Day worship—as you should
have—stick to it. If you have established a rule that the homeless
in your shelter must eat in a common dining hall, be accountable for their daily schedule, and abide by a curfew—as you
should have—stick to it. We all learn best and grow most when
we know our boundaries, when discipline is expected, when accountability is enforced, and when rules are applied. "Sin is law-
lessness" (1 John 3:4). Anarchy and autonomy are no help to
anyone.[7]

7. *Do* take precautions. Never put individual families in
physical or legal jeopardy. Thoroughly interview and investigate
each person who comes to the Church for help. The Scriptural
prerequisites of submission and obedience will instantly eliminate the professional panhandlers. Even so, every precaution
must be taken to ensure the safety of the families and workers in
the homeless ministry. Document every applicant with appropriate forms, documents, and legal liability releases. We
must be as innocent as doves, but we should simultaneously be
as wise as serpents (Matthew 10:16).[8]

8. *Don't* ever give up. You will undoubtedly have bad experiences. You will face difficult situations and heart wrenching circumstances. But we have been called to walk by faith and not by
sight (2 Corinthians 5:7). We have been commissioned by God
Almighty for our task. So, *we must obey*. No matter what.[9]

UNDERSTANDING THE STORY OF THE GERASENE DEMONIAC

by James B. Jordan

The story of the Gerasene Demoniac is of great value in understanding the plight of the chronically homeless in the world today, and I count it a privilege to be asked by George Grant to prepare this Appendix on the subject.

The Story's Context

The Gerasene or Gadarene incident is the first of three events recounted in Mark 5, all having to do with the subject of the resurrection. In the second half of the chapter we have the two stories of the woman with an issue of blood and of Jairus's daughter. The two stories are sandwiched together (Mark 5:21-43). The woman had been "ceremonially unclean" and thus untouchable for twelve years, and the child was twelve years old when she died (vv. 25, 42.) Both are called "daughter" (vv. 34, 35).

It is obvious that Jesus resurrects (or resuscitates) the child. It is less obvious to us today that the healing of the woman is also a resurrection, because we are not familiar with the laws of Leviticus. According to Leviticus 15:19ff., a woman with an "issue of blood" was "unclean." To be "unclean" is to be symbolically dead, and to be "cleansed" is to be symbolically resurrected.

The basic law of cleansing (or resurrection) is found in Numbers 19. The death of the "red heifer" substituted for the unclean person, and the ashes of the heifer, sprinkled on the unclean person, granted symbolic resurrection. The main cause of uncleanness, given in Numbers 19, is *contact with death* (v. 11). The sprinkling unto resurrection is made on the third day, and again on the seventh (v. 12), pictures of the first resurrection (that of Jesus, on the third day) and of the second resurrection (at the end of history).

Where does all this come from? Genesis 3:17 says that the soil of the earth is cursed for man's sake. Thus, people in the Old Testament always wore shoes, to keep themselves away from the cursed ground. That is why the Bible calls attention to the washing of feet in the Old Testament and right up to the Last Supper. That is why men only went barefoot on "holy" ground (Exodus 3:5; Joshua 5:15). In the New Covenant, however, the death of Jesus Christ removes the curse from the ground.

Since the ground was cursed, to be *dirty* or *unclean* was to have the curse on you. You needed to wash it off, to be cleansed. Now, precisely what was this curse? The curse was nothing other than *death*. God had told Adam and Eve that they would die (spiritually) on the very day they sinned. In their death they would return to the cursed dust.

Now we have the picture. Dust = death. To be dirty or unclean was to have death on you. To be cleansed was to be granted symbolic resurrection.

All the various kinds of uncleanness in the Bible are pictures of death and the curse. These are given in Leviticus 11-15. We cannot survey all of these, but let us note the one passage that is relevant—Leviticus 15:19ff. This passage tells us that the "issue of blood" is not an unhealed cut or wound. Rather, the issue is from the woman's private parts, the place babies come from. The fountain of life has become a fountain of death (Leviticus 20:18), for life is in the blood (Leviticus 17:11), and the continual flow of blood is a continual loss of life.

When Jesus healed the woman with an issue of blood, then, He was granting her symbolic resurrection. He was showing Himself as the True Red Heifer, whose death would cleanse the world.

Now with this context in mind, we are in a better position to look at the details of the story of the Gerasene Demoniac. From there we will move to a discussion of its relevance as a model for psychological dysfunction.

The Gerasene Demoniac

And they came to the other side of the sea, into the country of the Gerasenes (Mark 5:1).

This is Gentile territory, separated and removed from the "cleaner," holier land of Israel.

And when He had come out of the boat, immediately a man from the tombs with an unclean spirit met Him (Mark 5:2).

Notice the association of death (tomb) with uncleanness. The demons are called unclean because they are associated with death and curse. Indeed, God cursed Satan and his followers to "crawl in the dust" and to "eat dust" (Genesis 3:14). This means that the whole demoniac environment is an environment of death and "uncleanness."

And he had his dwelling among the tombs; and no one was able to bind him any more, even with a chain; because he had often been bound with shackles and chains, and the chains had been torn apart by him, and the shackles broken in pieces, and no one was strong enough to subdue him (Mark 5:3-4).

The emphasis here is on the demonized strength of this man. We are immediately reminded of the fact that Satan is bound with a chain in Revelation 20:1-3, precisely so that he might deceive the Gentiles (cp. Gerasenes) no longer. Moreover, Jesus had just finished teaching the disciplines that "no one can enter the strong man's house (the Gentile world) and plunder his property unless he first binds the strong man" (Mark 3:27). Here in this incident will be proof that Jesus Christ will bind Satan, the strong man, and set the Gentiles free from the chains of sin.

And constantly night and day, among the tombs and in the mountains, he was crying out and gashing himself with stones (Mark 5:5).

Satan's purpose is to destroy humanity, because humanity is the very "image" of God, and Satan hates God. Thus, those who are demoniacally possessed are destructive of others and of themselves. Jesus Christ, speaking as Wisdom in Proverbs 8:36, says, "All those who hate Me love death" and so it is. The Gerasene seeks to deface and destroy the image of God in himself.

The expression "night and day" is strange to us, and calls us back to the creation's "evening and morning." So does the reference to the mountains, for Eden was on a mountain. (Remember, four rivers ran out of it, and rivers flow downhill. Throughout the Bible, God repeatedly meets with men on mountains.) Here we have a pitiful picture of fallen humanity. Instead of serving God evening and morning, we seek to destroy ourselves night and day. Instead of worshipping God on His holy mountain, we defile ourselves there. Instead of an environment of life, we turn the world into a tomb.

> And seeing Jesus from a distance, he ran up and bowed down before Him; and crying out with a loud voice, he said, "What do I have to do with You, Jesus, Son of the Most High God? I implore You by God, do not torment me!" For He had been saying to him, "Come out of the man, you unclean spirit" (Mark 5:6-8)!

By the grace of God this man is drawn to Truth incarnate. He addresses Jesus by a Gentile name, Son of God Most High, the name by which the Lord was known among the nations. He recognizes that Jesus is Lord and Judge of heaven and earth, confesses that he deserves "torment," but pleads for mercy. He knows that Jesus can deliver him, and he begs for deliverance.

> And He was asking him, "What is your name?" And he said to Him, "My name is Legion; for we are many." And he began to entreat Him earnestly not to send them out of the country (Mark 5:9-10).

This man had many demons in him. So disintegrated was his personality that his body had become the house of many fallen angels. They knew that Jesus has come to judge the world, and to remove Satan from the nations. They also knew, however, that the time of the binding of Satan is not yet, so they asked that they not be sent "out of the country." Only after Pentecost would the triumph of the Crucified be published among the nations, and Satan's kingdom progressively abolished.

> Now there was a big herd of swine feeding there on the mountain side. And they entreated Him, saying, "Send us into the swine so that we may enter them." And He gave permission. And coming out, the unclean spirits entered the swine; and the herd rushed down the steep bank into the sea, about two thousand of them; and they were drowning in the sea. And those who tended them ran away and reported it in the city and out in the country. And the people came to see what it was that had happened (Mark 5:11-14).

Pigs were unclean animals, associated with death (Leviticus 11). It was entirely proper for these Gentiles to have pigs and eat them; only the Jews were restricted to "clean" foods (Deuteronomy 14:21).

When the demons entered the pigs, they drove them to their deaths in the sea. The pigs, like the other unclean animals, symbolized the nations of the world (Leviticus 20:22-26; Acts 10, 11). These verses show that the demons will drive the nations to destruction, unless Jesus conquers them. Just as the Gerasene demoniac was driven to live in a state of virtual death, so the pigs are driven to literal death.

> And they came to Jesus and observed the man who had been demon-possessed sitting down, clothed and in his right mind, the very man who had had the "legion"; and they became frightened. And those who had seen it described to them how it had happened to the demon-possessed man, and all about the swine. And they began to entreat Him to depart from their region (Mark 5:15-17).

Just as God clothed Adam and Eve, so Jesus clothes this man. He is restored outwardly as well as inwardly.

The Gentiles, however, are not ready for the Gospel. They do not rejoice that Satan has been driven from them. Instead they ask Jesus to depart. Not until the Holy Spirit is outpoured will the Gentiles as a whole be ready to hear the Word of Truth.

And as He was getting into the boat, the man who had been demon-possessed was entreating Him that he might accompany Him. And He did not let Him, but He said to him, "Go home to your people and report to them what great things the Lord has done for you, and how He had mercy on you." And he went off and began to proclaim in Decapolis what great things Jesus had done for him; and everyone marvelled (Mark 5:18-20).

Understandably the former demoniac wanted to remain with Jesus. First, he saw that his neighbors were not receiving the truth. Second, as a psychic cripple, he moved toward what appeared to be the easiest route to take: hanging around Jesus and the Twelve.

Jesus knew, however, that the kind of ministry He was conducting was not for an undisciplined man. Jesus had called hardworking, disciplined fishermen and tradesmen to follow him, men who knew how to work and how to budget time, men who would be able to withstand the psychological hardships of an unstructured life. Such a life was not for this new convert, fresh out of a totally disordered existence. What he needed was a restoration to family life, to a steady job, to friends and society. It would take a while to build him up to the point where he might be able to engage in the kind of work Jesus was doing.

The Gerasene's Condition and Schizophrenia

God is Three and One. He is both three Individual Persons, and also a Society. Human nature, imaging God, is to experience both integrity at the individual person level, and also to experience social wholeness.

The Christian finds that as he draws closer to God, he experiences more of the fullness of what it means to be the very "image" of God. He grows in both respects. People who have a tendency to be "loners" begin to become more sociable. They begin to enjoy the society of other people more and more, as they draw closer to the Triune God. Similarly, people who have a tendency to "follow the crowd" begin to find more personal integrity. They know more and more who they are, and they can "stand alone" if need be, and resist the crowd.

God is the Source of all life. As Christians draw closer to God, their personal as well as their social lives are enhanced.

In sin, men reject God. As sinful men mature, they move farther and farther away from God. As this happens, they lose their contact with society, and they also experience a loss of personal psychological integrity. They become asocial and schizophrenic. (Some schizophrenic disorders are chemically or dietetically induced, of course. We are here discussing schizophrenia due to sin.)

Loss of personal psychological integrity opens up the human personality to demonic possession. The fellowship and indeed inhabitation that a man should have of the Three Persons of God is replaced with fellowship and inhabitation of demons.

We see this in the story of the Gerasene Demoniac. Society had tried to help him, even to restraining him with chains, but to no avail. He had progressed in sin to the point of demonic inhabitation. He rejected society, and his personality had disintegrated.

This is exactly the plight of many of the chronically homeless people who hound our streets. They want to live in an environment of death. They are totally out of touch with the real world. It is impossible to converse intelligibly with them, because their personal psyches are so disintegrated. And, though secular workers will be slow to recognize it, many are inhabited by demons who drive them further and further into death.

Only the Gospel can save them.

END NOTES

Introduction

1. *Newsweek*, December 16, 1985.
2. U.S. Bureau of the Census, *Statistical Abstract of the United States: 1977* (Washington: U.S. Government Printing Office, 1977), p. 440.
3. U.S. Bureau of the Census, *Current Housing Reports: Home Ownership Trends 1983*, series H-121, No. 1 (Washington: U.S. Government Printing Office, 1984).
4. Ibid.
5. Kim Hopper and Jill Hamberg, *The Making of America's Homeless: From Skid Row to New Poor 1945-1984* (New York: Community Service Society of New York, 1984), pp. 17-19.
6. James F. Rooney, "Societal Forces and the Unattached Male: An Historical Review," in Howard Bahr, ed., *Disaffiliated Man: Essays and Bibliography on Skid Row* (Toronto: University of Toronto Press, 1970), pp. 13-38.
7. Hopper and Hamberg, pp. 21-38.
8. Kim Hopper, Ellen Baxter, and Stuart Cox, *Not Making it Crazy* (New York: Community Service Society of New York, 1981).
9. Jeffrey D. Blum and Judith E. Smith, *Nothing Left to Lose: Studies of Street People* (Boston: Beacon Press, 1972).
10. Ibid.
11. Ellen Baxter and Kim Hopper, *Private Lives/Private Spaces* (New York: Community Service Society of New York, 1981).
12. Ivan Illich, *Gender* (New York: Pantheon Books, 1982).
13. *Newsweek*, January 6, 1986.
14. Randall Rothenberg, *The Neo-Liberals: Creating the New American Politics* (New York: Simon and Schuster, 1984).
15. Michael Harrington, *The New American Poverty* (New York: Holt, Rinehart, and Winston, 1984).
16. Arthur Simon, *Bread for the World* (New York: Paulist Press, 1985).
17. Anna Kondratas, "Myth, Reality, and the Homeless," *Insight Magazine*, April 14, 1986.
18. Charles Murray, *Losing Ground: American Social Policy 1950-1980* (New York: Basic Books, 1984).
19. George Gilder, *Wealth and Poverty* (New York: Basic Books, 1981).
20. Mario Cuomo, *Forest Hills Diary: The Crisis of Low-Income Housing* (New York: Vintage Books, 1983).

21. Subcommittee on Housing and Community Development of the Committee on Banking, Finance, and Urban Affairs, U.S. House of Representatives, *Homelessness in America* (Washington: U.S. Government Printing Office, 1984).

22. *The Los Angeles Times*, October 27, 1983.

23. *US Magazine*, May 19, 1986.

24. *People Magazine*, February 3, 1986.

25. The full appellation given to the designation is, "The International Year of Shelter for the Homeless" (IYSH), but the popular press and even a majority of the monographs written in support of the "Year" use the abbreviated name, so that form has been adopted here throughout. See HABITAT "Press Kit," United Nations Centre for Human Settlements, Nairobi, Kenya, 1985.

26. IYSH Project Guidelines, *UNCHS/HABITAT*, Nairobi, Kenya, 1985.

27. Technical Co-operation Monograph Series, *UNCHS/HABITAT*, Nairobi, Kenya, 1986.

28. Housing America: Freeing the Spirit of Enterprise, UN IYSH Program, U.S. Department of Housing and Urban Development Office of Public Affairs, 1985.

29. John E. Cox, "Objectives of the UN International Year of Shelter for the Homeless (IYSH) 1987," *Ekistics 307*, July/August 1984.

30. Ken Auletta, *The Underclass* (New York: Vintage Books, 1983).

31. Lawrence M. Mead, *Beyond Entitlement: The Social Obligations of Citizenship* (New York: The Free Press, 1986).

32. *Newsweek*, December 16, 1985.

33. *US Magazine*, May 19, 1986.

34. *USA Today*, March 13, 1986.

35. *The Houston Chronicle*, May 26, 1986.

36. *Periodical Guide 1985*, for *The New York Times*.

37. Ibid., for *The Los Angeles Times*.

38. Ibid., for *The Washington Post*.

39. *Newsweek*, June 2, 1986.

40. George Grant, *In the Shadow of Plenty* (Fort Worth, Texas: Dominion Press, 1986).

41. George Grant, *Bringing in the Sheaves* (Atlanta: American Vision Press, 1985).

42. See the discussion in chapters 12, 13, and 14.

43. Herbert Schlossberg, *Idols for Destruction* (Nashville: Thomas Nelson Publishers, 1983).

Chapter 1 — The Drawing of the Dark: A Personal Look

1. Hampton Faucher and David Peoples, *Bladerunner: The Complete Screenplay* (San Diego: Blue Dolphin Enterprises, 1982), p. 51.

2. Ibid., p. 93.

3. Ibid., p. 58.

Chapter 2 — Duende Dancehall: The Crisis

1. Ira Bolston, *Homelessness: The Encroaching Crisis* (New York: Liberty Banner Press, 1986), p. 27.
2. Ibid., p. 28.
3. Ibid., pp. 30-31.
4. Ibid., p. 67.
5. Dan Salerno, Kim Hopper, and Ellen Baxter, *Hardship in the Heartland: Homelessness in Eight U.S. Cities* (New York: Community Service Society of New York, 1984), p. 112.
6. Ibid., p. 157.
7. Woody Guthrie, "This Land" (New York, Ludlow Music, 1956).
8. Bolston, p. 97.
9. Bolston, p. 98.
10. "Homelessness in Chicago," fact sheet published by the Chicago Coalition for the Homeless, November, 1982.
11. *The Chicago Tribune*, December 17, 1981.
12. Ibid.
13. Salerno, Hopper, and Baxter, p. 5.
14. Internal Memo, New York State Office of Mental Health, October 12, 1979.
15. *The Haven Newsletter*, May, 1986.
16. Mary Ellen Hombs and Mitch Snyder, *Homelessness in America* (Washington: The Community for Creative Non-Violence, 1982), p. 90.
17. Ibid., p. 91.
18. Subcommittee on Housing and Community Development of the Committee on Banking, Finance, and Urban Affairs, U.S. House of Representatives, *Homelessness in America* (Washington: U.S. Government Printing Office, 1984).
19. *The Wall Street Journal*, November 12, 1982.
20. Ibid.
21. Merril Goozner, *Housing Cincinnati's Poor* (Cincinnati: Wilder Foundation, 1983), p. 15.
22. Bolston, p. 107.
23. Salerno, Hopper, and Baxter, p. 148.
24. Hombs and Snyder, p. 124.
25. Salerno, Hopper, and Baxter, p. 91.
26. *Gleanings Newsletter*, HELP Services, Spring, 1986.
27. *People Magazine*, February 3, 1986.
28. Bolston, p. 164.
29. Ibid., p. 173.
30. Hombs and Snyder, p. 75.
31. Bolston, p. 21.
32. *Newsweek*, January 2, 1984.
33. *The Wall Street Journal*, November 12, 1982.
34. Bolston, p. 210.
35. *The Wall Street Journal*, December 15, 1982.
36. Bolston, p. 211.
37. Ibid., p. 212.
38. Task force on Joblessness and Hunger, U.S. Conference of Mayors, *Status*

Report: Emergency Food, Shelter and Energy Programs in 20 Cities, January, 1984.

39. Bolston, p. 11.
40. *The Haven Newsletter*, May 1986.
41. *Newsweek*, December 16, 1985.
42. *Insight Magazine*, April 4, 1986.
43. Ibid.
44. Ellen Baxter and Kim Hopper, *Private Lives/Public Spaces* (New York Community Service Society of New York, 1981), p. 8.
45. *Insight Magazine*, April 4, 1986.
46. *People Magazine*, February 3, 1986.
47. *Newsweek*, December 16, 1985.
48. *HHS News*, November 25, 1983.
49. U.S. Department of Housing and Urban Development, *A Report to the Secretary on the Homeless and Emergency Shelters* (Washington: U.S. Government Printing Office), 1984.
50. Kim Hopper and Hill Hamberg, *The Making of America's Homeless: From Skid Row to New Poor* (New York: Community Service Society of New York, 1984), p. 74.
51. Bolston, p. 62.
52. Hopper and Hamberg, p. 74.
53. *Newsweek*, December 16, 1985.
54. Ibid.
55. Hopper and Baxter, p. 22.
56. George Nash, *The Habitats of Homeless Men in Manhattan* (New York: Columbia University Bureau of Applied Social Research, 1964).
57. Jacob A. Riis, *How the Other Half Lives* (New York: Hill and Wang, 1957), pp. 1-2.
58. Howard Bahr, *Skid Row: An Introduction to Disaffiliation* (New York: Oxford University Press, 1973).
59. *The Haven Newsletter*, May, 1986.
60. Ibid.
61. Ibid.
62. *Life Chronicles Newsletter*, June, 1983.
63. Ibid.
64. Hopper and Hamburg, p. 58.
65. Ibid.
66. Bolston, p. 32.
67. Ibid., p. 261.
68. George Grant, *Bringing in the Sheaves* (Atlanta: American Vision Press, 1985), p. 34.
69. *The Wall Street Journal*, November 12, 1982.
70. Bolston, p. 14.
71. *The New York Times*, June 3, 1983.
72. George Grant, *In the Shadow of Plenty* (Fort Worth, Texas: Dominion Press, 1986).
73. Ibid.
74. *Good Morning, America*, January 31, 1984.

Chapter 3 — Making Hay: The U.N. Resolution

1. National Campaign for the Homeless, *Homelessness in the European Community* (Dublin, Ireland: NCH, 1985).
2. *Insight Magazine*, February 3, 1986.
3. Anna Le Ru, *Comment Devient-on "Sans Abri" en France en 1985?* (Dublin: NCH, 1985).
4. *Insight Magazine*, February 3, 1986.
5. Heinrich Holtmannspotter, *Bundesarbeits-gemeinschaft für Nichtsessaftenhilfe* (Dublin: NCH, 1985).
6. Ulf Hamilton Clausen and Bjarne Lenau Henriksen, *Missionen Blandt Hjemlose* (Dublin: NCH, 1985).
7. Rolf Boiten, *The Homeless in the Netherlands* (Dublin: NCH, 1985).
8. Shelter, *The Homeless in Britain* (London: Shelter, 1985).
9. *The Wall Street Journal*, April 25, 1983.
10. Brandon Tartellson, *Homelessness in Europe* (London: Gullison Publishing Ltd., 1985), p. 83.
11. John E. Cox, "Objectives of the U.N. International Year of Shelter for the Homeless (IYSH) 1987," *Ekistics 307*, July/August, 1984.
12. Ibid.
13. Brandon Tartellson and Lizabelle Tartellson, *Global Homelessness to the Year 2000* (London: Gullison Publishing Ltd., 1979), p. 118.
14. Ibid., p. 121.
15. Cox, p. 1.
16. Ibid.
17. Ibid.
18. Tartellson and Tartellson, p. 122.
19. Ibid., p. 118.
20. Arcot Ramachandran, "International Year of Shelter for the Homeless" (Nairobi, Kenya: HABITAT, 1985), p. 1.
21. Cox, p. 1.
22. Ibid.
23. Ibid.
24. Ibid.
25. CAUSA, *Lecture Manual Draft Edition* (New York: CAUSA International, 1983), p. 16.
26. Ibid., p. 18.
27. Lon Tal Ui, *Fire All Consuming: The Agony of the Pol Pot Revolution* (Paris: Exile Press, 1982), p. 74.
28. Ibid., p. 77.
29. Marekev Solzev, *Flee!* (New York: The Voice of Dissidents, 1969), p. 6.
30. Sven Rydenfelt, *A Pattern for Failure: Socialist Economics in Crisis* (New York: Harcourt Brace Jovanovich, 1983), p. 132.
31. *Insight Magazine*, May 5, 1986.
32. Sabutu Mariam, *The Eritrean Relief Association* (Djibouti: ERA, 1984), p. 6.
33. Ibid., p. 17.
34. Ibid., p. 19.
35. *Inside the U.N.*, April, 1985.
36. Cox, p. 2.
37. *Inside the U.N.*, May, 1985.

38. *The Wall Street Journal*, January 8, 1986.
39. Ibid.
40. Ibid.
41. Ibid.
42. *Inside the U.N.*, April, 1985.
43. *HABITAT News*, December, 1985.
44. *Inside the U.N.*, February, 1986.
45. *HABITAT News*, December, 1985.
46. Ibid.
47. *Inside the U.N.*, February, 1986.
48. Cox, p. 2.
49. Rydenfelt, pp. 104-109.
50. Ibid.
51. Tartellson and Tartellson, p. 187.
52. *Bulletin of the International Year of Shelter for the Homeless*, December, 1985.
53. Ibid.
54. *Inside the U.N.*, December, 1985.
55. *American Opinion*, April, 1985.
56. Ibid.
57. Tartellson and Tartellson, p. 203.
58. *HABITAT News*, December, 1985.
59. Tartellson and Tartellson, p. 206.
60. Ibid., p. 205.
61. *Inside the U.N.*, December, 1985.
62. European Economic Community Seminar Report on Poverty and Homelessness, Cork, Ireland, January, 1986, p. 5.
63. Ibid.
64. Ibid.
65. Ibid. p. 6.
66. G. Edward Griffin, *The United Nations: The Fearful Master* (Boston: Western Islands, 1964).
67. Ibid.
68. A. Ralph Epperson, *The Unseen Hand* (Tuscon, Arizona: Publius Press, 1985).
69. *Inside the U.N.*, July, 1982.
70. *Inside the U.N.*, September, 1984.
71. *Inside the U.N.*, May, 1983.
72. *Inside the U.N.*, January, 1985.
73. Epperson, pp. 367-371.
74. Paul Johnson, *Modern Times* (New York: Harper and Row, 1983), p. 689.
75. William M. Bowen, Jr., *Globalism, America's Demise* (Shreveport, Louisiana: Huntington House, Inc., 1984).
76. Ibid.
77. Dan Smoot, *The Invisible Government* (Littleton, Colorado: The Independent American, 1962).
78. Mel Hunter, "Freedom Report," *Inside the U.N.*, special issue, December, 1985.)
79. Johnson, p. 689.
80. Rousas J. Rushdoony, *The Nature of The American System* (Fairfax, Virginia: Thoburn Press, 1978), p. 116.

81. Ibid.
82. Ibid., p. 114.
83. Rousas J. Rushdoony, *Politics of Guilt and Pity*, (Fairfax, Virginia: Thoburn Press, 1978), p. 187.
84. Herbert Schlossberg, *Idols for Destruction* (Nashville: Thomas Nelson Publishers, 1983), p. 55.
85. *Inside the U.N.*, July, 1984.
86. Ibid.
87. Johnson, p. 691.
88. Ibid.
89. *Inside the U.N.*, August, 1979.
90. *Inside the U.N.*, March, 1984.
91. Ibid.
92. Ibid.

Chapter 4 — Still Crazy After All These Years: Mental Illness

1. Alfred Noyes, "The Highwayman," from *Collected Poems, vol. 1* (New York, Frederick A. Stokes Company, 1913).
2. Ibid.
3. Ibid.
4. Ibid.
5. Ibid.
6. Alfred Tenneyson, "The Charge of the Light Brigade," from *The Complete Works* (New York: Richard Worthington, 1913).
7. Kim Hopper, Ellen Baxter, and Stuart Cox, *Not Making It Crazy* (New York: Community Service Society of New York, 1981), p. 6.
8. G. Morse, "Conceptual Paper to Develop a Comprehensive System of Care for Chronically Mentally Disturbed Homeless Persons in St. Louis" (St. Louis: Community Support Program, 1982).
9. Covenant House, "San Francisco Support Services: A Comprehensive Aproach to Services for the Chronically Mentally Ill" (San Francisco: Support Services Association, 1982).
10. A. Arce et al., "A Psychiatric Profile of Street People Admitted to an Emergency Shelter," *Hospital and Community Psychiatry* 34:9 (September, 1983).
11. Chicago Task Force on the Homeless Report, *Homelessness in Chicago* (Chicago: Task Force on Emergency Shelter, 1983).
12. E. Bassik et al., "Back to Bedlam: Are Shelters Becoming Alternative Institutions?," *American Journal of Psychiatry*, (1984).
13. A. Presley, "Health Problems of Homeless People in the Denver Metro Area," paper presented at the American Public Health Association Meeting, Dallas, Texas, November 15, 1983.
14. J. Leach and J. Wing, *Helping Deinstitute Men* (New York: Ravistock, 1980).
15. S. J. Freeman et al. "Psychiatric Disorder in Skid-Row Mission Population," *Comprehensive Psychiatry* 20 (1979):454-462.
16. *Newsweek*, January 6, 1986.
17. *Insight Magazine*, April 14, 1986.

18. Hopper, Baxter, and Cox, p. 2.
19. *The Haven Newsletter,* May, 1986.
20. Ibid.
21. Rudyard Kipling, "The Ballad of East and West," from *Collected Works* (London: Allen, Sons Ltd., 1936).
22. Alfred Tennyson, "Crossing the Bar."
23. Mary Ellen Hombs and Mitch Snyder, *Homelessness in America* (Washington: Community for Creative Non-Violence, 1982), p. 44.
24. Kim Hopper and Hill Hamberg, *The Making of America's Homeless: From Skid Row to New Poor* (New York: Community Service Society of New York, 1984), p. 36.
25. Delvin Hartford, *The Plan for Deinstitutionalization* (New York: Talisman, 1961), p. 42.
26. U.S. Bureau of the Census, *Statistical Abstract of the United States* (Washington: U.S. Government Printing Office, 1984), p. 120.
27. *The Haven Newsletter,* May, 1986.
28. Ralph Altonrahd, *The Chronic Mental Patient in America* (Los Angeles: Bostwick Book House, 1984), p. 37.
29. Ibid., p. 42.
30. Ibid., p. 43.
31. *Newsweek,* January 6, 1986.
32. Ibid.
33. Ibid.
34. William Kirk Kilpatrick, *Psychological Seduction: The Failure of Modern Psychology* (Nashville: Thomas Nelson, 1983), pp. 30-31.
35. Ibid., p. 29.
36. Altonrahd, p. 62.
37. Ibid.
38. Ibid.
39. Ibid.
40. Ibid.
41. L. E. Garoni and J. E. Hayes, *Drugs and Nursing Implications* (New York: Appleton Century Crofts, 1971), p. 70.
42. Barbara B. Huff, ed., *Physicians' Desk Reference, 30th ed.* (Oradell, New Jersey: Medical Economics Company, 1976).
43. *Inside the U.N.,* December, 1986.
44. Ibid.
45. Ibid.
46. National Campaign for the Homeless, *Homelessness in the European Community* (Dublin: NCH, 1986), p. 6.
47. Ibid., p. 18.
48. W. B. Yarter, *Psychotherapeutic Treatment: A Study in Comparative Methodology* (Los Angeles: The Lafler Institute for Psychopharmacology, 1979), p. 12.
49. Ibid., p. 14.
50. Ibid., p. 15.
51. Ibid., p. 22.
52. Franklin E. Payne, Jr., *Biblical Medical Ethics: The Christian and the Practice of Medicine* (Milford, Michigan: Mott Media, 1985), p. 128.
53. Ibid.
54. Karl de Schweintz, *England's Road to Social Security* (Philadelphia: University of Pennsylvania Press, 1943), p. 18.

55. Llewen O'Casic, *Monastic Life* (London: Tallaec Row Publishers and Binders, 1951), p. 126.
56. Ibid., p. 129.
57. Ibid., p. 130.

Chapter 5 — You've Come a Long Way, Baby: Feminism

1. Sylvia Ann Hewlett, *A Lesser Life: The Myth of Women's Liberation in America* (New York: William Morrow and Company, 1986), p. 12.
2. See the endnotes in Hewlett's book.
3. See the endnotes in Weitzman's book below.
4. re: Lenore J. Weitzman, *The Divorce Revolution: The Unexpected Social and Economic Consequences for Women and Children in America* (New York: The Free Press, 1985). As well as, Mary Pride, *The Way Home: Beyond Feminism, Back to Reality* (Westchester, Illinois: Crossway Books, 1985).
5. Children's Defense Budget (Washington: Children's Defense Fund, 1985), p. 40.
6. Ibid.
7. Julia Wittleson, *The Feminization of Poverty* (Boston: Holy Cross Press, 1983), p. 19.
8. Ken Auletta, *The Underclass* (New York: Vintage Books, 1983), p. 68.
9. Ibid., pp. 68-69.
10. Kim Hopper and Jill Hamberg, *The Making of America's Homeless: From Skid Row to the New Poor* (New York: Community Service Society of New York, 1984), p. 24.
11. Auletta, p. 69.
12. Wittleson, p. 183.
13. Ellen Baxter and Kim Hopper, *Private Lives/Public Spaces: Homeless Adults on the Streets of New York City* (New York: Community Society of New York, 1981), p. 9.
14. *The New American*, January 20, 1986.
15. J. C. Wilke, *Abortion: Questions and Answers* (Cincinnati: Hayes Publishing Company, 1985), p. 90.
16. Ibid., pp. 90-91.
17. Ibid., p. 91.
18. Ibid.
19. D. Trichopoulos et al., "Induced Abortion and Secondary Infertility," *British Journal OB/GYN* 83 (August, 1976): 645-650.
20. Wilke, p. 92.
21. Ibid., p. 93.
22. W. Cates et al., *American Journal OB/GYN* 132:169.
23. L. Duenhoelter and B. Grant, "Complications Following Prostaglandin F-2A Induced Midtrimester Abortion," *American Journal OB/GYN* 46:247-250.
24. Wilke, pp. 103-104.
25. George Grant, "Saying Yes, Saying No" (Humble, Texas: The Christian Worldview, 1985).
26. Wittleson, p. 81.

27. Hardin Caplin, "Equality," *Journal of Business Policy Review,* 46:6, p. 77.
28. Richard Levine, "The Double Edged Sword," *Journal of Business Policy Review* 42:7, p. 41.
29. Hewlett, p. 71.
30. Ibid., p. 72.
31. Ibid., p. 71.
32. Ibid., p. 72.
33. Wittleson, p. 14.
34. Caplin, p. 76.
35. Hewlett, p. 71.
36. Ibid.
37. Thomas Sowell, *Civil Rights: Rhetoric or Reality?* (New York: William Morrow and Company, 1984), p. 100.
38. Hewlett, p. 71.
39. Ibid.
40. Peyton Moore, *Tales from the Front* (New York: L. L. Johnson and Sons, 1902), p. 215.
41. Auletta, p. 68.
42. Ibid.
43. Ibid.
44. Wittleson, p. 4.
45. *The American Spectator*, July, 1984.
46. Auletta, p. 69.
47. Ibid.
48. Ibid.
49. Weitzman, p. x.
50. Ibid., p. xii.
51. Ibid., p. xiv.
52. Hewlett, p. 51.
53. Weitzman, p. xvii.
54. Ibid.
55. Pride, p. 3.
56. *NGO: News on Human Settlements,* No. 3, 1985.
57. *Inside the U.N.*, December, 1985.
58. *Inside the U.N.*, January, 1986.
59. Ibid.
60. Ibid.
61. Ibid.
62. Ibid.
63. Note especially Mary Pride's *The Way Home*.
64. Hewlett, p. 32.
65. Ibid., p. 33.
66. Ibid.
67. Pride, back cover blurb.
68. See Ray Sutton's *Who Owns the Family?* (Fort Worth, Texas: Dominion Press, 1986).
69. Genesis 38:6-30.
70. Exodus 22:22.
71. Leviticus 22:13.
72. Numbers 30:9.

73. Deuteronomy 10:18, 14:29, 16:11-14, 24:19-21, 26:12-13.
74. Ruth 2:1-4:2.
75. 1 Samuel 27:3.
76. 2 Samuel 14:5.
77. 1 Kings 17:20.
78. Job 31:16.
79. Psalm 146:9.
80. Proverbs 15:25.
81. Isaiah 47:8.
82. Jeremiah 22:3.
83. Ezekiel 22:7, 44:22.
84. Zechariah 7:10.
85. Malachi 3:5.
86. Matthew 23:14.
87. Mark 12:42.
88. Luke 4:26, 7:12, 18:3.
89. Acts 6:1, 9:41.
90. 1 Timothy 5:9.
91. James 1:27.
92. Barbara Tuchman, *A Distant Mirror: The Calamitous 14th Century* (New York: Alfred A. Knopf, 1978).
93. Philip Ziegler, *The Black Death* (New York: John Day, 1969).
94. Karl de Schweinitz, *England's Road to Social Security* (Philadelphia: University of Pennsylvania Press, 1943), p. 15.
95. Wittleson, p. 17.
96. Antonia Fraser, *The Weaker Vessel* (New York: Alfred A. Knopf, 1984).
97. Morena Matthews, "Holy War: The Battle for Mercy to the Weaker Vessel," *Dulous* 14:2, pp. 16-19.
98. Ibid.
99. Ibid.
100. Pride, pp. 3-6.
101. Ibid., pp. 6-13. This is not to say of course that there is *no* remnant, but only that the Church has failed, as Mary Pride has so clearly asserted, to propose a "self-consistent" and dynamic "plan" for women; Pride, p. xii.

Chapter 6 — Time in a Bottle: Alcoholism

1. Jacob Riis, *How the Other Half Lives* (New York: Hill and Wang, 1957), pp. 158-159.
2. William J. L. Kevin, *Alcoholism and Skid Row* (Houston: Academie Lake Publishing, 1982), p. 43.
3. Ibid., p. 44.
4. Ibid.
5. Ibid.
6. Art Saleoid-Loal, "Alcohol Abuse and Homelessness," *Issues in Social Policy* 2:3 (Fall, 1981), p. 12.
7. Ibid., p. 13.
8. Valerie Thompson, "Family Life and the Escusive Syndrome," *Issues in Social Policy* 2:3 (Fall, 1981), p. 7.

9. *The Haven Newsletter,* April, 1986.
10. Ibid.
11. Mary Ellen Hombs and Mitch Snyder, *Homelessness in America* (Washington: Community for Creative Non-Violence, 1982), p. 133.
12. Ibid.
13. Ibid.
14. *The Report of the Coalition Network,* Homeless Coalition of America, 1984.
15. *The Haven Newsletter,* April, 1986.
16. Ibid.
17. Louis Jolyon West, "Alcoholism and Related Problems," in *Alcoholism and Related Problems: Issues for the American Public* (Englewood Cliffs, New Jersey: Prentice-Hall, 1984), p. 9.
18. Ibid., p. 10.
19. Ibid.
20. Ibid.
21. Ibid.
22. Stewart G. Wolf, "Alcohol and Health: The Wages of Excessive Drinking," in *Alcoholism and Related Problems*, p. 33.
23. West, p. 11.
24. Ibid.
25. Wolf, p. 32.
26. Ibid.
27. Kevin, p. 81.
28. Wolf, p. 31.
29. Ibid., p. 33.
30. West, p. 11.
31. Ibid.
32. Ibid., pp. 11-12.
33. George Gilder, *Wealth and Poverty* (New York: Basic Books, 1981), p. 68.
34. J. C. Ryle, *Christian Leaders of the 18th Century* (Edinburgh: Banner of Truth Trust, 1978), pp. 18-19.
35. Thomas O'Calthairn, *Revival in Their Midst* (London: The Gospeler Fund, 1957), p. 18.
36. Ibid., pp. 19-20.
37. Ibid., p. 22.

Chapter 7 — The Broken Citadel: Housing Regulation

1. Kim Hopper and Jill Hamberg, *The Making of America's Homeless: From Skid Row to New Poor* (New York: Community Service Society of New York, 1984), p. 31.
2. Ibid.
3. Cushing Dolbeare, "The Low Income Housing Crisis," in Chester Hartman, ed., *America's Housing Crisis: What is to be Done?* (Boston: Routledge and Kegan, 1983).
4. Ibid.
5. *Insight Magazine,* March 31, 1986.
6. Ibid.

7. Michael Stegman, "The Model: Rent Control in New York City" in Paul L. Niebanck, ed., *The Rent Control Debate* (Chapel Hill, North Carolina: University of North Carolina Press, 1985), p. 30.
8. Frank F. Kristof, "The Effects of Rent Control and Rent Stabilization for New York City," in Walter Block and Edgar Olsen, eds., *Rent Control Myths and Realities* (Vancouver: The Fraser Institute, 1981), p. 128.
9. Stegman, pp. 54-55.
10. Hopper and Hamberg, p. 32.
11. *Insight Magazine*, March 31, 1986.
12. Farber Lane, *Rent Controls and Construction Industry Reaction* (New York: Lane Textbooks, 1982), p. 61.
13. *Insight Magazine*, March 31, 1986.
14. Lane, p. 42.
15. Stegman, p. 30.
16. *Insight Magazine*, March 31, 1986.
17. Ibid.
18. Ibid.
19. *The Houston Chronicle*, May 30, 1986.
20. *Insight Magazine*, March 31, 1986.
21. Ibid.
22. Ibid.
23. Lane, p. 4.
24. *Insight Magazine*, March 31, 1986.
25. Hopper and Hamberg, p. 34.
26. Ibid.
27. F. E. Werner and D. B. Bryson, "Guide to the Preservation and Maintenance of Single Room Occupancy (SRO) Housing," *Clearing House Review*, April and May issues (serialized), 1982.
28. Hopper and Hamberg, pp. 32-33.
29. *Insight Magazine*, March 31, 1986.
30. *Inside the U.N.*, December, 1985.
31. Ibid.
32. Reuben Martinez, "Appendix on Statism" in Faber Lane, *Rent Controls and Construction Industry Reaction* (New York: Lane Textbooks, 1982), p. 186.
33. Gary North, *The Sinai Strategy: Economics and the Ten Commandments* (Tyler, Texas: The Institute for Christian Economics, 1986), pp. 139-140.
34. Ibid., p. 141.
35. Ibid.
36. Igor Shafarevich, *The Socialist Phenomenon* (New York: Harper and Row Publishers, 1980).
37. Sven Rydenfelt, *A Pattern for Failure: Socialist Economics in Crisis* (New York: Harcourt Brace Jovanovich, 1983).
38. Miron Dolot, *Execution By Hunger: The Hidden Holocaust* (New York: W. W. Norton and Company, 1985).
39. 16th Century England did *not* have a *fully* operative "free enterprise system." It was the era of merchantilism and high tariffs. But compared to today's brand of socialism and regulation, it was certainly as close to "free enterprise" as we presently have it.
40. Sidney Lens, *Poverty Yesterday and Today* (New York: Thomas Y. Crowell Company, 1973), p. 1.

41. Ibid.
42. Ibid., p. 2
43. Lucy Komisar, *Down and Out: A History of Social Welfare* (New York: Franklin Watts, 1973), p. 3.
44. Lens, p. 3.
45. Latimer Allwin-Jones, *The Industrial Revolution* (London: Crier Press, 1961), p. 129.
46. Ibid.
47. Ibid.
48. William Widowford, *The Keepers of the Poor* (New York: Carouthers Bindery, 1922), p. 86.
49. Karl de Schweinitz, *England's Road to Social Security* (Philadelphia: University of Pennsylvania Press, 1943).
50. See Jacob Riis, *How the Other Half Lives* (New York: Hill and Wang, 1957); and Alfred T. White, *Improved Dwellings for the Laboring Classes* (New York: Daybreak Books and Reprints, 1961).

Chapter 8 — Epitaph in Rust: Unemployment

1. Johnson Oatman and Edwin O. Excell, "Count Your Blessings," 1919.
2. Ibid.
3. Ibid.
4. Ibid.
5. Ibid.
6. *The New York Times*, November 28, 1979.
7. Harvey Olander, *The Rust Belt* (Cleveland: Treaty Township Press, 1985), p. 61.
8. Ibid., p. 62.
9. Ibid., p. 65.
10. Ibid.
11. Randy Barber and Jeremy Rifkin, *The North Will Rise Again: Pensions, Politics, and Power in the 1980s* (Boston: Beacon Press, 1978), p. 59.
12. John Naisbitt, *Megatrends* (New York: Warner Books, 1982).
13. Barry Bluestone and Bennett Harrison, *The Deindustrialization of America* (New York: Basic Books, 1982).
14. Barber and Rifkin, pp. 59-77.
15. Bluestone and Harrison, p. 4.
16. Ibid.
17. Ibid.
18. Ibid.
19. Ibid.
20. George Grant, *Bringing in the Sheaves* (Atlanta: American Vision Press, 1985), pp. 168-171.
21. Tom Peters and Nancy Austin, *A Passion for Excellence: The Leadership Difference* (New York: Random House, 1985); and John Naisbitt and Patricia Aburdene, *Reinventing the Corporation* (New York: Warner Books, 1985).
22. Lola Peterson, *Resistance to Change: Business, Family, and Faith* (Los Angeles: Peterson Publications, 1981).

23. Grant, p. 169.
24. Ibid.
25. Ibid., p. 170.
26. George Grant, *In the Shadow of Plenty* (Fort Worth, Texas: Dominion Press, 1986).
27. Peterson, pp. 43-56.
28. Ibid.
29. Bluestone and Harrison, p. 5.
30. Otto J. Scott, "The Lesson of OPEC," *Journal of Christian Reconstruction* 10:2 (1984).
31. Gary North, *Government by Emergency* (Fort Worth, Texas: American Bureau of Economic Research, 1983).
32. Peterson, p. 92.
33. Bluestone and Harrison, p. 9.
34. *Newsweek*, December 27, 1982.
35. Bluestone and Harrison, p. 9.
36. John Naisbitt, *The Year Ahead* (Washington: Amacom, 1984).
37. Ibid.
38. Olander, p. 82.
39. *The New York Times*, April 21, 1983.
40. Kim Hopper and Jill Hamberg, *The Making of America's Homeless: From Skid Row to New Poor* (New York: Community Service Society of New York, 1984), p. 53.
41. Henry Schechter, "Closing the Gap Between Need and Provision," *Society*, March/April 1984.
42. Hopper and Hamberg, p. 59.
43. *The New York Times*, April 21, 1983.
44. *The Wall Street Journal*, November 12, 1982.
45. *People Magazine*, February 3, 1986.
46. *The New York Times*, December 11, 1983.
47. *Rolling Stone*, May, 1986.
48. *Newsweek*, January 2, 1984.
49. *The Humble Echo*, November 24, 1982.
50. *The Christian Herald*, July/August, 1986.
51. *HABITAT News*, December, 1985.
52. *Fortune Magazine*, December 17, 1979.
53. Ibid.
54. Ibid.
55. Ibid.
56. *The New York Times*, November 28, 1979.
57. Olander, p. 114.
58. Ibid.
59. Ibid.
60. Henry Hazlitt, *The Conquest of Poverty* (New Rochelle, New York: Arlington House, 1973).
61. David Chilton, *Productive Christians in an Age of Guilt Manipulators*, 3rd ed. (Tyler, Texas: Institute for Christian Economics, 1981, 1985).
62. James B. Jordan, *Judges: God's War Against Humanism* (Tyler, Texas: Geneva Ministries, 1985).
63. Gary North, *Dominion Covenant: Genesis* (Tyler, Texas, Institute for Christian Economics, 1982).

64. George Gilder, *The Spirit of Enterprise* (New York: Simon and Schuster, 1984).
65. *Inside the U.N.*, January, 1986.
66. Ibid.
67. Ibid.
68. *Inside the U.N.*, November, 1985.
69. Ibid.
70. Ibid.
71. *Inside the U.N.*, January, 1986.
72. *HABITAT News*, December, 1985.
73. Ibid.
74. *Inside the U.N.*, November, 1985.
75. Ibid.
76. There is much more to the Biblical solution to the problem of unemployment than just gleaning. For instance, see chapter 4 in my book, *Bringing in the Sheaves: Transforming Poverty into Productivity* (Atlanta: American Vision Press, 1985), where I outline the doctrines of the alms tithe, private giving, and the charitable, interest free loan. Also, see James B. Jordan's provocative discussion of indenturation in chapter 5 of his brilliant book, *The Law of the Covenant: An Exposition of Exodus 21-23* (Tyler, Texas: Institute for Christian Economics, 1984).
77. As Christians, we must beware of humanism's rhetoric. It always runs opposite of the truth (Jeremiah 9:17; Proverbs 14:12). Thus, while both liberal and conservative humanists *claim* to be progressives, *only* Bible-believing, Bible-adhering Christians *can* be.
78. David Chilton, *Paradise Restored: A Biblical Theology of Dominion* (Tyler, Texas: Reconstruction Press, 1985).
79. Jeremy Rifkin, *Entropy: A New Worldview* (New York: The Viking Press, 1980).
80. See Chilton, *Paradise Restored*; and David Chilton, *The Days of Vengeance: An Exposition of the Book of Revelation* (Fort Worth, Texas: Dominion Press, 1986).
81. The humanist has no sense of the Fall, hence the Rousseauian naiveté about the Edenic condition of primitive fallen man.
82. Jeremy Rifkin, *Algeny* (New York: The Viking Press, 1983).

Chapter 9 — The Skies Discrowned: The Farm Crisis

1. *American Demographics*, May, 1986.
2. Ibid.
3. Ibid.
4. Herton Ford, *Belly Up in the Midwest* (Lincoln, Nebraska: American Farm Bureau Press, 1983), p. 14.
5. *Insight Magazine*, April 28, 2986.
6. *The New York Times*, January 16, 1983.
7. *The Houston Chronicle*, May 18, 1986.
8. *The New American*, May 5, 1986.
9. Ford, p. 17.
10. Ibid., p. 18.

11. *The Houston Chronicle*, April 4, 1986.
12. J. Tevere MacFadyen, *Gaining Ground: The Renewal of America's Small Farms* (New York: Ballantine Books, 1984), p. 26.
13. Ibid.
14. Ford, p. 18.
15. Ibid., p. 26.
16. Ibid., p. 42.
17. Ibid., p. 67.
18. Ibid., p. 83.
19. Ibid., p. 91.
20. Ibid., p. 106.
21. Bill Price, "America's Farm Crisis," *An American Farm Bureau White Paper, No. 3*, Lincoln, Nebraska, 1985.
22. *American Opinion*, May, 1985.
23. *The New American*, May 3, 1986.
24. Ibid.
25. Ibid.
26. Ibid.
27. Ibid.
28. MacFadyen, p. 26.
29. *The Houston Chronicle*, May 18, 1986.
30. *The New American*, May 5, 1986.
31. Ibid.
32. *American Opinion*, April, 1985.
33. Carlton Forbes, *Forgiving Souls: Paying the Way for Our Own Enemies* (Salt Lake City: Freedom Reigns Books, 1985).
34. Bumper sticker seen in Missouri.
35. *The Houston Chronicle*, May 18, 1986.
36. *The New American*, May 5, 1986.
37. Forbes, p. 41.
38. *The New American*, May 5, 1986.
39. Ibid.
40. Forbes, pp. 2-21.
41. Ibid., p. 16.
42. Ibid., p. 17.
43. William E. Simon, *A Time for Truth* (New York: Berkley Books, 1979), pp. 83-84.
44. Forbes, p. 87.
45. Ibid.
46. *The New American*, May 5, 1986.
47. Ibid.
48. *The Houston Chronicle*, May 18, 1986.
49. *Inside the U.N.*, October, 1985.
50. Ibid.
51. Ibid.
52. Ibid.
53. Ibid.
54. Arthur Cundall, "Baal," in Merrill C. Tenney, ed., *Zondervan Pictoral Bible Encyclopaedia* (Grand Rapids: Zondervan Publishing, 1975); and see the discussion of Baalism in James B. Jordan, *Judges: God's War Against*

Humanism (Tyler, TX: Geneva Ministries, 1985), pp. 34-38. Jordan's book is a sustained demonstration that ancient Baalism and modern secular humanism are identical at root.

55. John Whitehead, *The End of Man* (Westchester, Illinois: Crossway Books, 1986), pp. 37-38.

Chapter 10—Leave By the Dogtown Gate: Transiency

1. John Steinbeck, *The Grapes of Wrath* (New York: The Viking Press, 1939).
2. Alton Ford, *Transiency* (Santa Cruz: Del Radino Press, 1982), p. 7.
3. Tristran Holbeare, *Time Bomb: The Decline of American Industry* (New York: Singletary Publications, 1984), p. 202.
4. Ibid.
5. Barry Bluestone and Bennett Harrison, *The Deindustrialization of America* (New York: Basic Books, 1982).
6. *The Houston Post*, November 21, 1982.
7. Holbeare, p. 202.
8. Ibid.
9. Bluestone and Harrison, p. 99.
10. Ibid.
11. Ibid.
12. Holbeare, p. 202.
13. George Grant, "Boomtown to Bust-town" (Humble, Texas: The Christian Worldview, 1984).
14. Ibid.
15. Ibid.
16. Ibid.
17. Ibid.
18. Ford, p. 4.
19. Bluestone and Harrison, p. 100.
20. Ibid.
21. Emma Lazrus, "The Great Colossus," inscription on the Statue of Liberty.
22. Bluestone and Harrison, p. 100.
23. For a recent example, see Richard D. Lamm and Gary Imhoff, *The Immigration Time Bomb* (New York: Truman Talley Books, 1985).
24. Karl de Schweinitz, *England's Road to Social Security* (Philadelphia: University of Pennsylvania Press, 1943), p. 39.
25. Adam Smith, *An Inquiry into the Nature and Causes of the Wealth of Nations* (London: Penguin Books, 1962) I:170-171.
26. S. Humphreys Gurteen, *A Handbook of Charity Organizations* (Buffalo, New York: Charity Organization Society, 1882), p. xxi.
27. Ibid., p. xxii.
28. Ibid., p. xxiv.
29. *Inside the U.N.*, December, 1985.
30. *HABITAT News*, December, 1985.
31. See chapter 7.
32. See chapter 8.
33. See chapter 9.
34. Ford, p. 17.

35. *Inside the U.N.*, December, 1985.
36. *Inside the U.N.*, December, 1983.
37. Paul K. Conkin, *The New Deal* (Arlington Heights, Illinois: AHM Publishing Corporation, 1967), p. 57.
38. Ibid., p. 58.
39. Juan Luis Villiers, *The Influence of Fascism* (New York: Herald Booklist, 1941), p. 62.
40. Conkin, p. 58.
41. Gary North, *Moses and Pharaoh: Dominion Religion Versus Power Religion* (Tyler, Texas: Institute for Christian Economics, 1985), p. ix.
42. Gary North, *The Dominion Covenant: Genesis* (Tyler, Texas: Institute for Christian Economics, 1982), pp. 245-321.
43. Ibid., pp. 278-279.
44. North, *Moses and Pharaoh*, pp. 1-5.

Chapter 11 — Mama Don't Take My Kodachrome Away: The Media

1. Edward Jay Epstein, *Between Fact and Fiction: The Problem of Journalism* (New York: Vintage Books, 1975), p. 3.
2. Ibid., p. 4.
3. Ibid.
4. Ibid.
5. Ibid.
6. Francis A. Schaeffer, *How Should We Then Live?* (Westchester, Illinois: Crossway Books, 1975), pp. 242-243.
7. Ibid., p. 240.
8. Tom Goldstein, *The News AT ANY COST: How Journalists Compromise Their Ethics to Shape the News* (New York: Touchstone Books, 1985).
9. George Getschow, "Homeless Northerners Unable to Find Work Crowd Sunbelt Cities," *The Wall Street Journal*, November 12, 1982.
10. George Getschow, "Houston's Tent City Gets Into a Big Flap Over Publicity Blitz," *The Wall Street Journal*, January 14, 1983.
11. Ibid.
12. Ibid., and *The Houston Chronicle*, December 4, 1982.
13. Ibid., and *The Houston Chronicle*, December 6, 1982.
14. Ibid.
15. Ibid.
16. Ibid.
17. *Newsweek* has led the way with more than double the coverage of the other major media outlets.
18. UN-IYSH Press Kit, 1985.
19. *Inside the U.N.*, December, 1985.
20. Ibid.
21. Ibid.
22. See Gary North, *Conspiracy: A Biblical View* (Fort Worth, Texas: Dominion Press, 1986).

Chapter 12 — The Golden Ship: The Secular Shift

1. *Insight Magazine*, June 9, 1986.
2. Census Bureau estimate; accurate figures were not kept until 1961.
3. *Seeds: Christians Concerned About Hunger*, December, 1985.
4. Ibid.
5. Ibid.
6. Ibid.
7. *Insight Magazine*, June 9, 1986.
8. Ibid.
9. Fritz Lieberman, *Cutting the Fat: Why Congress Won't Listen to the Grace Commission Report*; (New York: The Liberty Trust, 1985), p. 24.
10. Ibid.
11. Ibid.
12. Ibid.
13. Charles Murray, *Losing Ground: American Social Policy 1950-1980* (New York: Basic Books, 1984), p. 14.
14. Lieberman, p. 24.
15. George Grant, *Bringing in the Sheaves* (Atlanta: American Vision Press, 1985), pp. 38-52.
16. Murray, pp. 154-177.
17. Walter Williams, *The State Against Blacks* (New York: McGraw-Hill Book Company, 1982).
18. Thomas Sowell, *The Economics of Politics of Race* (New York: William Morrow, 1983).
19. Henry Hazlitt, *The Conquest of Poverty* (New Rochelle, New York: Arlington House, 1973).
20. George Gilder, *Wealth and Poverty* (New York: Basic Books, 1981).
21. Lawrence Mead, *Beyond Entitlement* (New York: Free Press, 1986).
22. Clarence Carson, *The War on the Poor* (New Rochelle, New York: Arlington House, 1969).
23. David Chilton, *Productive Christians in An Age of Guilt Manipulators*, 4th ed. (Tyler, Texas: Institute for Christian Economics, 1981, 1986).
24. Michael Harrington, *The New American Poverty* (New York: Holt, Rinehart, and Winston, 1984).
25. Martin Luther, *The Books of Vagabonds and Beggars: With a Vocabulary of Their Language, "Edited by M. Luther in the Year AD 1528, Now First Translated into English, with Introduction and Notes,"* tr. John Camden Hotten (London: Reformation Binders, 1860), pp. 4-5.
26. Karl de Schweinitz, *England's Road to Social Security* (Philadelphia: University of Pennsylvania Press, 1943), p. 15.
27. Ibid.
28. George Grant, *In the Shadow of Plenty* (Fort Worth, Texas: Dominion Press, 1986).
29. Grant, *Bringing in the Sheaves*, pp. 54-63.
30. 2 Thessalonians 3.
31. See Alexander Toberts and James Donaldson, eds., *The Ante-Nicene Fathers*; and Philip Schaff and Henry Wave, eds., *The Nicene and Post Nicene Fathers*, both published by Wm. B. Eerdmans Publishing Company.
32. For a discussion of this matter, see James B. Jordan, *The Law of the Cove-*

nant (Tyler, Texas: Institute for Christian Economics, 1984), pp. 207-224.

33. Schweinitz, pp. 1-17.
34. Ibid.
35. See James B. Jordan, ed., *The Reconstruction of the Church*. Christianity and Civilization No. 4 (Tyler, Texas: Geneva Ministries, 1986).
36. See James B. Jordan, *The Sociology of the Church* (Tyler, Texas: Geneva Ministries, 1986).
37. Thomas Fuller, *The Church History of Britain from the Birth of Jesus Christ Until the Year MDCXLVIII* (London: Reformation Binders, 1655, 1859), book II, p. 126.
38. Stephen E. Ozment, *The Reformation in the Cities: The Appeal of Protestantism to Sixteenth-Century Germany and Switzerland* (New Haven: Yale University Press, 1975).
39. Fuller, II:307.
40. R. Tudur Jones, *The Great Reformation* (Downers Grove, Illinois: Inter-Varsity Press, 1985); W. Fred Graham, *The Constructive Revolutionary: John Calvin and His Socio-Economic Impact* (Atlanta: John Knox Press, 1971); and W. Stanford Reid, ed.; *John Calvin: His Influence in the Western World* (Grand Rapids: Zondervan Publishing, 1982).
41. Schweinitz, p. 19.
42. Brandon Tartellson, *Homelessness in Europe* (London: Guillison Publishing Ltd., 1985), p. 2.
43. Ibid., p. 3; also see William C. Innes, *Social Concern in Calvin's Geneva* (Allison Park, Pennsylvania: Pickwick Publications, 1983).
44. Luther, pp. xii-xiii.
45. Ibid.
46. Tartellson, p. 2.
47. Ibid., p. 3.
48. Ibid., pp. 4-5.
49. Luther, p. 6.
50. Ibid.
51. Tartellson, p. 4, in the case in Leisnig.
52. Ibid., in the case of Ypres.
53. Ibid., in the case of London.
54. Ibid., in the case of Paris.
55. Ibid., in the case of Rotterdam.
56. Ibid., p. 5.
57. James B. Jordan, *The Sociology of the Church* (Tyler, Texas: Geneva Ministries, 1986), pp. 137-138. Jordan's essay makes the point that statist philosophers during the middle ages had long advocated that the Church keep to "spiritual" things and leave society to the state. Luther stood in a long tradition on this point, and his innovation was to remove charity from the "spiritual" to the "secular" realm. On this tradition, see R. J. Rushdoony's remarks on Marsilius of Padua in his *Christianity and the State* (Vallecito, CA: Ross House, 1986), pp. 120ff.; and see also Leo Strauss, "Marsilius of Padua," in Leo Strauss and Joseph Cropsey, eds., *History of Political Philosophy* (Chicago: Rand McNally, 1963).
58. Ibid., p. 142.
59. Ibid., p. 143.
60. Schweinitz, pp. 39-57.

61. Ibid., pp. 58-68.
62. Ibid.
63. Tartellson, p. 7.
64. Sidney Lens, *Poverty: Yesterday and Today* (New York: Thomas Y. Crowell, 1973), pp. 4-17.
65. Ibid.
66. Lucy Komisar, *Down and Out: A History of Social Welfare* (New York: Franklin Watts, 1973), pp. 15-42.
67. Ibid.
68. Adam Smith, *An Inquiry into the Nature and Causes of the Wealth of Nations* (London: Penguin Books, 1962).
69. Joseph Townsend, *A Dissertation on the Poor Laws by a Wellwisher to Mankind* (London: McDoogle and Sons, 1786, reprinted 1817).
70. Rev. T. R. Malthus, *Selected Writings* (New York: Bethelridge Publishers, 1952).
71. Thomas Chalmers, *Statement in Regard to the Ramperism of Glasgow from the Experience of the Last Eight Years*, pp. 118-123 (from the *Select Works of Thomas Chalmers*, vol. X, London: Paternoster Publishers, 1856, 1909).
72. Thomas MacKay, *A History of the English Poor Law, in III Volumes* (London: P. S. King and Son, 1899) II:203.
73. Ibid., III:61.
74. Ibid., III:67.
75. Arnold Dallimore, *C. H. Spurgeon* (Chicago: Moody Press, 1985).
76. Octavia Hill, *Official and Volunteer Agencies in Administering Relief* (London: Wm. R. Hay, 1874, 1891).
77. Langdon Lowe, *The Work of God in the South* (London: Murray, Stockbrough, and Wilson, 1896).
78. Charles Kingsley, *Charities* (London: A Kingsley Monograph, 1911).
79. Paul K. Conkin, *The New Deal* (Arlington Heights, Illinois: AHM Publishing, 1967).
80. Komisar, p. 49.
81. Igor Shafarevich, *The Socialist Phenomenon* (New York: Harper and Row, 1980).
82. Murray, p. 17.
83. Grant, *Bringing in the Sheaves*, pp. 38-52.
84. Komisar, p. 52.
85. Albert Donaldson, *American History in Review* (Tulsa, Oklahoma: Christian Truth Publishers, 1971), p. 426.
86. Ibid., p. 521.
87. Ibid., p. 522.
88. Ibid.
89. Mead, p. 3.
90. Grant, *In the Shadow of Plenty*, chapter 11.
91. Ibid.
92. Ibid.
93. Ibid.

Chapter 13 — Recoverable Enchantments: A Biblical Perspective

1. For an in-depth discussion of the Paradise theme, see David Chilton, *Paradise Restored: An Eschatology of Dominion* (Tyler, Texas: Reconstruction Press, 1985), and Meredith G. Kline, *Images of the Spirit* (Grand Rapids: Baker Book House, 1980).
2. See Chilton's discussion of this "east of Eden habitation" in *Paradise Restored*, chapter 4, and in his superb commentary on Revelation, *The Days of Vengeance: An Exposition of the Book of Revelation* (Fort Worth, Texas: Dominion Press, 1986).
3. Chilton, *Paradise Restored*, p. 49.
4. See James B. Jordan's invaluable work on the Church and its heavenly connection in *The Sociology of the Church* (Tyler, Texas: Geneva Ministries, 1986).

Chapter 14 — The Instrumentality of Mankind: A Biblical Pattern

1. Gary North, *The Sinai Strategy: Economics and the Ten Commandments* (Tyler, Texas: Institute for Christian Economics, 1986), p. ix.
2. James B. Jordan, *The Law of the Covenant: An Exposition of Exodus 21-23* (Tyler, Texas: Institute for Christian Economics, 1984), p. 3.
3. Ray Sutton, *Dominion By Covenant* (Fort Worth, Texas: Dominion Press, 1986).
4. North, pp. xiv-xxii.
5. Sutton, chapter 6.
6. David Chilton, *The Days of Vengeance: An Exposition of the Book of Revelation* (Fort Worth, Texas: Dominion Press, 1986).
7. Sutton's work is absolutely invaluable in revealing this paradigm and how it appears in any number of Scriptural passages.
8. Herbert Schlossberg, *Idols for Destruction* (Nashville: Thomas Nelson Publishers, 1983), pp. 314-315.

Chapter 15 — Aubade: A Biblical Hope

1. John Bunyan, *The Pilgrim's Progress* (New York: Signet Classics, 1964), p. 17.
2. George Grant, *In the Shadow of Plenty* (Fort Worth, Texas: Dominion Press, 1986), chapter 2.
3. Thomas MacKay, *A History of the English Poor Laws, in III Volumes* (London: P. S. King and Son, 1899) I:37-46.
4. Octavia Hill, *Official and Volunteer Agencies in Administering Relief* (London: Wm. R. Hay, 1874, 1891).
5. Charles Kingsley, *Charities* (London: A Kingsley Monograph, 1911).
6. Arthur S. Link and Richard L. McCormick, *Progressivism* (Arlington Heights, Illinois: Harlan Davidson, 1962).
7. S. B. Frodeans, *The Legacy of Francis* (Nawtuck, Tennessee: Little Flowers Publishing House, 1951).

8. Mary Ellen Hombs and Mitch Snyder, *Homelessness in America* (Washington: Community for Creative Non-Violence, 1982).
9. David Chilton, *Paradise Restored: An Eschatology of Dominion* (Tyler, Texas: Reconstruction Press, 1985), pp. 215-216.
10. Arnold Dallimore, *C. H. Spurgeon* (Chicago: Moody Press, 1985).
11. John Perkins, *With Justice for All* (Ventura, California: Regal Books, 1982).
12. George Grant, *Bringing in the Sheaves* (Atlanta: American Vision Press, 1985).
13. A forthcoming work from American Vision (to be released in the spring of 1987) entitled, *To the Work: Ideas for Biblical Charity*, is designed as a practical manual for putting all of these principles into practice. Additionally, there are a number of practical and well-tested ideas listed throughout my other two books: *Bringing in the Sheaves* and *In the Shadow of Plenty*.
14. See Appendix 1 for more do's and don't's on caring for the homeless.
15. See chapter 10 in *Bringing in the Sheaves* and chapters 7 and 19 in *To the Work*.
16. See chapters 7 and 8 in *In the Shadow of Plenty*, and chapters 8 and 9 in *To the Work*.
17. See chapter 5 in *Bringing in the Sheaves*, and chapters 3-5 in *To the Work*.
18. See chapter 8 in *In the Shadow of Plenty*, and chapters 6, 8, and 9 in *To the Work*.
19. See chapters 3 and 4 in *Bringing in the Sheaves*, and chapters 3 and 7 in *To the Work*.

Chapter 16 — Proof in the Pudding: A Biblical Reality

1. *All* homelessness cannot be cured, of course. Sin is suicidal (Proverbs 8:36) and some sin-driven men will always reject the world and insist on living in the caves like the Gerasene Demoniac. My point, however, is that homelessness as a condition can be conquered on a person by person basis. It is not an unassailable social ill!

Appendix 1: Do's and Don't's

1. *Spin Magazine*, July, 1986. For more on how relief efforts have helped to bolster the communist government's deliberate triage in Ethiopia, see my forthcoming book, *Planned Famine*, due in the spring of 1987.
2. See chapters 3, 4, and 6 in my book, *Bringing in the Sheaves: Transforming Poverty into Productivity* (Atlanta: American Vision Press, 1985).
3. See chapter 8 in *Bringing in the Sheaves*.
4. See chapter 9 in *Bringing in the Sheaves* and parts 2 and 3 in *To the Work: Ideas for Biblical Charity* (Atlanta: American Vision Press, 1987).
5. See chapter 9 in *In the Shadow of Plenty*.
6. See James B. Jordan's valuable work, *The Sociology of the Church* (Tyler, Texas: Geneva Ministries, 1986), as well as the symposium he edited,. *The Reconstruction of the Church*. Christianity and Civilization No. 4 (Tyler, Texas: Geneva Ministries, 1986), for more on the importance of develop-

ing a strong ecclesiology for the task of renewing our culture.

7. If these concepts sound strangely monastic, they should, because they are. For more information on the Biblical basis of these kinds of programs, see *To the Work*, part I.

8. See chapters 10, 11, and 12, in *Bringing in the Sheaves.*

9. See chapter 10 in *In the Shadow of Plenty: The Biblical Blueprint for Welfare* (Fort Worth, Texas: Dominion Press, 1986).

SCRIPTURE INDEX